The Great American Chewing Gum Book

Eskimos now prefer bubble gum to blubber; Africans have traded wives for a wad; New Guinea headhunters demanded it in ransom for a diplomat; a group of Japanese has prayed to it. During the rubber-short days of World War II, black market bubble gum retailed for as much as $1 a chaw, and it's even saved a trans-Atlantic dirigible!

Probably nothing we put in our mouths has as strange a history as chewing gum. This illustrated look at its lore and technology explains the development of the product from the spruce resin the American Indians chewed to the tasty flavored concoctions manufactured today.

The Great American Chewing Gum Book tells you how chewing gum is made and about the inventors and entrepreneurs who've blown it into a billion dollar enterprise over the past century. It's a saga, too, of the battle of the brands and industrialists who go at each other with teeth and tongue.

And Bob Hendrickson tells all about chewing gum etiquette, record-holding chewers, the differences between regular gum and bubble gum, gum as a secret weapon in World War I, baseball cards and the games you can play with them, the surprisingly *happy* things gum can do for your teeth and mouth, and, finally, how to remove your misplaced gum glob from whatever it's stuck on.

Also by Robert Hendrickson:

THE GRAND EMPORIUMS: The Illustrated History of America's Great Department Stores

FOODS FOR LOVE: The Complete Guide to Aphrodisiac Edibles (published in hardcover as *Lewd Food*)

HUMAN WORDS: The Compleat Unexpurgated, Uncomputerized Human Wordbook

THE GREAT AMERICAN TOMATO BOOK: The One Complete Guide to Growing and Using Tomatoes Everywhere

RIP-OFFS

The
Great
American
Chewing Gum
Book

Robert Hendrickson

A SCARBOROUGH BOOK

STEIN AND DAY/*Publishers*/New York

FIRST SCARBOROUGH BOOKS EDITION 1980

The Great American Chewing Gum Book was originally published in hardcover by Chilton Book Company and is reprinted by arrangement with the author.

Copyright © 1976 by Robert Hendrickson
First Edition *All Rights Reserved*
Stein and Day/*Publishers*/Scarborough House
Briarcliff Manor, N.Y. 10510
Manufactured in the United States of America

Library of Congress Cataloging in Publication Data
Hendrickson, Robert, 1933-
    The great American chewing gum book.

    Includes index.
    1. Chewing gum.   I. Title.
TX799.H46 1976   641.3   76-6055
ISBN 0-8128-6050-0

To Joey, Eddie, Johnny, Beth, Eunice, Kevin, Snowball, Shadow, Poppy, *and* Piwackett—*who have all chewed it, detonated it, swallowed it, left it underfoot, parked it under tables and stored it used in the refrigerator.*

ACKNOWLEDGMENT

SINCE this is the first book on chewing gum and very little has been written on the subject anywhere, it was essential to interview many people who have had connections with or have great knowledge of the industry from its beginnings. I would especially like to thank the following people for their indispensable assistance: P. J. Brind Amour; Edward Berger; Dr. Basil Bibby; Edie Clark; Gerrald Carr; Gerard Cavanaugh; Walter Diemer; Dr. Ingemar Falkehag; Dr. Sidney Finn; Roger Fry; Les Levine; Ford Mason; Bob Murphy; Ed Pope; Steven Schwartz; David Sloane; Walter Weglein; and Bob Wherry. Many thanks also to my kind and astute editor, Benton Arnovitz, and to Dr. Heidi Rosenbaum, who helped in so many ways.

R. H.

Far Rockaway, New York

CONTENTS

*The
Great
American
Chewing Gum
Book*

"Some books are to bee tasted,
others to bee swallowed,
and some few to bee chewed
and digested."
—BACON,
Essential Studies, 1597

Choo Choo Choo Choo Choo Choo'n Gum

CHAPTER 1

THE Mayans manufactured it . . .

The Apaches, Commanches and Kennebecs chomped on it . . .

Columbus discovered it along with this brave new world . . .

Francis Parkman, seeking the origins of America, patched his canoe with it . . .

Tom Sawyer and Becky Thatcher chewed on the same piece of it . . .

England's King Edward VII was offered a hunk of it and nearly fainted . . .

Anna Held, America's "Won't You Come Play with Me?" girl, took communal milk baths chawing wads of it . . .

Anthony Comstock, prince of prudes, suppressed it . . .

1

Emily Post refused to even mention it . . .
Queen Sophia of Greece prescribed it for her troops . . .
Admiral Byrd chewed it for his nerves at the South Pole . . .
Jack Dempsey strengthened his jaw with it . . .
Mayor Fiorello Henry La Guardia cleaned New Yorkers' shoes of
it . . .
Jeremy Boob, Ph.D, repaired the Beatles' yellow submarine with
it . . .
The Astronauts munched on it in outer space . . .
Mickey Mantle blithely blew bubbles with it in the outfield . . .
Joe Namath blithely blew bubbles with it in the backfield . . .
Socialites now chew it . . .
Shady ladies still love it . . .
Kids are weaned on it . . .
Eskimos prefer it to blubber . . .
Headhunters have ransomed people for it . . .
Lyndon Johnson rarely chawed it, but he claimed . . .
Gerald Ford couldn't chew it and walk at the same time . . .

Chewing gum. Health-giving, circulation-building, teeth-preserving, digestion-aiding, brain-refreshing, chest-developing, nerve-settling, soul-tuning chewing gum. Clearly the fabled chew food—by now an American and international institution—has a long and fascinating history. A longer history, in fact, than we gumiverous animals generally realize, or admit. This was proved beyond a doubt back in 1932, when people all over the world were nervously chomping their way through the Great Depression. At the time, a team of respected anthropologists made a rather startling discovery: deep within a Texas mountain they came upon the skeletons of a family of primitive man, several well-chewed wads of tree resin gum beside them. The family may even have been sharing their ABC (already-been-chewed) gum, jawing away while trapped inside their cave by some persistent sabre-toothed tiger. Perhaps, lacking peyote or tobacco, they passed the cud around to pacify themselves while the feral creature paced back and forth by their portal, casting shadows on their bearskin rug. No one knows. But the discovery proved for the first time that peoplekind could be incontrovertibly classified as a gum-chewing species. *Homo chompit erectus* had evolved eons before Wrigley or Dubble Bubble, and the world's gum

The first chewing gum—at least the first commercial
chewing gum made of chicle. New York's City Hall is
pictured on the box. *American Chicle Company*

chewing, symphonic in volume, could no longer be reviled as a dirty *American* habit.

Some observers had known this years before. Christopher Columbus, for one, noticed people chewing gum when he discovered the New World and he mentioned this in a letter to Lord Raphael Sanchez, treasurer of Aragon and one of his patrons—emphasizing his discovery not because he stepped in a wad when he debarked from the *Santa Maria*, but because he hadn't found much gold to speak of.

There were many others before Columbus who remarked on man's love of chewing, *ad ridiculum*, everything from human gristle to chicle. It has been pointed out that all that remains of the brilliant ancient Mayan civilization are ruins and the chewing gum habit they passed on to their neighbors. Long before the American "chewing gum trust" was formed early in the twentieth century, people the world over were avid spruce gum chewers. Mark Twain, in fact, immortalized this practice in *Tom Sawyer* when he had Tom and Becky Thatcher share their chewed wad of spruce. What American entrepreneurs did was simply to capitalize on an obvious fact of life. They turned the natural process of chewing into a billion-dollar business, a major industry and (in the case of bubble gum, anyway) a minor art, by barely refining it, cleaning it up a bit, adding lots of sugar and softeners, and selling it hard.

Let the statistics carry the theme in this saga of sales and consumption. Probably well over a billion dollars' worth of gum is sold each year throughout the world, Americans consuming close to 800 million dollars' worth at the retail level. Roughly updating figures used by the official journal of the American Chemical Society some years back, the more than two pounds per person of chewing gum that Americans alone chomp on every year would make a stick nearly 3 million miles long, without even stretching it or blowing a bubble; long enough, that is, to reach about six times to the moon and back, or to hog-tie the planet about 150 times at its greatest circumference, or to almost wrap up the earth with an eight-foot wide pink-and-clay-colored ribbon at that same point. Another figure some mad mathematician concocted years ago proves that the energy Americans alone expend when chewing gum would be sufficient to light a city of over ten million people, for a year at the very least. Think of it. We chew gum at a force of from five to 100 pounds per square inch. If everyone put his and her teeth to the wad and chewed hard—all the gum chewers in the world—we'd be able to lift any Arab oil embargo, see the stars again in the cities, purify the waters, eliminate poverty. The possibilities are staggering. If all the politicians stopped talking and started chewing . . .

In America today fully half of us chew some gum, the national wad about equally divided among men and women—surprisingly, children don't "chicle" nearly as much as adults. One critic has labeled America's poor and inarticulate "The Wad," but the image is all wrong. In America *everybody*—rich, poor, reactionary, radical—constitutes The Wad. On her capture Patty Hearst was reported to be "chewing gum jauntily." Waiting in line for her diploma on graduation day, Caroline Kennedy obligingly blew a bubble for photographers. Then there is the exotic dancer Ms. Wriggley Gum ("She *giggles*/ She *jiggles*/ She *wriggles*!"), and the 350-pound, caped and gold-booted Captain Sticky, who is Supreme Commander of the World Organization Vs. Evil, and blows bubbles at villains in addition to squirting them with peanut butter from a peanut butter gun.

Whether President Gerald Ford really chewed gum or not, no reporter knows. Lyndon Johnson did say Mr. Ford couldn't chew the stuff and walk at the same time and a famous Oliphant cartoon depicts Mr. Ford trying to balance himself on a skateboard labeled "Vote Jerry" while Oliphant's little bird cries "Spit out the gum!" All evidence would indicate, however, that Gerald Ford was just accident-prone. During his travels he has bumped his head, slipped, fallen, been in an automobile accident, stumbled over the foot of a woman in a wheelchair and was almost poked in the eye by an American flag waved by an excited child. No gum was ever in sight.

If our glorious leader chose to chew in private, a number of lesser lights (including some Congressmen) are committed public chewers, and even prominent statesmen have been caught with their jaws coming down. Stage and screen idols beginning with Anna Held, the "Won't You Come Play With Me?" girl with the restless lips and hips that flowed like fine wine, have publicly indulged, and sports idols thrive on the sticky stuff. Willie Joe Namath popped gum in the backfield; there is a famous picture of Mickey Mantle blowing a bubble while awaiting a high fly ball; one major league catcher blew a bubble during the pitcher's windup, missed the pitch when the bubble burst all over his mask, and let the winning run score.

Gum does have its virtues. Back in 1921, Jack Dempsey so strengthened his jaw in training by constant gum chewing that when Georges Carpentier hit him, the blow broke Carpentier's thumb, Dempsey thereby winning the fight—at least so a British physician, Dr. James H. Doggart, told the American Medical Association convention in 1956. Gum has been used for many purposes. Admiral Richard Byrd insisted on carrying a large supply of it on his voyage to the South Pole (it calmed his nerves) and the Gemini V astronauts chewed it in outer space (it took the place of lost toothbrushes). Bubble gum has even been employed as an organic insecticide: certain bugs enjoy chewing on it—until their jaws stick together and they starve to death.

When Jeremy Boob, Ph.D., fixed the propeller on the Beatles' Yellow Submarine with chewing gum to help them escape His Meaniness and the Meanies, more than fantasy was involved. Everyone knows stories about spit, string and gum wads being used to patch engines, tires, life rafts, radio connections, and even hydraulic landing gear lines on bombers. These tales have a firm basis in truth. The British Royal Air Force Dirigible *R-34* couldn't have made its successful flight to America in 1911 if it hadn't been for chewing gum. In the middle of the Atlantic the craft's forward motor began hissing and grew very hot. A leak was discovered in its water jacket and after all the glues and putties aboard failed to repair it, ten crewmembers were given packs of chewing gum and told to chew as if their lives quite literally depended on it. This they did, and the leak was repaired with their collective cud when a thin layer of gum was smeared over the part, a strip of copper fitted to it and bicycle tape bound to the copper. Major H. C. Scott and his crew then knelt and "gave a vote of thanks to the gum man-ufacturers."

The uses of chewing gum have certainly been ingenious and myriad—ranging from its use as an aphrodisiac to its use as the basis for an international language. Recently, two smugglers chewed up 100 packs of Wrigley's Spearmint and carefully filled the empty packs with a fortune in "healthful, delicious, satisfying" marijuana. In another case, a tricky jewel thief asked to see some valuable gems at a leading diamond exchange. The stones were brought to his table and he palmed the largest one, covered it with a wad of gum he'd been chewing and stuck the wad to the underside of the table. When a thorough search of his person failed to turn up the missing gem, the owners apologized profusely. The next day his confederate retrieved the gum-wrapped diamond.

Some of us even remember the ragged coin fishermen of the Great Depression, who knelt over gratings with a string, a stone weight and a piece of chewing gum angling for small change passersby had lost. These sidewalk fishermen are back on the streets again with the return of hard times. They chew up their gum, stick it on the stone and with unerring aim drop it on a coin below—which sticks to the gum and is hauled to the surface.

Chewing gum has of course claimed its victims, too. No one was ever boiled alive in a vat of bubble gum, but in 1944, a piece of gum exploded in a Philadelphia man's mouth causing him to lose several teeth; police never solved the strange case of sabotage. Ten years earlier (stay tuned for The Great Chewing Gum Murder Case), some fiend tried to kill an entire Sacramento family by slipping them poisoned gum. This was an interesting case, unique in the annals of crime, but chewing gum has ruined far more rugs and seats of pants than it has lives. Entire cities have campaigned against gum as an ecological menace.

Chewing can indeed prove expensive. Ten cents' worth of gum cost one major airline $1,425.33. It seems that in 1959 a 10-year-old American chewer named Johnny Rand forced a big British Overseas Airways Stratocruiser bound for London to turn back for New York when 300 miles out. Johnny had stuffed 13 pieces of medicated airsickness gum into his mouth instead of the recommended one piece at a time. Fearing that the boy's life was in danger, the pilot headed back for New York, where Johnny received a stimulant shot to ward off the hypnotic drug in the gum. The airline estimated that a Stratocruiser costs $560 an hour to run, which figures out to $765.33 for the one hour and 22 minutes that the plane was airborne before returning. In addition, the pilot dumped 1,500 gallons of gasoline to make the unscheduled landing. At 44 cents a gallon for aviation fuel, this added $660 to make a total of $1,425.33. Johnny, who said the gum "tasted real good," apparently suffered no ill effects. At least he didn't become airsick.

Chewing gum is so honored in our culture that at least six songs have been written about it, classics that rank with such all-time favorites as "Abba-Dabba Honeymoon," "Cement Mixer, Putty, Putty," "Oh Mine Papa," "Shrimp Boats Is a Comin'," "Cry of The Wild Goose," and "Oh, How She Could Yacki Hacki Wicki Wacki Woo." The first of these seems to have been "Oh You Spearmint Kiddo With The Wrigley Eyes," from 1910. Others, ranging up to the Bubble Gum Rock genre, include "Chew Chew Chew (Chew Your Bubble Gum)," which the great Ella Fitzgerald somehow had a hand in writing (it advises us to blow our troubles away like bubble gum bubbles), and what is probably the second chomping song, "Chewing Gum," which was penned by the Carter Family in 1928 and tells about such things as a country girl chawing her chewing gum "right in the preacher's face"—in between inspirational choruses of "Chawing chewing gum / Chewing chawing gum." But the all-time favorite is "Choo'n Gum," written by Vic Mizzy in 1950, telling of a girl whose Ma gave her a nickel to buy a pickle, etc., but who bought choo'n gum instead—all to a chorus of "Choo, choo, choo, choo, choo choo'n gum / How I love choo'n gum." This classic is only approached in eloquence by the vaunted "Does The Spearmint Lose The Flavor (On The Bedpost Overnight)?" by Rose, Bloom and Breuer, whose lyrics amount to little more than the title.

Sculptor Les Levine has immortalized gum in what some critics think is a way far superior to song. Levine, an Irish Jew educated at Cambridge who works in his Greenwich Village Museum of Mott Art (it's on Mott Street), has, in the words of one art critic, "consistently dealt with new ideas in art and has endeavored to carry them to their logical or illogical extremes." But he has been a "king of *kitsch*," "seer of *shlock*," and a "Titan of trivia" as well. Levine has done a series of paintings depicting *used chewing gum,* and a number of sculptures of *gold-coated gum wads.* He believes that chewed chewing gum is sculpture made with the teeth, which are as viable a tool as the mouth. "It's a disgrace," he says, "that all those sculptors have

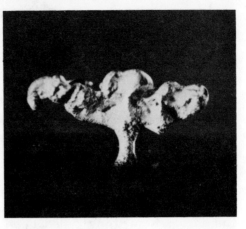

Artist Les Levine has done a highly acclaimed series of solid gold chewing gum sculptures that puts gum on the pedestal it deserves. *Museum of Mott Art, Inc.*

to work so hard to produce something that could have been done by sitting at home chewing gum." His miniature 18-karat gold chewing gum sculptures were exhibited in 1972 at the prestigious Fischbach Gallery in New York, among other places. For the record, the gold gum pieces were made the following way: Mr. Levine chewed a six-pack of Wrigley's Doublemint Gum. He chewed each piece for exactly two minutes. When he had chewed all 30 pieces, which was an hour's work, he sent them to be cast in 18-karat gold. Each gold gum piece is 1¾ inches tall, mounted on a ½-inch pin which holds it to a black marble base 2¼ inches square.

Mickey Mouse, Coca-Cola, the dread Swastika, a mushroom cloud, name what you will; chewing gum on a pedestal is as good a symbol of contemporary western civilization as any. Chewing, like having sex, is an instinctive process but a relatively modern industry. Its history is entwined with that of this great, often perishing, ever-rebounding Republic. The Mayans, Columbus, General Santa Anna (that arch-villain of the Alamo) all prominently figure in its story. We know the identity of the first chewing gum manufacturer, the inventor of modern gum, the first man to patent a chewing gum, even the inventor of bubble gum—who, by the way, is still alive and thwacking. Gum history is chock-full of gumsnapping good tales of chewing gum kings like William White, that bonkers Yank who tried popping gum into the mouth of England's astonished King Edward VII; of the irrepressible William Wrigley Jr., who bought red automobiles "so I can find them;" and of the fantabulous "King Bub," J. Walter Bowman, whose bubble gum picture cards caused an international incident and perhaps brought World War II a little closer. Then there are the spruce gum gatherers of New England and the chicleros or chicle gatherers of the tropics, who long took as many risks a day in Central American jungles as there are sticks in a carton of gum, in order to provide the base for our chewing habit. All are responsible for intriguing brands like Blibber-Blubber, Vassar, Kis-Me, Don't Let It Happen Over Here Gum, Love Gum, Passion Gum, Forbidden Fruit, Fight The Red Menace Gum, even something called Peerless Chips made down in Texas cattle country—not to mention old favorites like Chiclets, Wrigley's Spearmint and Dubble Bubble that are still on the market. These brave men and geniuses also brought us bright gumballs in every color of the rainbow; gumball machines that included an ill-fated pinball version which dispensed gum to high scorers; baseball cards that are often collectors' items worth thousands today; and gum shortages that caused "pink markets" like the one involving bubble gum after World War II.

The opposition to gum chewing here has included doctors, dentists and teachers, as well as puritans like Anthony Comstock and Carrie Nation, who were weaned on sour grapes and felt that gum was one of the most disastrous cultural influences ever to hit America. Across the Atlantic, Scotland Yard once forbade its Bobbies to chew gum (might get stuck in their whistles in an emergency, their chief argued). There have been major health scares concerning chewing gum, including charges that swallowed wads will cause the intestines to stick together and that gum is no good for the gums or teeth. Others have claimed that gum chewing made women's faces "hard" and old before their time, or that the product was made from horses' hooves, glue and old rubber girdles. Still others remarked on the similarities between the gum-chewing girl and the cud-chewing cow, pointing out that the major difference between the two was the "clear, thoughtful look on the face of the cow." But whether gum chewing constitutes an "adult pacifier," "oral masturbation," "a measure of sexuality," a way to fight boredom and tension, or simply a pleasurable exercise, what was once universally regarded as a bad habit has become an international custom. Even the Soviet Union, whose theorists once branded it as "just another opiate of the masses," now manufactures chewing gum. In some parts of the world storekeepers sell gum not by the pack, but by the half-stick, which lasts poor peasants two weeks or so. Then there are the Eskimos, who have switched from blubber to bubble gum, and the cannibal tribe so enamored of gum that they ransomed a captive doomed to the pot for a carton of Dubble Bubble. Brooklyn Bridge Gum in Italy, Pingi Pongi (Ping Pong) in Brazil, Hollywood Gum in France—all over the globe people are chewing hard today and all projections indicate that they're going to be chewing even more.

Though gum's popularity knows no racial or national boundaries, the chew food has special significance in America, where it has earned its unassailable place in the national diet and has more aficionados than anywhere else. Gum chomping is among the most pervasive images in American life. Everyone from the man in the street to Shipwreck Kelly up on his flagpole has chewed it and no one has ever demanded a refund. Chewing gum has earned an immortality here rivaling that of any food. For better or ill, gum's history is in great measure our own; at least four generations of Americans had gum in their bones, or mouths. We don't have too much else in the way of a common experience. In a pluralistic society, where our experiences of family, school and church are not common, you might say we are held or stuck together by chewing gum.

Gum chewing can, has and will be ignored by Comstocks and Emily Posts everywhere, but it does exist, on a grand scale, and has proved that it won't go away by being ignored; all the teeth of time have been unable to crush what is now a universal habit. The Japanese, who manufacture over 150 gum flavors, including pickled plum, probably best established the greatness of *gamu*, as they call it, in 1962, when the Let's Chew More Gum Association opened offices in Tokyo. The gala opening, attended by show people, politicians and baseball stars, amounted to a kind of religious ceremony during which a special prayer was intoned by a Shinto priest standing before an elaborate altar to *gamu*. It offers as good a note as any on which to launch out on this exploration of the legends, lore and cult of gum chewing, the rules of gummanship, and the modes of mannerly and unmannerly mastication:

O Great Spirit of the Chewing Gum, gum of diverse kinds, we offer this prayer to thee. There is grandeur in chewing gum. It is our marvellous pet, an important accessory of mankind in this modern age. Chewing gum sweetens the breath, imparts a pleasant feeling, strengthens the stomach and calms anger . . . It invites happiness. It attracts smiles. An enjoyable and intellectual life is made possible because of gum chewing . . . O Great Spirit of the Chewing Gum, rest in peace . . .

CHAPTER 2

Chewin' & Chawin': What The World Chews & Why

OBSERVERS from Charles Dickens to Emily Post have rather arrogantly assumed that chewing for the sake of chewing is "an exclusively American vice;" but in truth, people have been compulsively chomping on nonfood items, everything from each other to themselves, ever since Carlyle's "first hairy savage and chewer of acorns." The habit of ruminating on something besides food seems to be a curious demand of the human system that is universal in range, a practice that possibly, even probably, began with the first of us blessed or cursed with big mouths and a few trusty teeth.

But who knows why we chew gum and other nonfood items? There are lots of theories, but no satisfactory answer;

many counsels to be chewed but not swallowed. Scientists say that chewing is a sublimation of the fidgets, an outlet for nervous energy and such, yet even that's only one stick in the pack. People do chew (and chew gum especially) to ease tense nerves and muscles; a pencil, pipe stem, a blade of grass—anything handy will do. However, one panel of psychoanalysts, psychiatrists and psychologists that chewed over the unconscious emotional needs behind all our champing at the bit of reality found that the number one motive for gum chewing was to relieve feelings of loneliness and boredom. That gum chewing provided relief from tension by discharging nervous energy was the second most important unconscious motivation, and chewing to sublimate rage or to provide a quick socially acceptable outlet for anger and irritation came in a poor third.

Waverley Root, a noted food writer, charges that gum chewing "betrays the defective nature of our diet," that "working the jaws incessantly, uselessly and unbeautifully is an effort to deceive the body into the belief that it is being sufficiently well-fed when it isn't." But gum chewing isn't useless, to some it may be beautiful, and there is no correlation between malnutrition and chomping on even the bedpost spearmint. A mooning Henry Miller gave a sounder rationale for chewing in *Tropic of Capricorn* when he wrote: "I find a piece of chewing

Gum chewers used to look like this in the early days. *New York Public Library*

gum in my pocket—I chew it. I chew for the sake of chewing. There is absolutely nothing better to do unless it were to make a decision, which is impossible."

There are actually all kinds of psychological reasons for gum chewing (see especially Chapter 14). To cite another statistic, one out of one of us is affected by some form of emotional illness in this age of anxiety, so that alone leaves a large market for gum. Only the most meticulous, fastidious, exact, precise, orderly, accurate, organized, constant, unerring, disciplined, scrupulous, punctilious, particular and finical have no need to chew.

At least one psychiatrist way out there believes gum chewing may be "oral masturbation," fulfilling sexual hunger. This pronouncement necessitates "a stretch of belief which requires a more gumelastical faith than Heaven has allotted us," but masticatory masturbation might as well grace the list of all the other chewing bonuses. Besides knocking out fillings, getting all over shoes and pants' seats, and driving others up the wall, gum chewing can also, according to various studies: alleviate thirst and hunger; help workers concentrate; keep drivers alert at the wheel; moisten and refresh a dry mouth; sweeten the breath; keep teeth clean and strong; strengthen the jaws; aid in speech therapy; deter the smoker from smoking; pop ears on planes and in submarines; help maintain a dieter's weight at a

mere five to ten calories a slab; and even make women sexier and men more macho if they believe it does.

Nevertheless, most gum chewers would eschew any reasons for the relentless action of the molars and company. Since time unremembered people have chewed for pleasure alone, rarely because they considered chawing a chore. Never consciously so, anyway, unless they were into something like grinding grasses for basket weaving, or crushing up pap to feed their babies. First and foremost, chewing is pleasurable; often the rest follows, sort of the way nature set up reproduction. Doing what comes naturally was the chewing refrain ever since the first animal reared up and grabbed a rocklike glob of raw resin from a wound in a tree, or began ruminating on any nonnutritional substance. From the time we were red in tooth as well as claw we've been enjoying the "complicated concurrence of the jaw, the tongue, and the cheeks" that physiologists say is chewing, especially "the action of chomping and squeezing any substance between the teeth, without intending to swallow it." True, the overrefined and kinky souls among us haven't chewed much over the years. Many fastidious French ladies in the Middle Ages were dedicated nonchewers who subsided mainly on broths because they believed that the movement of the jaws "deformed the contours of their faces and detracted from the ethereal appearance of their beauty." But for the most part we've crushed, bruised, ground and chawed away with great enthusiasm on our sweet grasses, leaves, waxes, animal skins, human gristle, tree resins, and what have you—on myriad substances that have ranged from the sublime to the vile, many of which wouldn't be touched today by the veriest varlet that ever chewed with a tooth . . .

Some Old Chomping Favorites:
The Strangest Things Ever Chawed by Teeth

Odd, odious and plenteous indeed are the materials man has made mincemeat of. During World War II, for example, the Wrigley Company sent a botanist around the world to search out substitutes for their chicle gum base, which was then in short supply. His report, now in the company archives, filled several stout volumes. No one should have been surprised that he turned up so many chewy substances, for the variety of things gnawed for nonnutritional purposes by primitive tribes alone is extraordinary. Practically all peoples have practiced some form of "chewing without the intention of swallowing." Some, like the Tasmanians, were called "gum-suckers" because of their habit of chomping gum from trees. These gum suckers, whose name became a slang synonym for fool, were quite serious and industrious in their work, too, like gum suckers everywhere. Europeans, for instance, chewed grain and licorice, "to smellen sweet," as Chaucer put it. Then there were oddities like the spermacetti wax obtained from sperm whale oil, and "the bits of dirty chewed paper" Jonathan Swift described, or even materials like the one Hilaire Belloc mentioned in *Cautionary Tales*, when he wrote: *"The chief defect of Henry King/ Was chewing little bits of string."*

Figuratively, people have chewed the rag and chewed on iron and brass; literally, we've chomped up practically everything else around. Not too many years ago, Groucho Marx had a contestant on his *You Bet Your Life* show who chewed wood, any old wood. He is not alone. Among even odder substances man has munched on over the eons are tar, dirt and clay. Children everywhere are still attracted to tar as a kind of chewing gum, whenever it's available, and it does have a petroleum base, like many commercial gums today. Dirt and clay are a little harder to understand. Geophagists or dirt-eaters called the Ottomaques chewed "a fat, unctuous earth . . . tinged with a little oxide of iron," according to the explorer Humboldt. The chewy earth was baked into little balls and soaked in water before being used, each Indian chawing about a pound of it every day. The Ottomaques aren't isolated examples, either. Geophagists still chomp on dirt throughout the world and nutritionists tell us that they generally do so because they suffer from mineral deficiencies that the soil helps remedy. At least this is a better reason than the American historian Prescott had for gnawing on soap; one writer tells us this uncompromising moralist "ate soap under the theory that men should be clean inside as well as out."

If dirt has its reasons in the diet, so does chewing fare like blubber and gristle. But these are far better for the teeth, especially for those who don't brush after eating. All primitive races lived upon a diet that required vigorous chewing and kept their teeth well-exercised, sound and healthy. The Eskimos still chew blubber, the fat of whales and other animals, as well as *mutak*, the raw outer skin of the whale, and an eighteenth century Arctic explorer tells us how they passed around "the cartilaginous parts of the seal's fore-flippers . . . to be chewed upon." Recent studies show that Eskimos living upon such primitive diets have strong, sound teeth, whereas Eskimos who have learned to eat the soft, refined foods of civilization develop decayed teeth and unhealthy gums. Maybe that's why bubble gum has become such a great favorite among Eskimo tribes today.

In the past, superstition played a large role in determining what we munched on. "Chew on the bull's tail, son, and you'll be as brave as a bull," an ancient Druid might have advised her child. Likewise, cannibals often slashed off and chewed up the reproductive parts of their slain enemies to assume their sexual powers, using the flesh raw like plugs of tobacco. They did the same with cuts like filet of footsole and palm of hand, and no shaman ever chewed them out for this, either. Incidentally, many cannibals felt that tobacco smoking, meat-eating, and hypocritical white men were inferior in taste to locals; whites were too tough and often had to be repotted. Bearing this out is a recent report in the *Manchester Guardian* that Americans are "unfit for human consumption." It seems that the average Yank's bodily tissue contains 12 parts per million of D.D.T., the maximum level considered safe for consumption being 7 parts per million. Hardly fit for an organic chewing gum. So go catch a *Manchester Guardian* editor.

Human gristle probably isn't your dish as a chewing gum, but chewy plants like mints appeal to most everyone, which is one reason why they are the favorite chewing gum flavors today. Wild mint (*Mentha sativa*) has been chewed since earliest times and it, too, is often regarded as an aphrodisiac. Aristotle forbade the chewing of wild mint by Alexander the Great's soldiers because he felt it aroused them erotically and took away all their desire to fight. The same can't be said of the ancient chewstick or chaw-stick, the branches and sticks of the *Gouauia Domingenis* tree. These were and are still used in the West Indies exclusively for cleansing the teeth and sweetening the breath, just as the roots of the cola tree, called "chewed stick," are used in Sierra Leone.

Besides chewing on its roots, African natives chomp on stimulating nuts from the cola tree. It's said that Stanley was only able to find Dr. Livingstone in darkest Africa because his trusty bearers chewed on the strength-giving nuts or beans. In fact, cola beans were used by the U.S. military and in the early 1890's the Surgeon General of the Army said that chewing them enabled our foot soldiers to perform as well as anybody on forced marches. There used to be a considerable amount of cola beans in our national drink, Coca-Cola, but now they don't even constitute 1/100th of one percent of the brew.

Coca-Cola also contains minute percentages of coca, another chewing stimulant. Coca leaves are chewed by the Andean Indians, who seem to need them to get through the day just as westerners need cigarettes, Coke and chewing gum. Sometimes it's hard to balance physiological losses against psychological gains, for coca leaves constitute a euphoric that has its dangers. The leaves have nevertheless been used by South Americans since time immemorial as a masticatory, appeaser of hunger, aphrodisiac, and stimulant of the nervous system. "We should remember, however, that even Coca-Cola was flavored with coca extract until 1903," one writer notes, "by which time a growing body of medical opinion held that cocaine was a dangerous drug and the Coca-Cola Company decided to use only dealkaloided coca extract and substituted caffeine for the cocaine. Coca-Cola is still flavored with coca extract . . . though the cocaine is missing from the brew." Today U.S. law says that everyone must get no kicks from cocaine, but 8,000,000 South Americans still chew their coca leaves and we forget how in the late nineteenth century cocaine was so common that it was used here in cough syrups, tonics, cigarettes, cigars and (so I've been told) in at least one medicated chewing gum.

Maté, khat and mu-tir leaves are also chewed for their narcotic and aphrodisiac effects, but as an aphrodisiac masticatory no other chewable rivals ginseng, the chewed root of which has been touted as the ultimate turn-on for over 5,000 years. Ginseng (the Chinese call it "the elixir of life") is believed to be most potent when the roots are shaped like a man's body, complete with sexual organs, and are dug up at midnight during a full moon. Although "wild seng" is native to the U.S., the best kind is the Chinese "heaven grade root" which has sold in the past for $4,800 a pound, one Chinese emperor reputedly paying $10,000 for a perfect man-figure ginseng root of this variety. Many medical experts say that ginseng is no aphrodisiac or medicine at all, but other authorities vouch for it and to this day Chinese apothecaries prescribe the "herb that fills the heart with hilarity" or "the medicine of medicines" for strength, virility and longevity, citing it as the number one botanical drug in their most recent medical books. No wonder the South Koreans have begun to manufacture a chewing gum laced with the sexy herb. But then ginseng has always been chewed for the best results; experts advise that a small piece of the root be chewed an hour or so for the ultimate high because saliva helps to activate its aphrodisiac qualities.

Another famous masticatory people prize for the joy of a stimulating chew, even though it turns their teeth pitch black, is the betel nut. The betel nut comes from the areca or betel palm (*Areca catechu*); the tree's fruit, roughly the size of a hen's egg, contains the mottled gray seed or nut. The nuts are boiled, sliced and dried in the sun until they turn dark brown or black, when they are ready to be wrapped up in betel vine leaves and chewed. Native to Malaya and southern India, betel nuts are so widely used in Oriental nations that it is estimated that one-tenth of all the people on earth indulge in betel chewing. The introduction of modern chewing gum has cut into this figure slightly, but the betel chewers aren't easily discouraged. Not by the copious flow of brick-red saliva caused by chewing the betel nuts, which dyes the lips, mouth, and gums. Not by all those black teeth resulting from the betel nut habit. For betel is a true excitant and arouses a great craving in the addict. Legions of devotees—black-toothed, bloody-mouthed and bad-breathed—can be seen throughout the Orient chomping away and squirting scarlet juice all over walls.

Only the tobacco chewer would even consider using betel here. Tobacco chawing which turns the teeth black, yellow and green, is about the only habit that moralists have condemned as vociferously as they have betel chewing or chewing gum. Charles Dickens said that tobacco chewing was the cornerstone of American manners, and he didn't think much of American manners. Without mentioning that the quid had more than a few votaries in his own country, Dickens wrote in his *American Notes* of "The prevalence of those two odious practices of chewing and expectorating." But no spit-and-runner worth his plug cared a cud what Dickens thought. Americans have been chewing tobacco since the Indians taught us how and we still consume about 45 million pounds of it a year (without being prodded much by Madison Avenue), pots for tobacco spitters still lining the corridors of Congress. Far and above a male habit, chawing is considered emblematic of macho down South, just as it was among cowboys and seamen in the past. Prohibitionists have claimed that quidding is an acquired taste for a narcotic, but it is more likely an acquired taste with many purposes. For the cowboy choking on dust it was an oral cleanser he could apply without using his busy hands; it gave the sailor something to do while his hands were occupied and the wind blew too hard to light a pipe. Chawing may even prevent cavities. At any rate, despite their brown-stained shirts, bloated cheeks, and five-watt smiles, most chawers won't soon give up the plugs with the $C_5 H_4 NC_4 H_7 NCH_3$ in them. Stern rulers in the past have decreed that tobacco chewers be impaled or have their noses cut off when found indulging. But they're still with us, virile and vile as ever. There are even two annual contests for tobacco spitters, the National Open and the Missouri Open, featuring events such as spitting through the open door of a sizzling, pot-bellied stove, and hitting a dime from eight feet. An ole Miss man named Don Snyder holds the distance record—he let loose a juicy blast 25 feet, 10 inches long, and casually commenced chewing . . .

Tree Resins—
The First Real Chewing Gums

Judging by our heritage, primitive man must have ransacked nature for substances to chew on that would give him a lift or a high; there's no room here to list even the most important and unlikely materials we have chewed to rags. But tree resins have always been the most popular of the chewables, ultimately inspiring man to invent or perfect modern chewing gum. In the broadest sense, these resins have included the chewy bits of thickened gums, resins and latexes from almost any nonpoisonous plant species. For the last century or so chicle, a latex from the Sapodilla tree of Central and South America, has been the favorite among them, serving as the base of most commercial chewing gums until very recently. In the past, however, gums and resins were chewed far more widely than the latexes that give us rubber tires and girdles.

Resins have often been called gums in a general sense. An incomplete distinction between the two is that true gums are more or less soluble in water but remain insoluble in organic solvents, whereas true resins react in exactly the opposite way. Resins are particularly important in the making of varnish, and in the manufacture of paints, linoleum, soap and medicines. Their fragrance has long been valued and they have thus been used as incense for thousands of years.

Frankincense, though it is strictly speaking a gum resin, is probably the best known of the resin incenses. Obtained from various species of *Boswellia* trees (especially *Boswellia Carteri* or Birdwood), it is the incense mentioned so frequently in the Bible and was used by the ancient Egyptians in their religious rites. According to Pliny, the best frankincense is white, brittle and readily inflammable, and he remarked that breast-shaped "female" drops, formed by the union of two tears of the milklike juice, were superior to globular drops of "male" frankincense. Still widely valued as an aromatic, frankincense has had many uses over the years. It is considered worthless in modern medicine, but the ancients thought it cured hemlock poisoning, tremors, ulcers, vomiting, dysentery, fevers, carbuncles, gonorrhea, and leprosy, and also prescribed it as a stimulant, tonic, sedative, aphrodisiac and astringent. Small wonder people constantly chewed the substance. They still do, for that matter. This little-known fact was pointed out by Dr. Ingemar Falkenhag of the Westvaco Charleston Research Center, who kindly sent me a "tear" of genuine frankincense from the Valley of the Incense in Africa. Dr. Falkenhag advised that the Nomads in Italian Somaliland consider frankincense so indispensable that they have carried a pouch of it in their belts since prehistoric times, the pouch almost an artificial organ that perhaps quenches their thirst and makes up for the lack of water.

Encouraged by the Nomads, I experimented with the stuff. Crunchy at first, filled with bits of bark, the tan-and-white-colored tear broke apart into salmon-colored bits and it took about 10 minutes before the heat of the mouth made a passable gum of it. Even then the gritty wad tended to break apart slightly, never achieving a uniform consistency. The tear, roughly the size of a marble, was chewed up to nothing within 15 minutes. As for its taste, there was only the slightest hint of bitterness to what was a strangely refreshing woodsy flavor that lingered long, seemed to momentarily cleanse the mouth, and was definitely thirst-quenching. Compared to our sugary, highly flavored commercial gum, however, it resembled a chewed-out wad in taste and it even proved much inferior to spruce gum. It's safe to say that frankincense serves best as an incense and that it will never replace chewing gum here.

Unlike frankincense, the legendary mastic is a true resin still widely chewed today. Mastic, the chewing gum discovered by Columbus in Santo Domingo, is an exudation obtained from the six-foot-high lentisk or mastic shrub (*Pistacia lenticus*) cultivated mainly on the Mediterranean island of Chios. The resin, found in the lentisk's bark, speedily exudes when the bark is cut, hardening into oval tears the size of peas which are transparent and of a pale yellow or faint greenish tinge that darkens slowly with age. Mastic's primary use since ancient times has been as a masticatory to sweeten the breath and preserve the teeth and gums. People throughout southeastern Europe and the Near East have used it for this purpose and Dioscorides, the great Greek physician and medical botanist of the first century, refers to mastic's curative powers in his *De Materia Medica*. Today a chewing gum made with mastic and beeswax, a softening agent, is still enjoyed by many Greeks and Middle Easterners.

Mastic or mastiche (pronounced "mas-tee-ka") goes so far back that it may have constituted the Greek word *mastichon*, to chew, which is the root of the English word "masticate." This resin and all the other substances mentioned here (plus so many others) could certainly be classified as primitive chewing gums, proving conclusively that the chewing gum habit is hardly exclusively American. Yet it was in America that the first commercial gum came to be manufactured. Whether this was because we are the most inventive people on earth ever, or merely the most nervous, no one can really say. But the gum was spruce gum, another resin, and it came on the market at least 25 years before chicle even made the dictionaries.

CHAPTER 3

The Gumming Up of America: Of Spruce Gum Kings & Gum You Can Make In the Kitchen

SPRUCE GUM, which anyone can make on the kitchen stove, was the first chewing gum to be manufactured here, and for better or worse marked the rough beginnings of what is now a billion-dollar industry. Commercial chewing gum constitutes a uniquely American institution, a 100 percent Yankee "invention," unlike ice cream, soda pop or even baseball, a national pride of sorts whose origins are indisputable. But spruce gum itself was chewed long before anybody put it on the marketplace and isn't even unique to America.

Throughout Europe, there is a very old custom of collecting and chewing resin from the spruce. In Sweden, for example, spruce gum was thought to relieve a number of physical ailments and was so highly prized as a chewing gum that the *kada* (resin) was often given as a gift to a sweetheart. Germans, too, valued spruce gum, as would be expected in a land where so many of the *Picea* genus grow. It is, in fact, from Prussia that the spruce takes its common name. Courtiers in the reign of England's Henry VIII affected the dress of Prussian noblemen, those hautest of the haute who wore such fashionable attire as broad-brimmed hats with bright feathers, silver chains around their necks, satin cloaks and red velvet doublets. Anything from Prussia had been called "pruce" during the Middle Ages, but by the sixteenth century an *s* had somehow been prefixed to the word and dudes who dressed as elegantly as Prussian noblemen were said to be appareled in "spruce" fashion. Spruce soon meant a smart, dapper appearance, as is reflected in the phrase "to spruce up." The neat, trim form of the spruce tree may have suggested its name, too, but it could just as likely derive from the belief that the spruce was first grown in Prussia.

All types of *Picea* produce an abundance of resin, this genus name deriving from the Latin word for pitch. Here in America a number of our 30 or more cultivated spruce species—as well as other native trees like the Sweet Gum and Juniper—have been valued from colonial days for their chewy resins. But the black or bog spruce (*Picea mariana*), and the red spruce (*Picea rubens*) are the principal producers of resin gum. The Indians introduced us to chewing gum from these trees and they, in turn, may have emulated a bear or another animal "gumming up" on spruce resin in prehistoric times. Hunters say that bears customarily "gum up" before they hibernate by swallowing quantities of spruce gum as large as a man's fist. What's more, opossums and raccoons, when pursued by hunters, will fly for refuge to a gum tree in preference to any other, and hedgehogs feed upon the inner bark of spruces, their "hog cuts" causing injuries that are fruitful sources of gum. In an imaginary scenario we can visualize some Hiawatha of old shooting his arrow far into the air after some poor opossum who makes for a spruce, where a hedgehog has just finished gnawing a "hog cut" and a bear is pawing gum in his mouth as fast as it exudes. What's going down, Hiawatha thinks. He watches, from a safe distance, and when the bear moves on, he copies him, without swallowing the sticky stuff. Hey, this is pretty good, the great red hunter reflects, even cuts down on my thirst, and he keeps going back for more. Maybe Hiawatha eventually shares his secret with the tribe; perhaps he first shares his gum with the chief's sweetest daughter under a gum tree. Possibly another brave warrior spies him packing his mouth at the crotch of a spruce, thinks "What the hell is that dumb Hiawatha doing eating a tree?" and tries some himself. At any rate, chewing spruce gum for pleasure eventually becomes a tribal custom.

An unlikely story, but it dramatizes well and is probably as good an explanation as we have for the way man learned to chew spruce gum. After all, the first dog that buried a bone, the ants that stored provisions for a rainy day, the squirrels that hoarded nuts, the bees that gathered nectar and made it into honey—these were among the first creators of civilization; we watched them and learned. So why not a bear, or some other wild creature chewing gum? Anyway, the Indians used spruce gum as a refreshing thirst-quencher from earliest times. They often held it in the mouth without chewing it, provoking a flow of saliva and thus keeping the throat moist in the absence of water. No doubt they first introduced it to the white settlers along the North Atlantic Seaboard. The tribe responsible is hard to pinpoint, though it could have been the Maine Kennebecs, whom Champlain may have encountered when in 1604 he explored the long river, the cradle of Americans, that bears their name.

The Indians didn't introduce nearly as many vices as the whites, yet more than one moralist has condemned them not only for providing us with spruce gum to indulge our chewing habit, but for *causing* that habit as well. Toward the end of the last century an editorial writer blamed the entire "national gum-chewing disgrace" on the Indians. Let him tell the involuted tale in his own self-sure and inimitable manner:

> It is well known that all nerve tension or emotion finds vent or expression in muscular movement . . . In the early pioneer days of the country there were few idyllic pastoral conditions . . . The plowing of the settler had to be done while his rifle lay within easy reach, and at no time during the working day was there any relaxing of his constant, alert watchfulness for signs of the presence of the hostile

red man. Similarly, at night, when bolted and barred in
the bullet-proof security of his log cabin, he had no wak-
ing hour free from the nerve-racking alertness for the war-
ring whoop, or the silent dash. Eventually the enemy was
banished to remoter districts, and the nerve strain, as
such, became only a memory. But its effects remained
. . . In those early days the pleasures were limited and
primitive . . . hence it is to be surmised that the discovery
of spruce-gum conduced to the joy of the continent. And
thus it comes that in those early days of limited enjoyment, and under the widespread condition of a slightly
deteriorated nervous reserve, there grew into fashion the
use and practice of chewing gum. And this practice of
chewing gum is prevalent among us today; not for the
gustatory charm of the refractory mastic, but chiefly for
the unconscious nervous relief that the muscular act of
mastication provides . . .

Making Homemade Chewing Gum

If the Indians took a piece of our peace of mind while we
took large chunks of their land and livelihood, they at least
gave us a relatively harmless remedy and showed us where to
find it. We took everything from them in exchange for lies,
rotgut and reservations, while they pointed us into the woods
to search out the spruce tree and its consoling gum. The Indians had learned that trees on exposed ridges yielded more
resin than those in sheltered spots or on protected slopes and
that the best gumming was usually in mixed stands of spruce,
hemlock and hardwoods, not in pure spruce stands. They
taught the settlers to look for the drooping branches of the
black spruce or the tall, stately red spruce when they went
gumming and it was from the resins of these two trees that the
spruce gum industry evolved. New England settlers, and the
loggers after them, gummed all year round, but they soon discovered that spruce resin is too sticky in the summer and that
the best gumming time comes in early March, when the air is
redolent with the perfume of spruce and the denuded trees and
dead or dormant undergrowth make travel and visibility
easier. The highest quality gum, they found, usually comes
from the biggest trees. They also knew that every gum-

yielding tree has to have been wounded in some way—for when spruce bark is injured this touches off an alarm system in the tree, causing the pitch or resin to rush in and seal the break like a natural bandage until the tree can heal. Wounds can occur in numerous ways: hedgehogs feeding upon the inner bark of the spruces make hog cuts; there are lightning scars; forest fires; frost cracks; abrasions caused by neighboring falling trees; and even sapsucker drills. All provide fruitful sources for gum formation.

Although much gum is found high up in the spruces, a great deal occurs near the base and large quantities are harvested from the ground, where gum falls by frost action or the swaying of limbs in the wind. The gatherers tried to work systematically, each handling a strip of trees up to 70 feet wide, chopping off the gum with a long-handled axe where it could be reached easily or building staging on which to work if the gum was higher up. Only rarely was a tree cut down, as gummed woods of virgin forests are ready to work again five to seven years after a gumming.

The settlers had many other uses for the spruce besides chewing gum. Almost everything in the 30-to-90-foot-high tree was used except the wind in the boughs. The small globose cones made attractive decorations. Spruce masts for sailing ships were among the best and the black spruce was used for pulp in paper making, as it still is today. The red spruce became an important lumber tree and in later years the black spruce was put into service as a Christmas tree throughout New England. Settlers also imitated the Indians by using black spruce resin as caulking for their boats to prevent leakage. The pioneer American historian Francis Parkman wrote of such an experience on the Connecticut River in his 1842 *Journal*, describing how he and a companion took a makeshift leaking boat out of the water "and stuffed the seams with powdered spruce bark, chewed spruce gum and bits of cloth." The next day, however, "water spouted in like a stream from a pump" and the canoe "burst all to pieces."

Spruce boughs were used by the pioneers as mattresses and from the branches of the black spruce they obtained salves, medicines and stimulating spruce beer, a drink that dates back at least to the early sixteenth century in England ("Spruce beer . . . whyche makythe oft tymes men to stambur"). The colonists no doubt introduced this most potent of spruce products to the Indians. A fermented beverage made from the leaves and branches of the black spruce, and sometimes molasses and sassafras, spruce beer was said to be a powerful diuretic, "a kind of Physical Drink, good for inward bruises," an antiscorbutic, and "a wholesome beverage for the summer." It also got both whites and Indians high enough to have "more spruce beer in their bellies than wit in their heads . . ."

Gumming Up the Works

When the lumberjacks began to outnumber the settlers in the New England forests, the gumming tradition continued. Loggers collected the rocklike gobs of resin from the spruce and in their many idle hours by the campfire, whittled miniature barrels from blocks of cedar or white pine, hollowed them out, and filled them with the choicest gum the woods afforded as gifts for their wives, sweethearts, children or friends when they "came down" in the late spring. Many, of course, also went to the lively ladies and bartenders of Exchange Street and the Devils Half Acre in Portland, Maine and other logging cities.

The extent of loggers gathering gum across America is reflected in the language. Resins like spruce became widely available and "gum," for a chaw or piece of gum, was recorded in the dictionaries 50 years before chicle-based gum was invented. From chewing gum "gum-suckings" the word "gum-sucking" came to mean "soul kissing" and *Bartlett* defined it as "a disgusting word, applied to the tendency of lovers, young ones especially, to carry their innocent endearments to an excess that displeases a third party." One word detective even believes that the phrase "to gum up the works" derives from our early chewing habit. Trees like the spruce and sweet gum interested pioneers because of the fragrant resins they yielded, Webb Garrison notes in his *What's In A Word?* "Venturesome boys discovered the resin was pleasant to chew, so they frequently went on gumming expeditions. After gathering a quantity of the stuff, a youngster was likely to be daubed from head to foot. Gum was hard to wash from clothing—all but impossible to remove from one's hair. Indeed, an attempt to get gum off a person usually made matters worse. Proverbial sayings came to include many references to the stuff. Any person throwing a project into confusion was compared with a resin-smeared boy and said to gum up the works."

This theory may stretch the facts a little, but no better explanation has been offered for "to gum up the works." In any event, the lumberjacks, especially those along the Penobscot in Maine, still the best area for gumming in New England, created a market for resin chewing gum. Soon others were tramping out into the woods in early spring to supply this market. A gatherer, working from daylight to late afternoon, could gather 60 pounds of the gum in a good day's work. The demand was there, the supply seemed unlimited, and it wasn't long before an inventive Yankee took the initiative and became the first chewing gum manufacturer in the world . . .

Civilization's First Chewing Gum Maker

The man who started America and all peoplekind chewing gum on a grand scale was named John Curtis, a former seaman born in Bradford, Maine. In our best rags-to-riches tradition, he and his son John Bacon Curtis prepared the world's first commercial chewing gum in one of his wife's large pots on a Franklin stove in the small kitchen of their little Bangor home. It was the younger Curtis, a $5 a month swamper who cleared underbrush and blocked out roads through the woods, who first saw the possibilities for manufacturing spruce gum. His father, a cautious man, doubted that anyone would buy it and only after his family's prodding did he agree to make the first batch in the spring of 1848. From the beginning John B. handled the selling end of the business, while his father manned and managed the production line.

Sales were hard to come by at first. John B. walked the streets of Portland, Maine two full days talking spruce gum before he convinced a storekeeper to stock the family product. The gum quickly sold itself, but business was slow for the first few years, hardly enough to support a family, and young Curtis went on the road as a peddler, selling his spruce gum, patent medicines and whatever else he could take on. "Give a man all you can for his money, while making a fair profit yourself" was his motto, and he drove his team and cart throughout New England practicing what he pitched. He was so successful ("I was on the road while the other fellow was in bed") that he made the transition from peddler to commercial traveler, journeying all over the country selling his gum, which he carried with him, and as the representative of Eastern business houses. Indeed, some historians think John B. Curtis may have been one of America's first drummers, and he certainly traveled the West in advance of the railroads, using steamboat, canal boat, stage, horse, Shank's mare—whatever transportation he could get. "Many times I walked beside the stage with a rail on my shoulder, ready to help pry it out of the mud," he once said. "I passed hundreds of nights camping out with only a blanket for a covering and the ground for a bed. Did object to the rattlesnakes sometimes. It didn't pay to have them get too familiar . . . "

All for the glory of gum. The efforts of the young optimistic Curtis, who could have served as a model for William Wrigley Jr. in the future, introduced spruce gum to thousands of new customers. The product was made with great care. "State of Maine Pure Spruce Gum" wasn't sold fresh-picked, but was roughly refined first. Curtis and his son threw the raw gobs of gum, bark and all, into a big black kettle and boiled it into about the consistency of thick molasses, skimming the bark and other impurities as they rose to the surface. At this point, they may have added some lard or grease, or pitch and sap from other trees to the mix, and possibly even a little sugar (none of these would change the taste of spruce gum much, but would merely increase the volume and make the mixture thicker). For "State of Maine *Pure* Spruce Gum," however, no adulterants at all were added. The mixture was simply stirred until it became thicker and then poured out on a slab, where, while still hot, it was rolled out in a sheet about a ¼-inch thick and then chopped into pinkish pieces a ½-inch wide and ¾-inch long. These in turn were dipped in cornstarch, wrapped in tissue paper and sold as "State of Maine Pure Spruce Gum," about 20 pieces to the wooden box.

At two chaws for a penny (later a penny apiece) Curtis' spruce gum became a resounding success and he couldn't turn out his gum fast enough. He and his son advertised for more raw gum, which they bought in great quantities from lumberjacks, trappers, farmers, and a new breed of woodsmen who devoted themselves entirely to gum gathering in season and brought big bags of gum down to Bangor. The little Curtis Company grew so successful that Curtis was able to move into

Portland in 1850 to get closer to big city markets like Boston. There the younger Curtis invented a number of machines for making gum that formed the basis for the gum-making process in chewing gum plants everywhere. Other brands were added to the Curtis line: Yankee Spruce, American Flag, Trunk Spruce, and 200 Lump Spruce, the last a more natural-looking gum, though nearly all the brands were identical in flavor. One of these gums, C.C.C. (no one knows why it was so named, unless it simply meant Curtis Chewing Gum Company), was popular throughout America and the *Portland City Guide* notes that it "started the tireless wagging of stenographer's jaws throughout the world." Curtis made enough money to take on over 200 employees, who turned out nearly 1,800 boxes of spruce gum every day. Once he wrote a check for $35,000 worth (ten tons) of raw spruce gum—a record that has never been topped. In 1852 he erected the three-story Curtis Chewing Gum Factory, which, to quote the *Portland City Guide* again, was the first chewing gum factory in the world. Curtis & Son (the company kept its original name even after John Curtis died in 1869, aged 69) thrived until the early part of this century when it was acquired by the Sen-Sen Chiclet Company, which in turn merged with the American Chicle Company. The younger Curtis died in 1897, aged 70, a very wealthy man indeed.

Oddly enough, neither John Curtis nor his son ever patented their machines or their process for making spruce gum; they probably thought it was all too obvious. Hosts of imitations soon appeared on the market and they too sold well. Only in Maine, however, did the new firms rise up, mostly in the lower half of the state; other New Englanders appeared content just to gather their own spruce gum from the woods. Latecomers included the Maine Gum Company, the B.C. Oglivie Gum Company, Roudlett Brothers, Garceau and Thistle, The Happy Day Gum Company, and, naturally, the Hiawatha Gum Company.

One notable competitor was John Davis, who set up a small factory in Portland in 1850. Davis is said to have improved on his father's rudimentary attempts to prepare and market spruce gum and, but for a little luck, his father might have been the first man in history to manufacture chewing gum. Davis' business possibly survived until the late 1930's; at least a man by the name of Harry Davis was running the Eastern Gum Company at that time, employing some 20 gum gatherers, buying about 30,000 pounds of rough gum annually, and shipping his finished product out on the Monson-Maine Slate Company narrow gauge railroad, the only commercial line in New England. His was a fairly complex manufacturing operation, too, though on a much smaller scale than the Curtis firm's. But Davis found his market shrinking with each passing year; a lot of work was required for very small profits. Indeed, there were very few spruce gum manufacturers remaining toward the beginning of World War II. Except for workers at the Shaker Colony at Sabbath Day Lake, Maine, and perhaps a small firm in Canada, Davis seems to be the only maker of spruce gum left in the world at the time. In fact, if another Mainer hadn't stepped in to fill his shoes when he retired, the art of spruce gum making might have been lost forever . . .

"The Sole Remaining Maker of Genuine Spruce Gum Anywheres"

Spruce gum offers a good example of how popular tastes change. So many people were chewing the gum in the nineteenth century that according to Maine Forest Service records, the annual harvest of raw gum was estimated at over 150 tons and valued at $300,000, furnishing employment to hundreds. And these are very conservative figures; other writers put the yearly crude gum yield at closer to 1,500 tons. Gum chewing spread rapidly across nineteenth century America, long before chicle came on the scene. "There are the spruce gum-chewers, all backlotters; and vulgar," an early sermonizer despaired. "The careful observer cannot fail to note the prevalency of spruce gum chewing, and gum is universally chewed down East," a Maine newspaper pointed out a century later.

Today, only one spruce gum manufacturer remains in America, or in the world for that matter. He is the genial Gerrald F. Carr who lives in Portland, but does his gumming in Five Islands, Maine, which is near Bath. Carr, a Mainer from birth (60 years ago), is a railroad man "from way back," but has been making gum on the side since 1937, when he took over the C. A. McMahan Company owned by his wife's Canadian grandfather.

Conductor Carr is a hard man to catch between trains. Self-sufficient and low-keyed, his life-style is not a low-energy one. He commutes to his little factory in Five Islands, about 50 miles from Portland, "when the spruce is running," putting in about 30 hours a week in "a hobby that grew to be a monster." Still, this intrepid entrepreneur seems proud to be almost single-handedly keeping alive the age-old tradition of spruce gum chewing. He told me that he's held on to his business so he'll "have something to retire to in '76," not so much for the money as for his belief that spruce gumming kept both his father-in-law and father alive to ripe old ages.

Reading the scant literature on spruce gum and learning by trial and error, Carr built his Kennebec Spruce Gum Company up to the point where he now sells about two tons of processed gum every year. He makes only about $10,000 a year out of it, but the little business provides work for a dozen gatherers and satisfaction to thousands of customers who couldn't buy the gum anywhere if he didn't make it.

Carr can't collect much of the resin himself anymore, relying mainly on Nova Scotia gum hunters who would otherwise be unemployed during the winter months. The only reason he doesn't buy Maine spruce gum, he says, is because "It seems like nobody in the state of Maine wants to work too hard nowadays." One 82-year-old Maine man who lives in the Moose Head Lake area is an exception. This venerable gentleman sends Carr a large quantity of resin every year, even smelting it down first, shipping it out every week on the one plane connecting Moose Head Lake with the mainland. Another Mainer brought in 800 pounds of good gum last year, "hunks the size of your fist," but for the most part the Nova Scotians do the collecting. Carr pays them from 75 cents to $1.25 a pound, depending on the gum's quality, and takes care of all expenses, including shipping costs and the brokerage fee required. One can think of only a few occupations as lonely and unremunerative as gumming—beachcombing, "stooping" at racetracks, ragpicking, wormdigging, writing—but an industrious picker does make as much as $1,000 a year. Not by putting anything over on Mr. Carr, though. "Some of them try to sell me gum with the bahrk still on it," he says. "Think they're kiddin' me, but I know when there's bahrk—I've been smelting it out for fahty years."

Carr's gatherers work the woods with hatchets, hunting knives and sometimes a gum-gathering gadget that consists of a long hoe handle with a miniature basket attached to the end; the gadget is used to scrape higher-up portions of trees, gum falling into the basket. Coming down from the woods with their "nuggets" in their shoulder packs, the pickers mail their gum off when they have collected enough for a large shipment. Now that snowmobiles are being used extensively in place of snowshoes, and gatherers can work hitherto inaccessible areas, gum picking has picked up and so has Carr's work at Five Islands. But his business has always been an "up and down thing," as he puts it. Due to a box shortage in World War II and during a long illness he was forced to halt his operation entirely, but on the other hand he once had a number of salesmen working for him.

The spruce gum magnate, who runs a one-man factory, boils the resin he purchases in a "sixty gallon black kettle," adding oleo for a softening agent and pitch and sap from other evergreens to increase the volume. This brew is all melted, "cooking to 240° F, its top boiling point before it starts to go down," and then strained. It is next poured into a tub of ice water and strained again. Little pieces of bark still manage to get through ("cahn't be prevented"), but most are caught floating in the ice water. The next step is pulling the mixture over a hook by hand, similar to the way taffy is stretched, and the longer the gum is pulled the softer it gets. All that remains then is to let the gum harden, break it in pieces and roll it in cornstarch. Carr used to make rolled strips, individually wrapped in tissue, but paper is so expensive that he can't afford to anymore.

The small nuggets resulting from the refining process are packed in little 2½x½x1-inch boxes, which sell for 20 cents direct from Carr, but cost up to half a dollar in "some fancy tourist stores." The logo reads KENNEBEC SPRUCE GUM—FROM THE . . . FORESTS OF MAINE—PUT UP BY G. F. CARR & CO. FIVE ISLANDS, MAINE. A bright red Indian in war bonnet, battle axe in one hand and spear in the other, whoops it up opposite KENNEBEC.

Kennebec spruce gum is sold as a novelty item in many Maine gift shops and general stores, including the famous L. L. Bean's, but its mail-order market extends to Hawaii, Alaska and every state in the Union, as well as Canada, Mexico and England. Many customers are "displaced Mainers," but a number of out-of-staters have been converted to the chewable spruce. Carr's success is all the more unusual in this day and age because he doesn't believe in advertising and isn't much on pushing either his gum or himself. Wouldn't even go on "What's My Line?" His gum does get some plugs, though. "That entertainer Fred Allen," he told me, once sent a $10 check—"With his picture on it; they're all vain, y'know"—ordering gum to be sent to a friend who had had all his teeth yanked out. "Bragged about it on the radio, he did." Word-of-mouth is what sells the gum. Schoolchildren often write for a piece, enclosing a nickel, and Carr tries to oblige, though "the return postage is double that." One letter from New Jersey took just two days to reach him. It read: "To the sole remaining maker of genuine spruce gum anywheres, somewhere in Maine."

People may be chewing spruce gum for health reasons today, thanks to the "natural foods" craze. Carr says he's been told the spruce helps cure motion sickness, is good for the gums and aids digestion because it creates move saliva than sugar-based gums. But he makes no claims. "One woman tells me it's the only thing that helps her arthritis," he says. "Now that's ridiculous. I'm filled with arthritis myself—nothin' helps arthritis, 'ceptin' aspirin." On the other hand, spruce gum can't do a body no harm. "Some Florida woman was chewin' it years before she noticed the bahrk in it," he told me. "Wrote asking me if she'd been eating aunts all those years. Had to write back and tell her there's no way to get all the bahrk out and that it can't hurt you nohow." Carr never did answer the Connecticut woman who purchased his gum and wrote to him enclosing her picture and proposing marriage. "Could it be spruce gum is an aphrodisiac?" I asked. "Don't make any claims," he said. "How did your wife react to that letter?" I rejoined. "Get a lot of strange mail," said the gum czar.

Spruce gum isn't sweet like most commercial gums, to the displeasure of some Kennebec customers. It's also harder to chew. You have to patiently "tame" it, for after first chomping into the spruce nugget, you feel like you're sinking your teeth into frozen gasoline. But don't give up, keep on chewing. In a minute or so your teeth and the heat of your mouth may work a minor gustatory miracle. The amber and tan nugget, its texture like partially crystallized rock candy, will soften (though never like commercial gum) and turn a pinkish tan color. Gradually the turpentine flavor will become "woodsy," "wild," "tangy," "pungent," "clear," "refreshing." It's an acquired taste though, as with fiddleheads and other wild things, and some people never acquire it.

There are even people who like spruce gum because it's "foul-tasting." Many years ago, the manager of Durgin-Park, the venerable Boston restaurant opposite Faneuil Hall, had to find a replacement for the spruce gum brand it had traditionally sold as a confection at the cashier's desk. After tasting several sleazy imitations, the manager finally came upon a farmer who gave him a sample he knew was just right. "It tasted as rotten as the old stuff and it pulled a $6 filling right out of my tooth," he said. "Perfect."

No matter how it tastes, spruce gum does always give you a hard jaw-cracking chaw. You can chew it for hours before it loses its flavor. And it might well be just the thing for dieters, tobacco addicts, ulcer sufferers, neurasthenics, the weak-jawed, the big-mouthed . . . Just don't set your spruce gum aside chewed and expect to resume chawing on it later—it falls apart in the mouth like gravel the second time around. Mr. Carr should really put chewing instructions on each box, and I suggested this to him. "Cahn't, wouldn't know what to take off to make room," he said . . .

A Lament for Spruce Gum

Spruce gum is the gum of our ancestors, the link between Congressmen blowing bubbles in committee and the patriots chawing till they saw the whites of the other fellows' eyes on Bunker Hill. Abe Lincoln probably chewed it, or the resin of some tree, and the railsplitter only made four visits to the dentist in all his years. It is the gum of romance that Becky Thatcher gave to Tom Sawyer in Mark Twain's classic work of youth and love, which was set in the 1840's. Becky didn't care much for swinging dead rats around her head on a string, as Tom did. "What I like is chewing gum," she told him. "Oh, I should say so," Tom replied. "I wish I had some now." "Do you? I've got some," said Becky to her secret love. "I'll let you chew it awhile, but you must give it back to me." In Mark Twain's words: "That was agreeable, so they chewed it turn about, and dangled their legs against the bench in excess of contentment."

Tom Sawyer thought so much of the old-time gum that he

told Huckleberry Finn, in Twain's classic of that name, that
when a magician rubs a lamp and genies "come tearing in,"
they've got to do everything he says: "If he tells them to build a
palace forty miles long out of Di'monds, and fill it full of chewing gum, or whatever you want . . . " Di'monds and chewing
gum, one as valuable as the other; spruce gum was once that
important. If Mr. Carr ever goes out of business, we'll still be
able to walk in the woods and take our spruce gum straight
from the plated bark of the tree—and many people say it's
tastier that way, too; kids still scrape it off spruces with jack-
knives and after much labor reduce it to aromatic spruce-
flavored balls. But the demise of Carr's business will mark the
end of the commercial spruce gum industry, which for a brief
period of time monopolized the chewing gum trade and made
Maine the chewing gum capital of the world. Perhaps the industry will be revived, the American palate cultivated again to
the pleasures of spruce gum, but one doubts it. For better or
worse, Americans are into a sweeter, softer chew, as astute
businessmen discovered when the spruce gum industry began
to decline.

CHAPTER 4

The Genesis of a One-Cent Giant: Chicle Gum Is Born

IT was Richard Hoe's rotary printing press that sounded the death knell of the spruce gum industry. None was as yet obese as the Sunday *New York Times,* but as the nation's newspapers gained weight, publishers demanded more and more wood pulp to feed the greedy presses. All-out war was declared on the great spruce forests; the axes and saws sang their duet of destruction and raw gum became increasingly scarce, forcing the gum harvesters to flee the forest or take to cutting down trees themselves.

A few spruce gum manufacturers held out, but most had to find another way to satisfy the gnawing national need to chaw on something good. Though mastic gums like "Rose Mastic"

39

and "Mastic Hearts" were tried, the gum makers found their salvation in a substance that had been discovered in 1830: paraffin. This colorless, odorless and tasteless mineral wax would not seem to be an appetizing thing to chomp on, but it is really no worse than the synthetic–base chewing gums made today. Paraffin, like today's synthetics, is obtained in the distillation of wood, coal and oil shale, but its chief commercial source is the fractional distillation of crude petroleum, a process perfected and patented in 1850 by Scottish industrial chemist James Young. Young, of course, had no idea that his mineral wax—used mostly in making candles and in waterproofing—would be the basis of a chewing gum.

Paraffin manufacture falls into two broad steps: the distillation of the crude oil and then the extraction of wax from the distillate—the paraffin crystallizing out when the oil which remains after the gasoline and kerosene fractions have been distilled off is cooled. There were plentiful sources for the substance in the early nineteenth century; indeed, conservationists won't be overjoyed to know that in 1865, according to the London *Times*, "The hon. secretary to the River Dee Salmon Fishery had preserved a bottle of pure paraffin made from the waters of the Dee." In any event, with Young's refining of the white, waxy, translucent solid the paraffin gum industry briefly blossomed.

The first person to make chewing gum from commercial paraffin is a mystery, but it may have been the same John Curtis who made spruce gum a big business. Curtis and his son did start turning out paraffin-base gums in their Portland factory around 1850, no doubt due to the spruce gum shortage, and brands like "Licorice Lulu," "Four-in-Hand," "Biggest & Best," "White Mountain," and "Sugar Cream" helped them outlast all their competitors. Curtis' popular White Mountain was a stick about three inches long and half as thick as a lead pencil, wrapped in colored tissue paper. Scores of imitators like "Common Stick Gum," "Tin Foil Gum," and "Motto Gum," came on the scene, however, capitalizing on the abundance of paraffin and the discovery that Americans were beginning to like their chaws with a lot of sweet flavoring added. Paraffin also has the honor of being the first gum to attain the dignity of a fancy wrapper and carry the added lure of the "picture cards" that later became a staple of bubble gum. Made

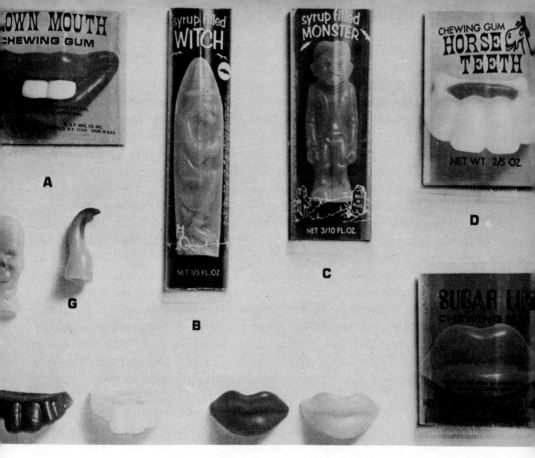

Paraffin gums, petroleum derived, were chewed long before chicle. A wide assortment of chewable paraffin novelties have been popular with kids for half a century. *W & F Mfg. Co., Inc.*

on greased marble tables, to keep the wax from sticking when rolled, it was sweetened, vanilla-flavored and wrapped in bright-colored paper. Most people did prefer it to spruce.

Nearly a century and a quarter has passed and today only one major paraffin gum firm exists in America. Aside from a few seasonal manufacturers, the W & F Mfg. Co. of Buffalo, New York comprises what was once an important industry. Mr. P. J. Brind Amour of W & F advises that the basic raw materials used in his gums are pure food-grade paraffin, sugar, coloring and flavoring. "The paraffin is supplied by refiners in tank trucks," he says, "and is stored in our plant in heated tanks. It is then pumped from the tanks into mixing vats where the proper amounts of sugar, color and flavor are added. The mixture is next piped into molds to form the different novelty shapes. The molds are chilled to harden the paraffin, then the figures are removed from the molds and taken to the packaging area."

W & F produces more than 1,000 variations of nearly 700 confectionary items. The operation began in 1926 with chewable penny paraffin when the company's founder, F. C. Gurley, Sr., mortgaged his home to buy a bankrupt candy firm a Canadian named John White had been forced to list in the papers under "Business Opportunities." White had invented a machine to make those tiny, edible wax bottles filled with a nip of sweet syrup that kids still enjoy everywhere, but though his machine was a success, sales weren't. Gurley's business acumen changed all this and within a year the company grew out of its loft and into a small plant, thanks mainly to a dainty "penny-nip" doll that he designed. Since then horse teeth, comic lips, wax mustaches, red noses and purple lips—all chewable— have been added to the line. The clown in every kid still loves them and parents still despair of them: Fangs, Buck Teeth, False Tongues, Wowee Wax Whistles, Slurpys . . . It's the ambrosia of youth, all that sticky sweet stuff, and it provides disguises to break up the class the instant the teacher's back is turned, but it isn't quite good enough for a chewing gum. Despite its attractiveness for use in children's novelty items, sweetened paraffin wax is not a very good chew. Unlike spruce gum, its sugary flavor quickly fades and like spruce it requires the heat and moisture of the mouth to render it suitable for chewing. Refined paraffin wax is now used as a chewing gum ingredient, but even as far back as 1850 people realized that it would have to be replaced by other substances as a base for regular gums. Spruce resin and paraffin had contributed the words chewing gum to the language, had begun the tradition of penny gum and brought pleasure to millions, but the search for the perfect chaw had to go on. . .

Chewing on Rubber—
The First Patented Gum

Among the first of Yankee inventors to pursue the golden gum grail was a "polished, genial, broadminded" dentist from Mount Vernon, Ohio. William F. Semple (not Simple or Wil-

liams & Semple, as many accounts have it) has the signal honor
of being the first person anywhere to patent a chewing gum
("It took an American to attach property rights to this universal
and timeless pastime," one writer notes). In 1869 Semple filed
the patent reproduced below with the U. S. Commissioner of
Patents.

A rather vague all-encompassing patent this, though acceptable to the Patent Office at the time, but, as the bubble gum
industry later proved, Dr. Semple was on the right track in
using rubber as his primary base. The trouble was that he did
nothing further with his invention, which included little flavoring and was to be used for jaw exercise and gum stimulation
as well as pure pleasure. The "industrious and frugal" Semple,
who was known for his "painful extractions" and his "midnight ramblings with a small dog," went on to file several other
patents based on rubber, and patented a stove, never even

United States Patent Office.

WILLIAM F. SEMPLE, OF MOUNT VERNON, OHIO.

Letters Patent No. 98,304, dated December 28, 1869.

IMPROVED CHEWING-GUM.

The Schedule referred to in these Letters Patent and making part of the same.

To all whom it may concern:

Be it known that I, WILLIAM F. SEMPLE, of Mount
Vernon, county of Knox, and State of Ohio, have invented a new and improved Chewing-Gum; and I do
hereby declare that the following is a full, clear, and
exact description of the same.

The nature of my invention consists in compounding with rubber, in any proportions, other suitable
substances, so as to form not only an agreeable chewing-gum, but also, that from the scouring-properties of
the same, it will subserve the purpose of a dentifrice.

It is well known that rubber itself is too hard to be
used as a chewing-gum, but in combination with non-
adhesive earths may be rendered capable of kneading
into any shape under the teeth.

In the manufacture of this improved chewing-gum,
no vulcanizing-process is employed. It is produced
by simply dissolving the rubber in naphtha and alcohol, and when of the consistence of jelly, mixing with
it prepared chalk, powdered licorice-root, or any other
suitable material, in the desired proportions, and subsequently evaporating the solvents.

I do not, however, confine myself to this method
alone for the manufacture of the gum. For commercial
purposes, other equally effectual processes may be used
for the uniting of the rubber with suitable substances.

Instead of the solvents named, any other that will
soften the rubber, without being offensive, may be employed, such as paraffine, spermaceti, wax, gums, resins, and the like. Any of the materials commonly used
for the manufacture of dentifrices may be combined
with the rubber, such as orris-root, myrrh, licorice-
root, sugar, barytes, charcoal, &c.

By the term "rubber," I wish to include the allied
vegetable gums, which are ordinarily known as the
equivalents of caoutchouc.

Having thus fully described my invention,

What I claim as new, and desire to secure by Letters Patent, is—

The combination of rubber with other articles, in
any proportions adapted to the formation of an acceptable chewing-gum.

W. F. SEMPLE.

Witnesses:
    O. MAGERS,
    T. V. PARKR.

attempting to market his gum, which might have brought him a great many new patients if nothing else. In any event, his idea became no more than an historical curiosity and for a time it looked like the mouths of America might be forever sealed shut. Luckily, however, another inventor had already made the connection that was to provide the cornerstone for the modern chewing gum industry . . .

The Chicle Connection

Thomas Adams Sr. is not listed in the *Dictionary of American Biography* along with John, John Quincy, Charles Francis, Franklin Pierce, James Truslow, Hannah, Maude, Henry, Samuel and other great Adams. But surely the man who gave us penny chicle sticks of "health-giving, circulation-building, teeth-preserving, digestion-aiding, brain-refreshing, chest-developing, nerve-settling, soul-tuning chewing gum" deserves a few lines therein. His connection with Mexican General Antonio Lopez de Santa Anna is a story in itself.

Unlike Adams, General Santa Anna has no publicity problems with posterity. He saw to this from the moment he entered politics, stage right; exposure, as we call it today, was in fact a guiding principle of his life. Exposure and expedience. Joining the Spanish army at the age of 14, Antonio Lopez de Santa Anna became a violent partisan against Mexican independence, but quickly changed sides when he found that there was little hope of real personal advancement under the Spanish despotism. So he reentered the political world, stage left. His actions were always to be governed by opportunism rather than any fixed principle. Cruel, fiery, even heroic, blessed with a shrewd political sense and magnetic personality, this handsome part-Indian was to become Mexico's most unpredictable *caudillo* or boss, and was probably the chief contributor to the disturbed condition of Mexico for over 30 years. An early victory over the Spanish earned him the title of "the hero of Tampico," which he relished ever afterward and used to help win him the presidency of his country in 1833. Not a big man, but imposing like Bonaparte, he fancied himself a western Napoleon, with a Napoleonic belief in his star and a Napoleonic lust for power. Perhaps this is why he resigned the presidency temporarily in 1836 to lead the campaign against Texas, then trying to gain its independence from Mexico.

Santa Anna led a force of over 6,000 men across the Rio

Grande to storm the Alamo at San Antonio with its relative handful of defenders. After several days' siege, he massacred the survivors, Davy Crockett and Jim Bowie among them, and a month later, under his express orders, a Texan force of 300 was brutally massacred at Goliaid after it had unconditionally surrendered. Because of these slaughters he justly became an ogre in America and the slogan "Remember the Alamo! Remember Goliaid!" became the battlecry of the victorious Texans when they defeated him under General Sam Houston at San Jacinto. Why General Houston did not execute this self-styled Caesar after taking him prisoner remains something of an historical mystery, but Houston always claimed the safety of "the little scoundrel" was necessary to insure peace between Texas and Mexico. What Santa Anna did was to buy his freedom by signing a treaty recognizing Texas' independence, although his government predictably repudiated both him and the treaty soon after.

This did not faze the unscrupulous Santa Anna. Back in Mexico he took part in the defense of Vera Cruz against the French in 1837, losing his leg in the battle and becoming something of a martyr. Within a few years he was in control again and became dictator of his country. Santa Anna, however, was the original revolving president of Mexico. In 1845 he was deposed and exiled to Cuba for ten years, the first of several exiles and triumphant returns that eventually found him aboard a U.S. warship sailing for New York. Why, no one knows, but Secretary of State William Seward furnished him passage to New York, where he lived on Staten Island for five years, "spending his time in cock fighting and playing Spanish monte," according to one account.

Staten Island seems to have been a haven for political exiles in the last century—Garabaldi was another notable who found refuge there. No doubt Santa Anna did his share of cock fighting and card playing, hard drinking and womanizing while at Sailors Snug Harbor. But he still planned a return to power, and that is where Thomas Adams Sr. and chewing gum entered the story, stage center. It's said that Adams Sr. had made Santa Anna's acquaintance briefly during the fifties, but there is no mention of this in the general's memoirs and it hasn't been proved one way or the other. The chance meeting is actually only one of a number of possibly apocryphal tales attached to the story of the first chicle gum. The human mind, being part of nature, abhors a vacuum, and where few facts exist, legends grow. We can only make the best of it. What we do know is that Adams was born in New York City in 1818, was orphaned at the age of nine, later married Martha Dunbar, and sired seven children, four sons among them. An intelligent, inventive man of many talents, he seemed unable to find anything worthy of his genius until, well into his middle age, he became America's first chicle gum czar. Adams had been something of a daguerreotypist, good enough to have been appointed a military photographer when he enlisted at the outbreak of the Civil War. He served in that position for three years, assisted by his son Thomas, taking a lot of pictures of men in uniform to be sent home as mementoes, but soon switched from photography to a number of other trades, trying all the while to find the proper outlet for his inventive streak. A burner for kerosene lamps and a horse feed bag that Adams invented did come into wide use, but most of his gadgets brought him little or no return. The restless Yankee finally became a wholesale glass merchant, opening a store on Cortlandt Street in Manhattan, just a block from where the Staten Island Ferry docked then at Liberty Street, but he always remained an inventor at heart.

It so happened that Adams was the right man in the right place at the right time. For Rudolph Napegy, General Santa Anna's personal secretary, traveled regularly between Staten Island and Manhattan on errands for *el caudillo*. One day he was attracted by a display in Adams' window and entered his store to make an enquiry. This was the beginning of a series of visits that led to a pleasant acquaintance, if not a deep friendship, in the course of which Napegy became aware of Adams' inventive talents. As fate would have it, Napegy also knew that his boss, like most deposed dictators, needed money for his perpetual plan to raise an army which would march on and "liberate" his country, not to mention money to pay his secretary's salary. Napegy reported back to Santa Anna, who thought that Adams would be just the man to do something with the chicle he had brought with him from Mexico.

Chicle had for some years been gathered from sapodilla trees in Mexico and shipped to the U.S. in an effort to induce rubber manufacturers to mix the latex with rubber or use it as a rubber substitute. All previous attempts had failed, but Santa Anna was convinced that a good Yankee inventor could do the job. The profits would be enormous: wild crude rubber (rubber plantations weren't conceived until the early twentieth century) then sold for one dollar a pound, the dried sap of the sapodilla going for only five cents a pound. Some gum historians say that Santa Anna was so confident that he brought 500 pounds of chicle with him into exile, sacrificing many of his personal belongings in order to do so, but the evidence is that he brought only a large hunk of the stuff. At any rate, early in 1869, he either arranged for his aide to bring Adams a chunk of chicle to work with or to have Adams visit with him on Staten Island. Since Adams did visit Santa Anna there on several occasions, the historic meeting on the island probably did take place.

So one fine morning Adams and his son Thomas Jr. boarded the Staten Island Ferry (until recently still a nickel, as it was in those days) and called upon Santa Anna in Sailors Snug Harbor. Adams wasn't, as various accounts say, Santa Anna's landlord, didn't run a boarding house where Santa Anna roomed and find a chunk of chicle in the dictator's dresser drawer. Adams' youngest son John hadn't been Santa Anna's secretary and didn't steal any chicle from him. Neither did Santa Anna visit Adams and bring some chicle to chew in an overnight bag which one of Adams' children ransacked. It was in Santa Anna's little stone house in Sailors Snug Harbor that the two men met, and from the testimony of an Adams' grandson, combined with contemporary descriptions of the general, we can attempt to reconstruct that historic scene on Staten Island.

Adams and his son were greeted by a fine-looking old gentleman not yet bowed down by the weight of age in his seventy-fifth year of life. Santa Anna's upright, shoulders-back military carriage prevailed still, his hair abundant and jet black, his oil-black gleaming eyes confiding that the fires of his life were far from spent. Still slim-built, with no trace of a paunch, the generalissimo was as smooth-skinned as he had been in earlier days, and his face had a kindly expression strangely at variance with the almost universal idea of his character and the psychopathology of his will. But the man's great pride was obvious. When he sat on the sofa, he hid his false leg, throwing it out directly before him, covering it with his left leg, and never moving from that position for the entire visit. Slightly deaf, he simply ignored anything he didn't hear, never apologizing, and his regal manner precluded anyone from even smiling at the badly fitting set of false teeth he wore. He talked freely and vivaciously, Napegy translating (for *el caudillo* had never bothered to learn English), but he already lived at present in the past, perhaps knowing deep down that the future held little for him. He delighted to recount his own exploits in the minutest particulars, but as to passing events of the day, he didn't even know that Ulysses S. Grant was president. Adams listened as he explained the one thing in the future that did interest him, even obsessed him.

"I need millions, Señor Adams," Santa Anna confided. "To equip a new army and march on Mexico City. I shall be presidente again!"

Adams blinked when the general commanded Napegy to bring him his bag and he plunked down on the table what seemed to be a large lump of soil covered with bark and pebbles. "Millions, millions of dollars!" Santa Anna declared, greedily fingering the stuff. "We can make millions, Señor Adams. Here is the treasure of Mexico. You are the Yankee inventor. This is chicle, the latex of the sapodilla tree which we have in great abundance in my country—and you can convert it into a rubber substitute!"

Here we might add that some gum historians claim Santa Anna first chewed a pinch of the chicle and that "the inquisitive Adams asked to see the stuff." But a man with badly fitting false teeth wouldn't likely be chewing chicle and one imagines that a request to see what a distinguished host was chewing would have to be delicately put (though people used to walk up to Charles Lindbergh in restaurants and peer in his mouth to see what he was eating). More likely Santa Anna just mentioned the fact that Mexicans had chewed chicle from the time of the Aztecs, taking great pains to conceal his own teeth as he spoke. From all the information available it would seem that Adams simply agreed with the presidente-in-exile that chicle could be a big money-maker, or had possibilities, and took home a large chunk to experiment with. Santa Anna's handing over of that ball of chicle was to become by the irony of time a more far-reaching act than any in his long, tempestuous career . . .

The Adams' Idea

After arranging with friends in Mexico to send Adams a ton or more of chicle, which Adams paid for, Santa Anna seems to fade from the chewing gum picture. Fuming at first over the inventor's lack of progress in devising a rubber substitute, the general lost all interest within a few months. Several years later he took advantage of a political amnesty and returned to Mexico, where he died in poverty and neglect, aged 81, never even suspecting that he had made a great contribution to the chewing gum cause. Meanwhile, Adams and several friends, a chemist among them, continued his secret experiments in the kitchen of his home on Palisade Avenue (near Hoboken Avenue) in Jersey City Heights, New Jersey. Adams ruined all his wife Martha's pots and pans in the process. Experimenting on the kitchen stove like Firestone a quarter-century before, he had visions of chicle bicycle tires, chicle carriage tires, even thought his "new kind of rubber" might work as a setting for false teeth—an idea a dentist friend scornfully rejected. Yet try as he did, he couldn't vulcanize the sapodilla latex. If he had been able to, the world might now be wearing spearmint bras and chiclet girdles, driving cars that roll on Juicy Fruit tires, and Adams would have become even richer than he did. But no matter how the sap was boiled and refined it never acquired the characteristics of rubber, lacking its elasticity, resiliency and wearing power. The stuff shredded to pieces, wouldn't bounce, wouldn't erase. According to his son Horatio, Adams was ready to quit until fate intervened in the form of a gum-chewing little girl. A document unearthed from the archives of the American Chicle Company gives the full story for the first time. Horatio, who died in January 1956, aged 103 (see what gum chewing can do for you!) told the tale at a banquet given for American Chicle Company managers in 1944.

After about a year's work in blending the chicle with rubber, the experiments were adjudged a failure. The gum chicle was in a warehouse on Front Street in New York City. My father, Mr. Thomas Adams Sr., had about made up his mind to throw the whole lot into the East River, as it had no value for any purpose known at that time. But it so happened that before this was done, Thomas Adams Sr. went into a drugstore on the corner of Chambers Street and Broadway to purchase something. [In another account Horatio put the store at Newark Avenue, Jersey City.] While there, a little girl came in and asked for a penny's worth of chewing gum. It was known to Mr. Adams that chicle had been used as a chewing gum by the natives of Mexico for many years, and as they themselves had been chewing it while experimenting with the rubber blending scheme, the idea struck him that perhaps they might be able to make chewing gum out of chicle and so salvage the lot in storage. After the child left the store, Mr. Adams Sr. asked the druggist what kind of chewing gum the little girl had bought. He was told that it was made of paraffin wax, was called White Mountain, and was 'pretty poor gum.' When he asked the man if he would be willing to try an entirely different kind of gum, the druggist agreed. When Mr. Adams arrived home that night, he spoke to his son, Tom Jr., my oldest brother, about his idea. Junior was very much impressed and suggested that they make up a few boxes of chicle chewing gum . . .

All five Adams men then went to work on what became known as "the Adams' idea." Everybody had a hand in the pot: Adams Sr. and Jr.; John; the baby Garrison; and Horatio, only a boy of 16 at the time. "That evening," Horatio confided to a reporter on another occasion, "my father and I took some of the chicle and put it into hot water. We left it there until it was about the consistency of putty. Then we wet our hands, rubbed and kneaded it and finally rolled it into little balls—two hundred of them. It was no longer brownish black, but a kind of grayish white." Modern chewing gum, down to the exact color, was finally born to this little gleam of time between two eternities!

Adams' unsweetened grayish white chewing gum balls were sent to his druggist friend in Jersey City, who took them on as he had promised. Adams told him the supply would "probably last three months," but the owner turned on local schoolchildren to the two-for-a-penny item and it sold out before noontime. This encouraging news sent the inventor trotting back to his stove to cook his chicle to an even smoother consistency and package some more. The Adams family pooled their resources, $35 to $55, according to the gum ur-materials, and went into business. As Horatio told the American Chicle managers, it was decided to give the gum a name and Thomas

Adams Jr., then a salesman in wholesale tailors' trimmings who traveled as far West as the Mississippi, agreed to hawk it on one of his sales trips. The brand name chosen was Adams' New York Gum No. 1—Snapping and Stretching. Recalled Horatio:

> It was made in little sticks, and wrapped in various colored tissue papers. The retail value of the box (200 pieces), I believe, was one dollar. On the cover of the box was a picture of City Hall, New York, in color. My brother started on his regular trip through the West with about 25 boxes of the gum. He did not succeed in selling a single box to the drug trade, which he saw every day after visiting his regular customers in the tailors' trimming business. On returning home, of course, he had to report that he had been unsuccessful, but he was certainly not discouraged and was determined to take it out again on his next trip. He said at that time if he could not sell any of it, he wouldn't bring it home. He would give it to the druggists if they would promise to display it on the counters. This

Adams made drugstores the primary outlet for his Adams #1, the first modern chewing gum. *American Chicle Company*

time he succeeded, and left on consignment all the boxes of gum that he took out. Before his return to New York, reorders for chewing gum were coming in to his father in New York City to the amount of 300 boxes in total. This was very encouraging to both of them, and Mr. Thomas Adams Jr. decided to leave his job and devote himself to building up a business in chewing gum . . . Of course, he did not fail and the business grew very rapidly. A small building [actually a loft of 725 square feet] in Jersey City was rented and 25 girls were hired to wrap the gum by hand. Later other gums were brought out, such as Adams' New York No. 2. This was a larger package. There also was Adams' Sapota and two or three other brands . . .

"Immoral" Gum and the Immovable-Jawed

The "Adams' idea" proved a success from the very beginning, but there were some sticky problems during the early chewing gum years, especially from immovable-jawed moralizers. Erstwhile scientists spread rumors that chicle gum was really made of horses' hooves and glue, that if one swallowed a chunk it would make the intestines stick together, causing appendicitis or instant death. Puritans convinced many parents that gum was a "vice," schoolteachers rapped pupils' knuckles for chewing it in class, and actresses playing ladies of loose morals on the stage early adopted gum chewing as an obvious mannerism. Even Anthony Comstock got into the act. Comstock, who had destroyed some 160 tons of books, stereotyped plates, magazines and pictures in his 40-odd year career as a self-appointed crusader against "immorality," was chief special agent for the New York Society for the Suppression of Vice, which he had founded, giving him the power of an inquisitor general. His name, in the form of comstockery, became a synonym for narrow-minded, bigoted and self-righteous moral censorship, the word coined by George Bernard Shaw after Comstock vehemently objected to Shaw's play *Mrs. Warren's Profession*. It's apparent that Comstock would hate anything as voluptuous and juicy as someone smacking his lips and sucking on a piece of gum, but he couldn't do anything about it until Thomas Adams Sr., in an attempt to build up his business, came up with the "prize package." The idea was to insert a ticket in each box of gum, each ticket redeemable for prizes ranging from a tin whistle to a grand piano. "Sales soon boomed," Horatio Adams recalled. "Then along came a reformer named Anthony Comstock, who came to the conclusion that the prize package business was a violation of the lottery law in New York City . . . " The Adams' concern was summoned to court for trial and the court ordered that the prize packages had to be discontinued.

Comstock had his small victory, though it didn't matter much. Adams' chicle gum was too firmly entrenched in the mouths of America. In fact, by 1871 the inventive Adams had devised the first patented gum-making machine, which kneaded and ran the chicle out in long thin strips notched by a toothlike attachment so that a duggist could break off penny lengths. Next he turned his efforts toward putting some taste in the chicle. He tried sassafras first and then shredded licorice into the puttylike mass, perfecting a licorice-anise flavor called Adams' Black Jack, which is still made by the American Chicle Company and is the oldest flavored gum on the market today.

American Chicle Company

Adams and Sons did so well that they moved from their plant in Jersey City, which was, oddly enough, next door to a candy store run by George William Loft, who went on to make a fortune with Loft's Candy. They moved to new, larger quarters at 58-60 Vesey Street in New York in 1876 and to still larger quarters on Sands Street in Brooklyn 12 years later. Finally, the company settled at a plant in Manhattan at 77 Murray Street. By that time Adams gums, including a fruit-based Tutti-Fruitti, were even a smash in vending machines. Tutti-Fruitti, incidentally, was probably the first gum to be widely advertised. Horatio Adams noticed that euchre, an immensely popular card game at the time, was being advertised on simple posters bearing two crossed euchre hands, the words "Which Hand Wins?" printed beneath them. He promptly had a photographer make a reproduction of one of the signs and the euchre hands soon appeared on wrappers of Tutti-Fruitti gum. Euchre hands had nothing whatsoever to do with chewing gum, but placards bearing the same logo were strung up all along Broadway.

Chewing gum patriarch Thomas Adams Sr. died of pneumonia in 1905, aged 87, at his home on Washington Avenue in Brooklyn. He had retired only six years before when his company was merged with eight others into the American Chicle Company, his son Thomas Jr. becoming the first chairman of the Board of Directors of this new organization. For many years his widow, four sons and three daughters received handsome dividends from American Chicle and when Thomas Jr. died in 1926, 80 years old, he left a fortune of nearly $2 million. Not bad for a $35 business begun on a kitchen stove.

Which is all in the best tradition of American capitalism, but which is getting ahead of our story. More important is the fact that what is decidedly America's zaniest and most secretive industry had been born from a ball of chicle, which was to remain the base of all chewing gums for almost a century. Chicle, chewed neat, tastes like nothing so much as chewed-out chewing gum—there's no other accurate comparison. But its resilient chewing quality and ability to carry flavor won preference for this type of gum and paved the way for the billion-dollar business that began in the early 1900's and spawned a host of inventors, promoters and con men the likes of which few other industries can match. The substance and the romantic lore surrounding its gathering certainly rate closer scrutiny.

CHAPTER 5

Chewing Gum In the Raw From the Chewing Gum Tree

LITTLE remains of the ancient Mayan civilization created by the most brilliant aboriginal people ever to populate this peculiar planet. The Mayans tamed the all-encompassing jungles in Southern Mexico and Central America, building great cities connected by intricate highway systems. They achieved a degree of civilization unequaled anywhere else at that time, constructing beautiful spacious temples whose ruins are still a marvel to behold, surpassing the ancient Egyptians and Babylonians in astronomical knowledge and devising an accurate calendar. They developed an arithmetical system involving the concept of zero and invented New World writing. Then, in about the year 800 A.D., some unknown calamity all but destroyed their civilization and the jungle slowly took re-

venge on its monuments. It is one of the great ironies of history that the most conspicuous evidence of the Mayan's heroic
efforts remaining today is the chewing of gum. It is as if
Americans will be remembered one day for the Hula-hoop, the
pogo stick, the Frisbee, or . . . the chewing of gum.

But chew gum the Mayans did; their habit can be traced
back at least to the second century, when, as if to forecast the
modern gum stick, they rolled up hunks of chicle and wrapped
them in wild banana plant leaves for an edible package—the
first 100 percent American masticatory. The chicle was the
same used today in many gums (the thick creamy latex of the
Achras sapota, more commonly known as the sapodilla), and
was likely discovered centuries ago by a Mayan gatherer unin-
tentionally injuring a sapodilla tree while climbing it to collect
some fruit. The Mayans rather impulsively invented uses for
other latexes. In fact, they concocted primitive rubber shoes or
galoshes by dipping their bare feet up to the ankles in rubber
latex. Perhaps that first Mayan gatherer popped the sapodilla
latex into his mouth as soon as the stuff thickened into a
gummy mass when exposed to air; more likely time to find a use
for the gum was to be measured in centuries. At any rate,
when the Spanish conquerors of the New World descended,
swords clanking ominously, they found descendants of the
Mayans and many other Indian tribes stoically popping their
chicle gum to ease their inevitable nervous tension over these
steel-white brutes riding their four legged slaves. The Con-
quistadores even ascribed the gleaming teeth of Aztec maidens
to their chewing gum habit.

The Mayans had many other uses for the real-life counter-
part of Wrigley's "Juicy Fruit Tree." Surpassing mahogany in
durability, red in color, fine-grained and so hard that a splinter
of it can be driven like a nail into a pine plank, the wood from
the chewing gum tree was valued more than any other timber
for construction. Intricately carved lintels of zapote, as the
wood is called, still survive in ancient Mayan doorways, the
finest examples found in the ruins of the great pyramid temples of Tikal. Besides chopping it down with their stone axes,
the Mayans also cultivated the sapodilla as a shade tree, its
dense, well-proportioned crown and evergreen laurellike
leaves making it a favorite still in ornamental gardens. In so
doing they learned that under cultivation the tree not only

branched out more freely, but produced far more fruit than under wild conditions. The fruit, variously known as naseberries, marmalade plums, sapodillas, and sapodilla apples, became a staple of their diet. Rough-skinned, russet-colored and about the size and shape of a small apple, it has long black seeds at its core and sweet granular flesh that is highly valued for its delicate flavor. "Small, very sweet and delicious to eat," Fray Diego de Landa, second bishop of Yucatan, wrote of the fruit of the chewing gum tree in 1566. Sapodillas, which are strictly speaking a berry, are now occasionally available in some New York City markets and the tree is grown in frostfree parts of Florida for its tasty fruit, the climate in the Florida Keys so much to its liking that it has become naturalized there.

The Mayans found, however, that cultivated sapodilla trees do not produce as much latex. They planted many trees around their settlements, enjoying the fruit, shade, and small white flowers, but gathered most of their chicle from the jungles. Tapping the sapodilla bark, they coagulated the milky latex by boiling, chewing the velvety, smooth and almost tasteless gum that resulted. The tree they named the *ya*, an obsolete name today, but their word *tsictle* became our chicle. When tapped from the tree, the latex was simply called *itz*, yet after being prepared it was dubbed *cha*, a jaw-chomping sound as obviously related to chomping as our chaw or chew. "Chicle, or *cha*, was well known to the ancient Mayas," an early anthropologist wrote, "being chewed to quench thirst and also as an accompaniment of meals and to relieve exhaustion." It is still chewed by the ancestors of the Mayans, the handful of Indians living crudely in the jungle today, many of whom make their living as chicleros, or chicle gatherers, in the Mexican territory of Quintana Roo and other parts of the *tierra caliente*.

Less than half a century ago it was estimated that over a hundred million chewing gum trees were growing in Yucatan alone, many of them dating back to the time of the Spanish conquest. The sapodilla (also called the sapota, the chicozapote, the naseberry and the bullytree) remains the commonest tree on the limestone plains of the Mexican Yucatan and is one of the tallest trees in the jungle, reaching a height of over a hundred feet and a diameter of up to four feet. Though this member of the family Sapotaceae grows in all tropical lands,

being particularly abundant in states bordering on the Gulf of
Mexico and the Caribbean, practically all the gum gathered
comes from Yucatan, the large adjacent area called El Petén in
Guatemala, and British Honduras. Numerous varieties of the
sapodilla exist, but only the red and white species are of commercial importance, and the best specimens of these are found
at an elevation of from 500 to 1,000 feet above sea level in the
heart of wild jungles. Several 1,000-acre sapodilla plantations
have been started, but they haven't proved particularly successful . . .

Chewing Gum Wars and
Chewing Gum Murders

The sapodilla is one of the most ornery trees ever to be
tapped by man. Not only are they relatively unproductive
when cultivated, but chewing gum trees can't usually be
tapped successfully in the wild until they reach about 70 years
old, and they are generally vastly older when "milked."
Neither will the sapodilla cooperate in any but the rainy season, from June to February, when the latex from the cortex of
the tree flows abundantly: "Without rain, there is no chicle,"
is the saying in the Yucatan. All an average tree will yield is
2½ pounds of latex in a 24-hour tapping. After that it must be
allowed to rest from four to eight years before being tapped
again, and even with such care some 15 percent of all sapodilla
trees tapped each year are so badly damaged that they either
die or can never again be bled for chicle.

Working under such handicaps has always made it difficult
for the chicleros who gather the gum to make a decent living,
but their perpetual depression is not the most important of
their problems; they have a hard time just staying alive. Many
chicleros are distant descendants of the Mayans who invented
chicle gum, though the breed is a dying one. Those living in
the jungles of Quintana Roo resisted European civilization
longer than any New World people. In 1847, in the cruel,
bloody conflict called The War of the Castes, the Mayans even
took back their Quintana Roo homeland, coming close in the
process to wiping out the entire population of the Yucatan
Peninsula. They retired into the jungles, but it was many years
before any outsider would venture into Quintana Roo. Mexico
finally made peace with her refractory territory in 1915, but
today Quintana Roo still lies in the heart of darkness. Long

A chiclero scaling a sapodilla tree in Central America to obtain chicle for use in chewing gum. The latex runs down through interconnected crosses to a bucket on the ground.
Wm. Wrigley Jr. Company

impossible to map properly because villages disappear and new ones take their place every four months or so, the jungle is impenetrable to all but native guides. When Mexico made peace with the Mayans, she adopted the old policy of divide and conquer, recognizing various native chiefs as sovereign. The chewing gum business was already developed and large concessions in chicle were given to the chiefs, who enriched themselves and did little for their people. The gum that we chewed in those days came just as much from native slave labor as from nature's bounty.

After many years of exploitation, the Mayans finally rose up against their employers on the chicle plantations of Quintana Roo during the late 1920's—in what might be called the Chewing Gum War. The rebellion was quelled, though, and by the time conditions were reformed significantly the Mayans had largely died out as a power in the territory. Today, remnants of them, bearing little outward resemblance to the proud warriors of the past who built Chichen-Itza, Uxmal and other great cities, still gather chicle in the jungle, exposing themselves to death and diseases that literally eat them away every day. Considering their need for the money, it seems a shame that chicle is gradually being replaced by artificial substitutes; considering their lot, it may be just as well.

Supplementing the ranks of the native chicleros, whose numbers grow smaller every year, are Spanish Indian and Carib laborers imported from South America by *contratistas* or contractors. Criminals and drifters from all over the world have also found a haven in the Quintana Roo and El Petén, violent hard-drinking types straight out of the pages of a Conradian tale. Their numbers, too, have dwindled, but less than 50 years ago it was reported in several American archaeological journals that "all the fugitives from Latin American justice end in the Quintana Roo chicle trails." Another writer observed that "It is not uncommon to see Englishmen, Scandinavians and Americans working in chicle camps. They are on the 'dodge' for some crime and hiding out until conditions get less dangerous. The criminal world knows the Petén for a haven, and several murders have occurred in its depths, when crooks trailing some enemy came upon him in a chicle camp—and left him there forever." Voodoo practices also flourished in the camps, especially among the Carib laborers. Doctors making their rounds reported that many a worker with a serious injury only reluctantly accepted modern medical treatment but always insisted upon using some charm or amulet to effect a cure.

Criminal elements still thrive in the chicle jungles, but today they are busy looting the thousands of archaeological sites in the vast area, often employing motor-driven saws to slice off the sculptured faces of monuments and smuggling out their loot aboard helicopters. Tourists, however, are a far more common sight nowadays in the heart of the forest. In the Petén, for example, thousands of foreign visitors fly in from Guatemala City to visit the ruins of Tikal, an ancient Mayan city that flourished until about 900 A.D. Tikal, lying at the end of a road that winds through the jungle like a dark green tunnel, is among the grandest of archaeological sites, its lofty, limestone pyramids gleaming with ancient majesty. One almost expects to see the ancient Mayan priests intoning incantations to the gods of rain, sun, wind and vegetation.

When a chiclero works on his own in the bush, he'll sometimes leave his family behind in a town at the edge of the jungle ruins, like Flores, the capital of Petén State, which is connected to the mainland by a causeway. "It is a town squatting on a tiny island in the middle of Lake Petén," a visitor wrote not long ago. "At one time the island was much larger, but the lake rises several inches each year, swallowing up part of the land and engulfing a few more houses. The streets of Flores branch out from a central point, like a wheel's spokes, and if you walk down any one of them you can stroll right into the water. Even if you're entirely submerged, you'll see the street going on under water lined with houses on either side. The farther out you go, the more ancient the buildings are. Someday the isle may vanish." Flores, with its picturesque pastel-colored houses and stalacite cave of Jabitsimal, is also noted for the stone image of conquistador Hernando Cortes' horse that is said to be buried at the bottom of Lake Petén Itza. Legend has it that Cortes' horse went lame and that he left it at Lake Petén hoping it would recover. The Indians tried to care for the horse, the first one they had ever seen, even offering it flowers and birds to eat, but the animal died. Frightened of Cortes, they made an image of stone, hoping to fool him when he returned. He never did and in time the Indians came to worship the stone horse as a deity, until a Spanish missionary consigned it to the bottom of the lake, where it lies buried in the silt today . . .

Fer-de-Lances, Tigres and
Man-Eating Chicle Flies

Rather than leave his loved ones behind, the chiclero often elects to transport his family and all his meagre belongings into the jungle for the entire rainy season. The family usually lives under a hastily built "hato" or palm roof which protects their hammocks, cooking fire, and supplies, and is close-by a *cenote* or waterhole. Supported by upright timbers and frequently without walls, these shelters in the heart of the jungle offer little protection against insects and the weather. The women in the group remain in the clearing at all times while the men go out to hunt chicle. Food is simple, scanty and monotonous—tortillas, red beans and coffee for three meals a day, week in and week out, except when the chiclero can spare a few hours for hunting and brings down an occasional wild turkey or peccary. Then there is the problem of getting food for the mules. Green pasturage is all but lacking in the forest and leaves must be cut off breadnut trees to serve as browse for the animals. Except for the cash he'll make, the native chiclero would much rather be back home tending his small patches of corn in forest clearings.

Things are no better in the chicle camps that the *contratistas* provide for their workers. Gangs of 10 to 20 workers and their little mules go off together, hacking their way through the jungle at the start of the rainy season, each man staked by his employer and responsible for gathering his own chicle, but all of them living together in rude shelters. The only woman in each party is a cook, who gets no share of the chicle. Life is just as hard and monotonous in the camps and for diversion there is only gambling with dice and perhaps drinking when liquor is available. The contractor often erects a hut in a suitable clearing and makes this his base of operations, sending the chicleros out in different directions to set up their own little camps not too far distant. He supplies them with provisions on a weekly basis: coffee, beans, flour, perhaps some canned meat and a tot of lime juice to combat scurvy. He will be more than amply paid for whatever he supplies, their one-man company store. On the other hand, the chicleros seldom cheat each other. By some inscrutable process they even seem to know their own particular trees and never poach on another man's territory.

For every stick of gum we chew, the chiclero has probably taken more chances than we will in a lifetime. Their occupational mortality rate in the tropical rain forests is higher than any steeplejack's. Before reaching nature's rudimentary gum-slot machine, the chiclero must cut his way through a maze of poisonous plants and the well-guarded homes of many reptiles. Hurricanes are a normal hazard of the business, as are myriad forms of jungle death. The venomous fer-de-lance, whose bite is usually fatal, slithers along the forest floor with a number of deadly companions, against whom the chicleros have only a rude, native antidote. Then there is the constant menace of tigres, ferocious cats almost as dangerous as Asiatic tigers. The chicleros are constantly exposed to great clouds of malarial mosquitos, most of the men shaking with fever on alternate days, and in the high humidity pneumonia takes a heavy toll. They routinely have to climb the sapodilla trees to heights of 70 feet or more and sometimes cut their own ropes with their machetes while working the trees, diving to their deaths below.

Insects are ravenous in the green hell of the forest. When a mule falls dead in his tracks from exhaustion there is nothing left of him in a few hours but bare bones. The chicle or chiclero fly is doubtless the worst of the swarms of insects, causing horrible disfigurements to the workers. The disease caused by this fly dates back to ancient times, examples of ravaged faces found on figures on pre-Spanish pottery. In 1911 it was discovered that the parasitic fly caused cutaneous leishmaniasis or "chicle-gatherer's ulcer" as it is popularly known. The voracious chicle flies buzz around the busy chiclero working up in a tree and he is too occupied to swat at them while aloft. The fly almost always lays its eggs in the chiclero's ears or nose, and the lobes of the ears and cartilage of the nose are gradually eaten away. As a result chicleros are frequently poor, multilated persons who lack part of an ear or the nose, an entire ear, and sometimes both ears, "having the appearance of being victims of that medieval justice which used to punish certain crimes by amputation." At one time fully five percent of all gatherers ended the season with the fearsome chiclero's ulcer. Presently various antimony preparations can halt the disease if it is caught in time, and the chiclero often takes preventative steps like wearing a helmet that protects the ears and nose, or wrapping a protective cloth around the head. But there are still many casualties. Quite a price to pay so that we can take out our frustrations on a hunk of chewing gum and stick it on the bedpost or under our seats at the movies . . .

Gather Ye Chicle While Ye May

If the chiclero survives the terrors of the *tierra caliente*, if he can painstakingly hack his way through the bewildering oppressive jungle curtained with lianes and epiphytes, where it is always twilight, where paths become mazes within hours, only then can he get down to work that is arduous and dangerous in itself. He must first distinguish the chewing gum tree from the hundreds of tree species in the forest. Then he must select those trees he believes will bear prolifically. No one knows why all sapodilla trees won't yield chicle, but several trees in a clump of 30 or 40 invariably refuse to oblige. Some Indian chicleros have a theory or superstition that the barrenness of certain trees can be accounted for by the absence of bird droppings on the branches, and make their selections accordingly. Most gatherers simply experimentally whack the trunks of likely trees with machetes until suitable yielders are found.

As soon as he is ready to bleed a tree, the chiclero ties a rope around his waist and slips it around the trunk. With the aid of the rope, sometimes telephone linesmen's spurs, and always simian agility, he scrambles up the chewing gum tree, making gashes in the rough oaklike bark from bottom to top as he climbs up to one hundred feet in the air. The slanting, crisscross machete cuts, or gullies, one above the other, extend almost around the trunk, and when the tree is cut from base to top, it resembles a long set of interconnected Xs leading from the bough to the roots. Through these deep zigzag channels the very viscous latex or "milk" runs down to a small rubber-lined and watertight canvas or linen bag tied beneath the last cut and resting on the ground.

When the chiclero's machete first hacks the bark, the milky chicle juice spurts forth for an instant, as if confined under pressure, but it soon begins oozing out, slowly flowing through the grooves or tracks to the bag below. The chiclero must be careful in cutting, because channels cut by unskilled hands often not only fail to reach latex, but kill the tree as well.

What the sharp edge of the machete does is to cut into the bark of the sapodilla, severing hundreds of microscopic tubes turgid with latex, from which fluid is freed to fill the wound. The mother vessels dry up and are useless for further latex production once the milky juice is drained out; latex forms again only after four years or so when the wound heals over with new bark that contains new latex-producing cells. No Band-Aids can be put on the trees (though surgeon's tape, incidentally, has a chicle base). If the chiclero cuts too deeply and injures the delicate renewal layer of cambium, the tree either dies or can never be bled again. Unfortunately, defoliated chewing gum trees, their bare arms stretching to the sky, can be seen throughout the forest.

Once the chiclero has finished bleeding a tree, he moves on to his next charge; he can generally work up to ten trees a day in this fashion, depending on their size. Another peculiarity of all chewing gum trees is that they will run latex only during the daytime, the dripping always stopping at sunset and resuming again at sunrise. So the chiclero collects the chicle from his "walk" of trees once a day, moving on to another location when an area is "milked dry." Each tree yields from 2½ to 4 pounds of chicle, though really large ones can yield 20 pounds' worth or more, and a man can gather about a ton per season from 200 to 300 trees.

The latex looks like milk as it flows from the tree, but it afterward takes on a yellowish color and thickens until it is about the same consistency as molasses, averaging about eight pounds to the gallon. Fresh chicle ferments readily and therefore spoils quickly, so Sunday of every week is devoted to boiling down or cooking the harvest to get it into a solid and easily transportable mass. After the latex is gathered it is carried to the boiling shed where a great steaming cauldron hangs over a low fire. The chicle is poured in, strained through cloth, and boiled from three to six hours until coagulation takes place and it turns a light chocolate color. Constant stirring is required, for chicle scorches as easily as animal milk and scorched latex is inferior in grade, failing to bring premium prices. As the operation continues it is necessary to knead the mass from time to time in order to extract the water; properly cooked chicle loses two-thirds of its original water content and acquires the ability to keep almost indefinitely.

In the past (when they were paid ten cents a pound for their labor) chicleros often "padded" the latex while boiling it, adding foreign substances such as stones, dirt and leaves in order to increase the weight and make a few extra centavos. Because of these practices chicle had such a bad reputation by the 1920's that it was being blamed for the great influenza epidemic circumnavigating the globe and responsible for the death of millions. An article by Dr. Paul Bartholow in the *New York Times* examined this rather vague and capricious theory. It seems that investigators "had been stirred to unusual interest by the discovery of 'flu' among the 'chicleros' or chicle gum gatherers of Mexico and Yucatan." Furthermore, "tests of the chicle showed that various germs, bacteria and molds grew in the commercial product" and were carried from country to country. "It is certainly more than a coincidence that the spread of influenza and the discovery of germs in the crude gums of commerce have occurred at the same time," Dr. Bartholow wrote. But just as good a case could be made for the coincidental and the doctor failed to mention the fact that chicle had actually been in worldwide commerce for nearly a century.

In any event, chicle is now thoroughly inspected before being shipped out. The chiclero pours his processed latex into greased wooden molds rectangular in shape but with rounded tops, each mold holding roughly ten kilos (22 pounds) of crude chicle. Each slab must bear the date of gathering and the mark of both the chiclero and the contractor, who until recently bought it from the chiclero and sold it to chewing gum company representatives or middlemen. At the base camp the contractor passes the blocks, or *marquetas*, to a cutter and a chemist for a careful examination. The cutter looks for any foreign matter, often cutting open the slabs, and the chemist examines the chicle for moisture and adulterants, rejecting those blocks that are too "milky," dry or dirty. If a chiclero is caught cheating, he isn't hired the next season. The blocks of chicle are finally canvas-wrapped in bales of four and shipped to ports like Belize in British Honduras. Not many years ago, long arduous mule trains made these journeys, but today small airstrips dot the Yucatan peninsula and the chicleros need only drive their mules, laden with two or three bales of chicle, to these close-by loading areas. There, cargo planes transport the chicle to ships that will carry it to manufacturing centers in America and other countries . . .

The Decline and Fall of Chicle

From the time when the first sapodilla cutting was opened in 1866 the chicle gatherer's lot has been a hard one. In the early days millions were spent by the chewing gum companies in a chicle chase that sent their agents on expeditions all over Central and South America. More millions were spent on futile efforts to tame the chewing gum tree on plantations. Companies like Wrigley, the Mexican Exploitation Company, and the Chicle Development Company (a joint subsidy of Beech-Nut and American Chicle) all bargained for concessions from year to year with whatever government was currently in power. American Chicle alone once controlled over 5 million acres of chicle-producing land in Mexico, Guatemala and British Honduras. But while *los caudillos* and the capitalists made millions, the chiclero's condition never appreciably improved. By 1930 some 15 million pounds of chicle were being imported into the U.S. alone. Chewing gum consumption was growing at a fantastic rate here and it took over 13 pounds of chicle to make 5,000 pieces of gum. Then the chicle boom ended with the advent of World War II and life got even harder for the chiclero. Chicle became scarce during the war because it was difficult to ship into the country and huge supplies lay rotting in jungle warehouses. The chewing gum manufacturers began a search for new natural resins and perfected synthetic resins similar to tree latexes. After the war many companies forsook chicle for these substitutes. By 1948 travelers coming North from the jungle-clad mountains and remote swamp-lands of Quintana Roo and Campeche in the Yucatan peninsula were telling alarming stories of famine and depression among the natives there. "My people are starving," warned a Mexican priest in an appeal for help. "There is no work anywhere."

Today things are looking up for the people in chewing gum country, no thanks to the chewing gum tree. In the Petén, for example, Guatemala has encouraged immigration and the area's population has risen from 15,000 in 1950 to today's 65,000. Diversification of the economy has been encouraged and although fields are still set aflame in the age-old ritual of slash-and-burn agriculture, the people are being educated in modern farming methods and there is promise for the future. Never again will chicle dominate the economy; those colorful, cruel days are gone.

America imported about six million pounds of chicle from the Yucatan in 1974, but chicle is a government monopoly there now and was selling at $1.25 a pound at last report. This is too expensive for any company to use it as the major ingredient in gum base. Gum formulas are jealously guarded secrets, but modern chewing gum consists roughly of 60 percent sugar, 20 percent gum base, 19 percent corn syrup, and one percent flavoring. Of the gum base, one expert assures me, the "natural ingredient mix" is today generally only about 10 to 20 percent of the total. Sometimes, too, the nonsynthetics in the gum base are composed not of chicle but of substances like jelutong from trees in Malaya. Even more frequently the base is made entirely of synthetics and this seems to be the trend in the industry (see Chapter 8).

At the turn of the century chicle was so important in gum making that "chicle-gum" became a synonym for chewing gum and the verb "to chicle" meant to chew ("Fifty percent of our population chicles," an editorial writer claimed). Today these usages are obsolete, but the gum companies still keep the switch from chicle to a synthetic base something of a trade secret. From its earliest days the chewing gum industry has thrived on romance and glamour, rising to power in roughly the same years that the advertising industry became so important in the economy. And so chicleros will be braving the green hell of the jungle to bring chicle back alive long after the last sapodilla has been tapped. "After all," says one chewing gum executive, "there's romance in a jungle tree's sap and none at all in a test tube."

CHAPTER 6 *America's Greatest Movement: The Jaw Movement*

WITH chicle as king during the infancy of the chewing gum industry, America's greatest movement, as Robert Benchley called it, was the jaw movement, a movement made by millions of molars chomping on gum. Americans had become gumniverous animals: chawing, munching, scrunching, nibbling, gnawing and gnashing their way to Nirvana on every conceivable variety of gum. Before the Gay Nineties were out we had Chiclets, Blibber-Blubber (the first bubble gum), and Dentyne, the original dental gum. There were even gums like Kis-Me and Goody-Goody, not to mention one brand featuring a pig on the wrapper. Congressmen, kings and playmates were chawing—and giving testimonials. The first gum millionaires were made, the "chewing gum trust" was born, industrial espionage came into its own. The chewing gum industry is far more conservative and much fatter today, many times the former shadow of itself; but in those formative years, full of hoopla and humbug, it was to American big business what Barnum was to circuses.

In the early years many small manufacturers contributed to gum's growth, rivaling Thomas Adams in their innovations. Among them were a number of druggists with easy access to flavor extracts, the most successful of the lot being John Colgan, a hustling Louisville, Kentucky pharmacist. This peppy posologist had been selling a gum extracted from the balsam tree and sweetened with powdered sugar, his store on the corner of 10th and Walnut Streets a popular pit stop for Louisville children on their way to school whose wads had lost their flavor on the bedpost overnight. Hearing about Adams' success with chicle, Colgan decided to go him one better and put a tastier chicle gum on the market. First he had to buy the chicle, which proved something of a gamble. A shipment from Central America was available, but the druggist learned that he

An early gum, Colgan's Taffy-Tolu being hawked on the streets of Louisville. *American Chicle Company*

couldn't order 100 pounds of the stuff as he wished. "You want any at all," he was told, "you'll have to take the whole ton of it." Somewhat reluctantly, Colgan decided to take the chance. Purchasing the chicle, he blended it with the spicy aromatic sap of the balsam tolu tree, which had long been used as a basis for cough syrup mixtures. By early 1879 he was marketing Colgan's Taffy-Tolu Chewing Gum, "The Tolu-flavored chew." It proved an overnight success. Boys peddled Taffy-Tolu from baskets on the streets and rode the horse trolleys hawking it. Colgan quickly sold out his drug business and turned his entire attention to the manufacture of chewing gum, tackling Chicago, Cincinnati and Cleveland. When merchants in those cities warned him that gum chewing wasn't considered quite nice thereabouts, he replied that mannerly mastication was "only a matter of education" and proceeded to educate them by chewing a few slabs "politely." Proof of his success is the fact that within a year or so there were ten other companies making tolu-flavored gum. Proof of how fickle tastes are is the fact that within ten years not one gum company bothered making the flavor anymore.

California Fruit, the first fruit-flavored gum, proved a more lasting early favorite. California Fruit was pioneered by Elkhorn, Indiana manufacturer Jonathan P. Primley, an advertising genius who soon dubbed his product Kis-Me in an attempt to capture the romance market in the early 1800s. At the time, according to *Harpers*, chewing gum was "mainly a female accomplishment," the few men who chewed gum "supposed to do so by reason of gallantry." Kis-Me gum gave the boys still another reason: "sparking." If a sweet young thing asked for a stick of Kis-Me, her escort could always claim she'd said, "Kiss me!" and proceed to honor her request. Other cut-ups of the day liked to test whether the gum was really "Far Better Than A Kiss," Primley's slogan. At any rate, the brand was so successful that Primley named his concern the Kis-Me Gum Company.

Goody-Goody gum obviously aimed for a more inhibited market. Originally manufactured by the C. T. Heisel Company of Cleveland, Goody-Goody became the property of Stephen Toghill Britten, a traveling salesman for Heisel, who convinced his employer to establish a factory in Toronto, which he managed and later purchased as the basis for S. T. Britten and

Company. Britten, a self-made man orphaned and self-supporting from the age of 11, chawed his way to the top in the best chewing gum tradition and came to be one of the most widely known figures in the industry when his firm merged with four others into the "chewing gum trust." A technical virtuoso, he remained vice-president of American Chicle until his death in 1934, aged 72, and was particularly active in setting up new plants for the giant company throughout the country. His Goody-Goody, however, wasn't a brand name that many people identified with.

If chewers were indifferent to a gum like Goody-Goody, they were completely turned off by Beeman's Pepsin Gum—at least when it featured a contented pig on the wrapper. Beeman's was the brainchild of Dr. Edward E. Beeman, a Cleveland druggist. Goody-Goody's S. T. Britten, a lean gumstick of a man, seems silent and sour when compared to jolly, bubble gum-bubble-paunched Dr. Beeman. A former Civil War doctor and the son of a pharmacist, Beeman had been operating a fairly successful drugstore on Superior Avenue in Cleveland when he invented a pepsin compound powder that he marketed as a remedy for the national epidemic of heartburn made common by the gargantuan dinners of the period. One story has it that the idea of combining his pepsin with gum was suggested to him by an impoverished young woman who worked at a newsstand where he occasionally bought a stick or two, and that he always took care of her after he made millions. Another claims that Beeman's bookkeeper, named either Nellie Horton or Jane Harton, suggested that he put the pepsin into gum "since so many people buy pepsin for digestion and gum for no reason at all," and that he rewarded her with a large block of stock in his company that made her rich ever after. Pepsin gum was an innovation that Thomas Adams had tried and set aside. In any event, Beeman succeeded in blending his pepsin powder with chicle—only to market his gum in what must be one of the worst merchandising moves in history. The doctor's pepsin compound wrapper had featured a pig's picture—implying that if you took his pepsin powder, you could eat like a pig without suffering indigestion. Dr. Beeman simply put the same pig's picture on his gum wrapper! The only worse choice would have been the picture of a cow chewing its cud. Predictably enough, the gum

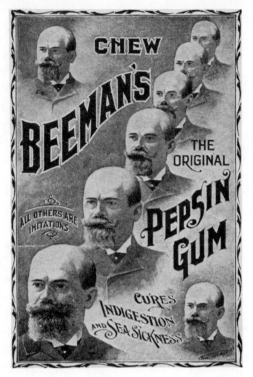

This 1898 ad shows pioneer gum manufacturer, Dr. Edward E. Beeman, for a time the most famous face in America—save for the Smith Bros. of cough drop renown. *American Chicle Company*

didn't sell very well, and if it hadn't been for the efforts of Cleveland financier George Worthington, both the pig and Dr. Beeman would soon have been forgotten.

George Heber Worthington, who later became the guiding jaw of the chewing gum trust, figures so prominently in the saga of gum that he deserves closer attention. The portly banker demonstrated his business acumen when little more than 18 by taking over a small family stone quarry and turning it into the Cleveland Stone Company, the largest producer of building stone and grindstones in the world. His nose was to the grindstone ever after and his interests reached out in all directions—including real estate, mining, explosives, chemicals and medicines—over 50 commercial and industrial enterprises in all, 8 of which he headed as president. Sound judgment and keen insight characterize his success, which made him a millionaire many times over, but none of his contemporaries could describe him as much more than a disembodied brain. Worthington did own the *Priscilla*, America's cup defender for 1885, and his stamp collection was recognized as one of the three greatest in the world, selling for one million dollars just prior to his death in 1924. Yet he seems not to have been much of a social animal—he certainly wasn't a glad-hander and Casanova like his arch rival chewing gum king William White. "All business" best describes Worthington. "In his entire career," writes his biographer, "there is no esoteric phrase . . . He lives in an atmosphere of self-repression and reserved force—a grave, modest, low-voiced, conservative man . . . [whose] interests are to him as the mover of the pawns and kings upon the chessboard and it is recognized fact that he is never checkmated . . . "

Worthington began his chewing gum career when Dr. Beeman, an old acquaintance, told him that his new business had been meeting with heavy losses. The banker examined Beeman's books and, impressed at the low cost of chicle and the large profits to be made in gum, immediately offered to refinance and reorganize the company. The first thing he did when Beeman accepted was to take the contented pig's portrait off the package and substitute the good doctor's. This was to make Dr. Beeman's the most famous face in America, excepting possibly the black-bearded Smith Bros. of cough drop fame—for his picture remained on the cover of Beeman's Pepsin Gum until 1955. Beeman's visage was everywhere on posters and handbills, with words telling the virtues of pepsin gum. The doctor, however, couldn't handle his overnight celebrity. Setting aside his practice of medicine, he devoted himself to indulging in all the frivolities known to man, trying to spend each $5,000 check he received before next month's came. Plump, convivial old "Doc" Beeman, as he was called, became a familiar sight on the downtown streets in Cleveland; his comic stories and antic adventures were long repeated there. But when he took to drinking heavily, his family left him and he eventually became afflicted with paralysis. In 1906, 25 years after he made his discovery, the first chewing gum millionaire died. Several years before he had sold Worthington his gum interests—just after the Beeman Chemical Company became part of the new chewing gum trust and Worthington had begun his assault on the throne of William White in earnest . . .

America's First Chewing Gum King

Thomas Adams' discovery of chicle as the ultimate gum base marked the beginning of America's greatest movement, but the gum business might have bogged down like cranberries if it hadn't been for the flavoring innovation of a former popcorn salesman named William J. White. The man who put the flavor and gumption in gum, obscure as he is today, stands out as one of the most colorful kings in chewing gum history, rivaling even Wrigley the Great in this regard. White, who had the soul and drive of a carnival barker, with a touch of the poet thrown in, was born in Allenwick, Canada in 1850, but brought to Cleveland when his father died while he was still a child. He had to depend on his own wit and hard work to support himself from the time he was barely six years old, passing his early days, it's said, "amid scenes and companions well calculated to debase and ruin a person of less natural strength of character." White wandered from place to place, working on farms, at odd jobs in cities, even drifting to the plains of the Far West. On turning 18, he headed back to Cleveland and worked as a carpenter, mason, bridge builder, sailor, and manufacturer of popcorn before having any connection at all with gum making. However, shortly after he married in 1873, he became partners with a confectioner named Dimmock, who provided him with a horse and wagon and a stock of candy which he sold to retailers for one-half of the profits. When Dimmock relocated to Detroit, White went along, gaining a practical insight into the manufacture of candies—thanks mainly to his wife Ellen, who managed to steal the secrets of that then mysterious business right from under Dimmock's nose.

Armed with proven candy formulas, White went into business for himself in Cleveland. In 1876 he bought a plant belonging to George E. Clark, manufacturer of a paraffin-base gum called Busy Bee, and began his first experiments to turn out an improved brand of chewing gum. A brand called The Diamond that he put out proved phenomenally successful and he soon devoted himself entirely to the manufacture of gum. Chewing gum only enjoyed a ready sale of about three months of the year in those days, but White traveled from small store to small store obtaining orders for brands like Mammouth, White Mountain, Picture Tablets, and Cleveland Belle. Ill health forced him to take in C. T. Heisel as a partner in 1885, yet after a few months the maverick found that he couldn't work in harness with anyone else (a lesson he unfortunately didn't remember in later years) and he sold the business to the original Goody-Goody man.

The irrepressible White sold his first chewing gum business to Heisel at 11:00 A.M. on November 14, 1885 and by 3:00 the same day he had leased a factory and ordered printed announcements for a new chewing gum concern. Within the course of a week he drummed up his first orders, manufactured his gum, and made his first shipments. Little more than a year later he was manufacturing the immensely successful Yucatan gum that was to revolutionize the industry.

Yucatan gum, like Adams', had a chicle base, but White solved the mystery of how to put and keep flavor in the mix. He came upon the chicle when a neighborhood grocer received a barrel of the latex instead of an ordered barrel of nuts and gave it to him in disgust. White took the chicle home with him. To the inquiries of a curious neighbor as to just what the stuff was, he retorted grandly: "It's bread. Petrified bread. Found in a baker's oven in the ruins of Pompeii!" "I believe it," said the neighbor. "Looks like it might be at that."

Putting their knowledge of the confectionary trade to good use, White and his wife experimented with the free chicle on their kitchen stove. The major problem with the substance was that it wouldn't absorb flavors. White found that more sugar was the answer to this conundrum—that by combining flavors with corn syrup, any flavor could be obtained, the syrup blending instantly with the latex. He chose peppermint for his gum, first calling it Yellow Band and settling on the name Yucatan to capitalize on the romance of chicle. Peppermint proved a wise choice—even today some 50 percent of all gum has a peppermint flavor—but as it hadn't been tried before, White had to educate the public to its use by some adroit advertising. He also flattened his gum into sticks and wrapped it in pink paper—the typical gums of the day came in tiny rods wrapped in plain tinfoil, half as long and half as thick as a cigarette. Yucatan proved such an instant success that the tolu gum companies collapsed practically overnight, those gum makers who survived, including Adams, making it only because they adopted White's flavoring technique. Within months White's gum was so heavily in demand that he had to erect a much larger four-story chewing gum factory employing some 300 people. The building, once a two-acre site on Detroit Avenue, in Cleveland, is still standing today.

Yucatan became famous throughout the world, the first American gum that stretched and popped across national boundaries. White sold some 5 million sticks of it in 1887, 150 million sticks six years later. For almost a decade his operation was the largest of its kind anywhere. He amassed a fortune of over $5 million and enjoyed every penny of it. His estate, Thornwood, situated in a grove on the banks of Lake Erie, was the most magnificent of the 12 homes on Cleveland's "Millionaire's Row-West;" the 52-room mansion was a showplace containing one of the finest collections of paintings and tapestries in the country. The Whites and their seven children lived and entertained lavishly at Thornwood, trying to outdo the established snobs of the city, including the automobile Whites, who snubbed them to the end. For an added diversion they had Two Minute Villa, a 455-acre stock farm and race track nearby, which was a veritable horse paradise, and the *Say When*, the largest, handsomest yacht on the Great Lakes.

America's first chewing gum king almost always had a broad smile on his face, a broad-beamed girl on his arm, a large drink in his hand, and a grandiose scheme in his head. In 1889 he decided to run for Mayor of West Cleveland. He won handily. Four years later, after devising a promotion stunt of personally delivering a box of Yucatan to every Congressman in Washington, he figured the time had come to run for Congress himself. Handing out gum and promises by the ton, he got himself elected as a Republican from Cleveland's 20th district. Serving well, if erratically, he was responsible for a federal bill providing for a signal system on the inland lakes, which he successfully steered through the house. But his heart wasn't in politics and he refused to accept another term, in face of the fact that he had no opposition for the Republican nomination.

White preferred to devote his time to less prosaic pursuits. It was aboard the steam-powered *Say When* that he sailed to England to promote his chewing gum. There an audience was arranged with King Edward VII, but White didn't bow humbly and speak only when spoken to. The chewing gum king barreled right up to the King of England, pushing his flunkies aside, and launched into a sales-pitch for Yucatan. "Your

William White, America's first Chewing Gum King, who forced a piece of gum on the King of England. *New York Public Library*

American Chicle Company

Majesty," he began, "I'd like you to have a box of my chewing gum. You've never tasted anything as refreshing. Here, try a piece, Ed . . . " When he finished, the king had all he could do to remember that this chap was a former American congressman. Though he firmly refused to chew any Yucatan just then, he took the gum White had practically shoved in his mouth and thanked him politely. So unnerved was the stuffy Edward, however, that he called off all audiences for the day and left the room, "mopping at his brow." For his part, White was elated. He wired back exaggerated accounts of how Edward had chewed up his gum; bathed in the warm glow of the publicity and increased sales; and sailed on to conquer more kings.

The potentate of peppermint also created something of a scandal when he became the constant companion of America's Aphrodisiac, the luscious long-legged actress Anna Held. Miss Held, famous for her milk baths on stage and her rendition of "Won't You Come And Play With Me?", had begun her stage career as a street singer in her native Paris when only eight years old. She was a renowned muscial comedy star by the time she turned sixteen, Flo Ziegfeld discovering her during one of his European visits, marrying the siren and starring her in many of his lavish productions. Anna easily pulled down over $1,000 a week in productions like *The Parisian Model* when White first met her, and went on to earn $5,000 a week in the early silent movies, but the handsome fun-loving emperor of chewing gum more than matched this. It's said that White at one time spent up to $100,000 a month helping promote Anna Held's stage career, completely backing at least one play of hers, and that he became so enchanted by his Lorelei that he gave her a string of matched pearls worth $120,000. No one can say what went on in private, but Anna certainly chewed his gum vigorously in public. She also endorsed Yucatan as a way of keeping your teeth bright, your breath kissing-sweet and as a way to strengthen sagging chin and bust muscles.

The chewing gum king's descension from the throne began when he joined in the organization of the new chewing gum monopoly, the American Chicle Co., which was engineered by that enigmatic "father of the trusts," Charles Ranlett Flint. Though American Chicle made millions for the other companies that joined it, the idea proved to be White's undoing. In

1899, shortly after the combine was formed, he did succeed
Samuel B. Lawrence as its president. The profits from the
merger were indeed tremendous, but White straightaway ran
into resistance, especially from the conservative banker
George Worthington, who headed Beeman's. Worthington disliked White's life-style; behind his back he accused him of
playing around, loving and living it up instead of devoting his
time to matters of mastication. The banker saw little sense in
White's policy of big advertising campaigns; he believed that
once you had a monopoly you increased your profits by cutting
costs and raising prices. William Wrigley Jr. was later to prove
White absolutely right as regards advertising, much to American Chicle's misfortune, but for the moment White's liberal
spending ways gave Worthington the ammunition that he
needed. He constantly criticized White, spread more stories
about his wild champagne parties and womanizing. The other
directors, knowing full well that White had the biggest share of
the company (every member shared according to the percent-
age of the market he had when the monopoly was organized),
were more than glad to have a reason to force him out. In 1905
they piously voted his dismissal and split his millions of dollars' worth of shares between themselves.

White was penniless again, yet far from ready to give up
gum. The world, he knew, was indifferent, brutal and benevo-
lent, in turn—and he had great patience. Within five years he
had organized the W. J. White Chicle Company and built a
new plant and fortune at Niagara Falls. Personal problems
abounded, though. His admiration of beautiful shades and
shapes figured in his divorce from the long-suffering Ellen in
1906, and the day after his sensational divorce trial he married
the elegant and wealthy divorcée Helen Sheldon. The two built
an imposing home on Riverside Drive in New York, but this
marriage failed also. Still, White tried to hang in there, even
after he lost his business a second time when his old partners
swamped him with lawsuits. Returning to Cleveland again in
1922, he went into business with his eldest son, renting a room
on the top floor of the National Tool Company building.
Though he had almost no capital, and was sapped as a tapped
sapodilla, he set up a small factory and might have been well
on his way to making a fourth fortune at the age of 72, when he
slipped and fell in an icy Cleveland street. He died from in-

juries suffered in the fall four weeks later on February 17, 1923 and was buried in Lakewood Cemetery, Ellen White joining the celestial hierarchy a few months later. Of all the chewing gum kings, William White was the most engaging and only William Wrigley Jr. proved more deserving of the crown, yet the big gum monopoly just chewed him up till all the flavor was gone . . .

"The Chewing Gum Trust"

William White helped effect American Chicle's formation in 1899, but the financial wizardry behind the chewing gum trust merger was worked by financier Charles Ranlett Flint, dubbed "The Father Of The Trusts" by the muckrakers of his day. Flint was active in business almost until his death in 1934, at the age of 84. He always firmly believed that many economies and greater stability resulted when business units became larger. In the 1880's he made the first public speech advocating this idea, earning his sobriquet, many admirers and even more enemies in the process. Flint, the son of the owner of a Maine clipper ship fleet, was by instinct a trader and loved a good deal; in fact, to him the deal was the thing, not the fame that came with it or the money to be made. Although he earned a large annual income ($80,000 a year in those nontaxable days), he never tried to accumulate great wealth and was always a shadowy, enigmatic figure little-known to the public. But those in power knew him well. For a time Flint held the title "Rubber King of America" for his activities in arranging the importation of Brazilian rubber. His firm of commission agents, Flint, Dearborn and Co., often acted on behalf of foreign governments, particularly in providing warships, guns and ammunition. They were agents for the sale of the first practical Wright Brothers' airplanes abroad and also for Simon Lake's submarines. Flint himself had acted as consul for Nicaragua and as consul general for Costa Rica. Inextricably mixed up in the intrigue that underlay revolutionary movements abroad, supporting a tottering throne or pulling it down, this quiet American promoted Pan-American unity and is said to have advised his intimate friend Secretary of State James G. Blaine on tariff matters and treaties of reciprocity. Later in his career he furthered American aid to the Russian revolutionary government.

An impressive man who wore sideburns to conceal a large scar on his cheek, Flint, in the words of one who knew him well, was "a man of action little given to reflection, religion, or charity." Something of a sportsman ("Mix sunshine with your blood instead of moonshine!"), he owned America's fastest sailing yacht and the world's fastest steam yacht. But his life consisted mainly of round-the-clock business deals that made him the darling of the likes of old J. P. Morgan, Mark Hanna and President William McKinley. Whatever the shortcomings of the trusts he formed, he was doubtless sincere about the advantages of such horizontal combinations. Flint believed that the consolidated companies would compete with one another and that stockholders, consumers and workers would all profit. His chief service consisted of discovering possible consolidations, getting together the persons concerned and suggesting terms and compromises. At this he was a master without peer, putting together what reads like a *Who's Who* of American business of the time: a score of enterprises, or more, including The United States Rubber Company, The American Woolen Company, and the International Business Machine Corporation. Naturally, he saw great possibilities in organizing a chewing gum monopoly. There would be substantial economies in shipping and advertising, and production would be much simpler—flavors could simply be added to the chicle base as needed and there would be no duplication of expensive machinery. In 1899, after a year of negotiations, Flint and White drew the five largest U.S. gum companies into the combine—Adams' Sons & Company; Worthington's Beeman Chemical Company; W. J. White & Son; the S. T. Britten Company; and Primley's Kis-Me Gum Company. American Chicle, by far the largest chewing gum company in America at the time, had an initial capitalization of $6 million Common Stock and $3 million Preferred. Thomas Adams Jr. became its first chairman of the Board of Directors and Flint fast disappeared from the scene to search out new hunting grounds . . .

Chiclets, Blibber-Blubber, and the Lady in Red

After William White and Flint departed from American Chicle, the chomping giant continued to grow, gorging itself on the Sen-Sen Company with its four constituent companies

(T. B. Dunn & Co., Curtis & Sons Co., The Grove Co., & Frank H. Fleer Co.) as well as Sterling Gum and the Dentyne Company. From Fleer came American Chicle's most famous product, Chiclets. This first candy-coated gum was conceived around the turn of the century by Henry Fleer, Frank's brother, who based his idea on a then popular confection, candy-coated almonds. Henry supposedly showed his brother a sample of his gum pellets one day, remarking that the "little chiclets" were coming along just fine. "That's it!" Frank cried. "That's what we'll call them—Chiclets!" Chiclets were an instantaneous success, and have become the only gum distinctive enough to be widely known by a name of its own. When Frank Fleer sold them and his company to American Chicle in 1914, he was allowed to go into business again for himself, provided he didn't duplicate any of the products he had previously manufactured. No one could foresee that he would later make a fortune in the bubble gum business (see Chapter 10). Fleer had already invented the first bubble gum in 1906, but few, including American Chicle, saw much hope for it. Made of synthetics, his Blibber-Blubber had only its name going for it. Far too sticky, it didn't hold together and it had a "wet" bubble that usually burst and stuck to Junior's face so stubbornly that only

America's first candy-coated gum. This billboard ad was displayed in 1929, "when chicle was a nickel." *American Chicle Company*

hard scrubbing with turpentine could remove it. "Dry" bubble gum would not make its debut until 1928.

As for Dentyne, the first dental gum, it had made its name long before joining the chewing gum trust in 1916. Dentyne, hard or "chewy" and low in sugar, is supposed to be twice as efficient as other gums in reducing the acid in tooth film if chewed directly after a meal. Its inventor was Franklin V. Canning, the young manager of a New York drugstore. After discussing the matter with a dentist friend, Canning decided to try to develop a chewing gum with properties beneficial to the teeth. A long series of experiments resulted in the pink chewing gum that he named Dentyne, a contraction of "dental hygiene." Canning and his wife spent a lot of time advertising their gum before selling out to the trust. They pasted 40 of the rectangular gum packs on cardboard easels, embellished with an actress' sparkling teeth, and peddled their wares on street corners. Soon there were enough funds for bigger stunts. In 1908, the New York *Journal* headlined a story "Mysterious Lady Dressed In Red Blocks 5th Avenue." The "mysterious lady" seated in a red hansom cab, it turned out, was an advertising woman named Margaret Sullivan handing out samples of Dentyne to passersby.

American Chicle (nobody calls it or has reason to call it the chewing gum trust anymore) has been responsible for many innovations in gum making. Under Amos Urban Shirk (1890-1956), director of research, the company developed a synthetic chicle for a chewing gum base, a nonoxidizable chewing gum base, and new chemical analyses and testing control methods for chewing gum. Shirk also planned the giant $3 million American Chicle plant in Long Island City, New York, a spotlessly bright building five stories high and covering a city block. At one time the company alone controlled more than 5 million acres of chicle-producing lands in Central America and was far and away the largest gum manufacturer in the world.

Today American Chicle, which was merged into the giant Warner-Lambert Pharmaceutical Company in 1962, is second only to Wrigley in the industry. Another major competitor is Beech-Nut, which has always given the bigger company a run for its money. Beech-Nut, now a division of the Squibb Corporation, was founded by Bartlett Arkell in Canajoharie, New York in 1891. President Arkell, a sharp-witted jovial type who had been editor of both *Judge* and *Leslie's Weekly* magazines, founded his company as a distributor of ham and bacon, but in 1911 gum was added to its product line. Legend has it that Frank E. Barbour, Yale's All-American quarterback in 1888, had a lot to do with this. The Frank Merriwell of his day had coached the University of Michigan football team after graduating from Yale, but in 1908 he married Arkell's daughter and the following year he joined Beech-Nut as secretary. It's said that one night an American Chicle executive was drinking with Barbour, got drunk and blabbed about the true profit rate of the chicle trust. The next morning Barbour promptly went to his father-in-law and talked him into taking on gum as a sideline. Arkell believed from the beginning that a chewier gum made with more chicle would outsell all others and soon adopted the slogan "There's more chicle in it!", selling his product at a premium price as a quality gum and eventually outstripping his venerable rival American Chicle for a short time in the race for second place behind Wrigley. For his part Barbour was rewarded with a vice-presidency of the company.

There were well over 50 gum makers sharing the field with the chewing gum trust by the end of the first decade of the twentieth century; the gum business was, in fact, over-crowded. Gumball machines were everywhere, gums of every conceivable flavor were on the market, every advertising gim-mick imaginable had been tried, to a limited extent, and the annual market value of gum easily exceeded $25 million at the time. But American Chicle, Wrigley and Beech-Nut were al-ready gumdom's Big Three. The invincible William Wrigley Jr., however, was to lead Wrigley far ahead of all its rivals. Full-blooded, masterful, dramatic, back-slapping, cigar-bestowing Wrigley the Great was a survival of the frontier age, when men and not corporations were dominant, when Babbit was in the future, the last of those super-salesmen, super-showmen, super-self-made men whose impassioned per-sonalities once colored the business scene. More than anyone he was to give the world the Greatness of Gum.

The Man Who Taught The World To Chew

IF William White is remembered as the Huck Finn or Peck's Bad Boy of chewinggumdom, then William Wrigley Jr. will go down in history as a kind of reformed Huckleberry: somewhat more "sivelized," almost as carefree, even more imaginative and $200 million richer at the end. A soul brother of the perpetually unwinding Teddy Roosevelt, whom he greatly admired, the Great Wrigley was the foremost huckster of his day and brought uninhibited salesmanship to chewing gum, changing the character of the industry and the chewing habits of the world in the process. Wrigley had class, sass, brightness—and bite befitting a chewing gum czar. This complete extrovert boasted that he could sell pianos to the armless men of Borneo. That may be extreme, but no one could doubt that the man who built a company which has since sold trillions of sticks of the stuff could and did sell chewing gum to the toothless men of America (even if his company did have to invent a brand that wouldn't stick to their dentures).

Like more than a few millionaires, masterminds, mahatmas and mafiosi, Wrigley the Great galloped onto the field of his triumphs as a grammar school dropout. The sheer romance of his career commenced when teachers began sending long letters home to his father. Pleasant enough, but so energetic and restless that he was unruly, the curly-haired, blue-eyed boy managed to get expelled from classes on the average of once every three weeks by the time he turned eleven. William Wrigley Sr., a Philadelphia soap manufacturer, scrubbed out his mouth and brushed his bottom a number of times, yet the father of nine didn't have the time or heart to do much more with his eldest underachiever. Weekends, the boy had sold a lot of soap on Philadelphia street corners, but that was about all he'd accomplished. Things got worse when he ran away to New York for three months in his eleventh summer. Investing his last five cents in a few papers, young Wrigley tried making his fortune as a "newsie" along Manhattan's Park Row. On cold nights he slept on a grating of the old *Tribune* building, the heat from the pounding presses curling up around him; rainy nights found him wrapped up in newspapers under a wagon parked in the street. When the lot of a newsboy palled on him, he tried his hand as a seaman. His first job, peeling potatoes in the galley, proved disastrous—he was fired for peeling as generously as an Army K.P. A job on board another ship appealed to him even less. He was sent aloft in the rigging with a sharp knife to cut away pieces of tarred rope which the sails had been tied with. One day up there was enough to convince him to steal ashore under cover of darkness and begin making his way home.

Back in Philadelphia, Wrigley's parents quickly forgave him and had him reinstated in school. Somehow he had advanced to the eighth grade and it looked like he might even graduate—until he noticed the imposing nameplate on the school building one afternoon and decided that a cream pie plastered all over it would depict his sentiments exactly. The outcome: his final expulsion. Wrigley had joined the ranks of

Einstein, Poe, Shelley, Röntgen, Whistler and other greats expelled from one school or another over the years. "Your school life hasn't been a success," his father sighed, in one of history's great understatements, and it was the soap factory for his scion. William drew the hardest job in the place—stirring the thick contents of soap vats with a paddle—at a salary of $1.50 a week. For one full year, ten hours a day, he stirred like a mechanical crutcher, laying the foundation for the physical strength and stamina he would maintain all his life. But the more he paddled, the more he planned. His father, who held that kids who run away from home and never finish school turn out to be very bad or very potent, and had no doubts that his son was heading in the first direction, now seemed impressed by his industry. It was time to make a move. Wrigley pleaded to be put on the road as a soap salesman. At first his father protested that he was only 13 but when he countered that he was big for his age and had taken care of himself before, nothing remained but to consent to a trial.

Before long the boy salesman was driving a spanking four-horse team with bells jingling on the harness through all the "high-grass" towns of Pennsylvania, New York and the New England states. Wrigley soap was shipped by rail to stations along his route and he picked it up and sold it for cash. At this young Wrigley immediately showed the optimism, tenacity and imaginativeness that were to help him stretch gum to its limits. Around him centers a whole cycle of tales that used to be told (and told well in a big booming voice) by himself. With his first customer he spent a full two hours. "Well, sonny," the grocer said at last. "I see that I'll have to buy some of your soap if I expect to do any business today." The yarns above all show his ingenuity and flair for dealing with people. Once he won over a storekeeper (who had irritably criticized his selling technique) by asking for instruction in salesmanship, receiving it on the spot and getting an order for a year's supply of scouring soap. Another cranky customer was a wholesaler whose outstanding characteristics were a dislike of drummers and a habit of being at his store every morning at 6:45 sharp. Wrigley got up early every day for a month in order to meet the man outside his office at opening time, often when temperatures were well below zero. Just before he left town, the wholesaler gave him a large order and told him he could count on him as long as he was in business.

For 16 years Wrigley the Great wasted his considerable talents as his father's star traveling soap salesman. In this time he only abandoned his fascination with selling once—when at 19 he and a friend headed West to seek their fortunes mining gold and silver. Unfortunately, Wrigley's straw hat, both tickets tucked in the band, blew out the open coach window when a gust of wind swept past and the two young men were kicked off the train at Kansas City. Wrigley took a job as a waiter in a run-down coffee shop and managed to make several hundred dollars selling rubber name stamps in his spare time, but Kansas City seemed to cure him of his wanderlust. Especially when he and his friend awoke one night to see their two boardinghouse roommates sorting out a pile of expensive silverware. These roomers, who had claimed to do "regular night work," were in fact seasoned burglars . . .

The Slippery Road
from Soap to Spearmint

Wrigley's travels at least gave him the confidence that he could survive wherever he landed and bounce back from anything—which served him well in the future. In 1885 he married his 18-year-old sweetheart, Ada Foote, working all the harder for her. After selling all the soap his father's factory could produce year after year, he set out for Chicago six years later to open a new branch of the family firm. He made about $10 a week at the time and had only $35 capital, but an uncle soon loaned him $5,000 to get started. Wrigley's first move was to raise the price of his soap, increasing the dealer's profit, and to offer each dealer a few cheap umbrellas which he could either keep or sell over the counter. This started a system that made him the largest distributor of premiums in the world, and was to become a cornerstone of his chewing gum business as well. "We must give dealers the thick end of the stick," he used to say to his assistants in later days. "No matter how thin our end is, remember we have thin ends coming in from everywhere. And many littles make a lot . . . "

Wrigley's premiums ranged from lamps, clocks, counter scales, and cash registers, to guns and free accident insurance. They give a fair picture of life in the Gay Nineties, including mandolins, slot machines, pink lemonade sets, solid brass cuspidors, coffee mills, a baby carriage complete with a lace-edged parasol, and fancy petticoats. The premiums introduced many new inventions such as fountain pens, Graphophones, cameras, even a home motion-picture machine and safety razors several years before the Gillette Company was incorporated. Some were complete failures. A carload of 65,000 umbrellas with decorated china handles proved to be fine so long as the sun was shining—the moment water touched one it began to drip red dye. One hundred thousand green handbags also did very poorly, for few women wanted to carry a distinctively colored bag that was a duplicate of bags carried by hundreds of other women in the same town. But every time Wrigley lost, he plunged in deeper. Most of his premiums were successful. Topping them all was a cookbook featuring recipes using a baking powder that he had added as a sideline to his soap business. The 150-page cookbook, offered free with each can of baking powder purchased, was distributed at the rate of 50,000 a week, baking powder sales soon running so far ahead of his other business that in 1892 he dropped soap all together.

Among the premiums Wrigley offered with his baking powder were spruce and paraffin chewing gums; two packs of chewing gum came free with each can of ten-cent baking powder. The offer proved a huge success and when he saw that the tail was wagging the dog again, the maestro of merchandising turned his attention completely to the tail, dropping baking powder that same year. Deciding to make chewing gum his life's work and pleasure, he picked a gum manufacturer and went around to close the deal. Wrigley himself boasted that he'd never been late for an appointment and when this man kept him waiting ten minutes he stalked out of his office and found another manufacturer—giving the little Zeno Gum Company business which came to millions over the years.

Certain that "the Adams' idea" was gum's hope of the future Wrigley changed Zeno's paraffin product by making chicle the main ingredient. His first brand was Vassar; the name of this elite women's college both appealed to the "carriage trade" and took advantage of the fact that women chewed much more gum than men at the time. Then came Lotta, for those who wanted "a lotta gum," and something called Sweet Sixteen Orange. Juicy Fruit and Wrigley's Spearmint made their debuts in 1893. The spearmint gum constituted a vast improvement over rival brands—spearmint odor had been so strong and unappealing due to early flavoring methods that merchants rarely ordered it. Nevertheless, Wrigley couldn't have

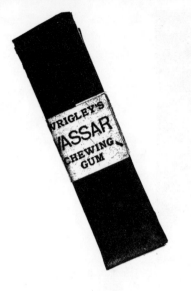

Vassar, the Wrigley Com-
pany's first gum, its name
designed to capture "the
classy trade," and Sweet 16
Orange, an early precursor of
Juicy Fruit. *Wm. Wrigley Jr.
Company*

picked a rougher time to start selling chewing gum. The field
was crowded and whenever a new flavor came on the market,
scores of imitators rushed in. Operating out of a little
storeroom on East Kinzie Street, Wrigley had all he could do to
stay solvent; only the premiums he offered to induce dealers to
handle his gum saved his business. But in 1898 he formed the
William Wrigley Jr. Company and when the newly merged
"chewing gum trust" offered him a chance to join the following year, he refused, preferring as always to go his own way.
These were the days when he served as his own salesman,
sales manager, packer and bookkeeper. During the new firm's
first year he spent 187 nights on sleeping cars traveling around
the country to show dealers how to best display his gum . . .

Tell 'Em Quick and Tell 'Em Often

From the beginning Wrigley emphasized ADVERTISING.
"Anybody can make gum," he held. "Selling it is the problem." Even when he couldn't afford to advertise, there were
the ads of others to capitalize on. One time the bigger gum
companies were touting chewing gum as an aid to digestion.
Wily Wrigley promptly had his own brands placed in restaurants next to the cash register, a space still vied for today by the
gum and antacids people. Gradually, other fields of advertising were tried and finally, in 1902, the fledgling gum maker

The Great Wrigley—William Wrigley Jr., flamboyant founder of America's greatest gum dynasty. *Wm. Wrigley Jr. Company*

decided to "make one heap of all winnings and risk it all on one turn of the wheel." He proceeded to invest $100,000 in a New York City ad campaign that was a total failure, tried a second time on Broadway with another $100,000 and again failed utterly. "Nothing to sweat about," the gum man with gumption told everyone. Investing still another $100,000 in a campaign aimed at the smaller cities in upstate New York, Wrigley bought up every square foot of available billboard space, every vacant space in streetcars, and contracted for spreads in all the major newspapers. This time the campaign triggered an avalanche of sales that more than paid for it. "Now I'm gonna pick up that $200,000 I dropped in the big town," he told his associates.

Sheer nerve was the collateral behind Wrigley's 1907 advertising campaign, the first spectacular one in American history. He decided to concentrate on selling his spearmint-flavored gum and designed the spearlike, grinning gnome that still adorns the Wrigley gum pack. One million dollars had to be invested on ads, but he didn't have the million or anything like it. Few companies were advertising at the time. The Panic of 1907 had resulted in a recession which found most advertisers trying to back-pedal on their contracts, and even the vaunted "chewing-gum trust" had pared its advertising to the bone. But this only encouraged Wrigley more. Besides, he believed that "people chew harder when they are sad," an intuition later substantiated by increased gum sales during a great depression and four wars. Wrigley begged, borrowed and mortgaged everything he owned to raise $250,000, which enabled him to buy $1.5 million worth of ad space at Panic rates. He immediately extended his campaign by distributing coupons that entitled any dealer in the country to receive a box of Wrigley gum gratis from his jobber. Business soon tripled. Within a year spearmint sales zoomed from $170,000 to well over a million. More ads and profits followed. By 1910, Wrigley's Spearmint was America's favorite brand of gum.

A year later Wrigley bought the Zeno Company for $250,000 and thereafter the William Wrigley Jr. Company produced all its own gum. Soon the Great Wrigley's liberal advertising policies had seized over 60 percent of the market from under the nose of the dozing gum trust. "Get a good product," he later told a reporter in explaining his coup, "it's easier to row downstream than up. Then tell 'em quick, and tell 'em often . . . keep everlastingly coming at them. Advertising is pretty much like running a train. You've got to keep on shoveling coal into the engine. Once you stop stoking, the fire goes out. The train will run on its own momentum for a while, but it will gradually slow down and come to a dead stop."

Wrigley himself kept on stoking. As the result of one advertising contract, each of the 62,000 street, subway and elevated cars in America carried a Wrigley poster. His flashing electric sign in New York's Times Square cost $104,000 a year to run but reached millions. There were a few stumbling blocks. The courts, for example, ordered the Wrigley Company to pay the L. P. Larson Jr. Company one million dollars because Wrigley had used a color scheme for a wrapper that the Larson concern had first used. But more than anyone before or after him The Great Wrigley taught America and the world to chew gum. People complained that they couldn't get away from the smell of spearmint—"the Wrigley smell of success." In 1915, the suzerain of spearmint mailed four sample sticks of his gum to all 1.5 million subscribers listed in America's telephone books; four years later he duplicated the campaign, reaching 7 million homes this time. Along the Trenton-Atlantic City railway in the New Jersey meadows he erected an outdoor chain sign half a mile long advertising all his products—including Wrigley's Doublemint, introduced in 1914, and his 1921 introduction, P.K., a candy-coated gum like Chiclets (named not for his son Philip K. Wrigley, as is generally believed, but from the gum's slogan "Packed tight—Kept right!"). There were 117 separate bulletins and cutouts in the chain sign, the bulletins shaped like gum wrappers in the Wrigley line and the cutouts showing the grinning Wrigley sprite standing or riding a donkey cart, elephant or automobile while holding one brand or another.

The greatest gum maker in the world also cultivated the chewers of the future, sending more than 750,000 two-year-olds two sticks of gum every year on their birthdays. Among the radio programs he sponsored was a show called "The Lone Wolf;" eventually some 100,000 boys enrolled in the program's "tribe," making it the largest Indian tribe on record. Then there were his Mother Goose books, rewritten to tie chewing gum into nursery jingles and dedicated "To the children of the world—from 6 to 60." Over a two-year period beginning in 1915 he distributed about 14 million of these. Featuring the Sprightly Spearmen, Wrigley's sprites, the rhymes were often crude but always made their point:

The most famous Wrigley advertisement, the "mile long" sign along the railroad tracks in the Atlantic City Meadows. *Wm. Wrigley Jr. Company*

Jack be nimble
  Jack be quick
Jack run and get your
  WRIGLEY stick!

One, two—it's good to chew,
Three, four—they all want more,
Five—six, it comes in sticks,

Seven, eight—the flavor's great,
Nine, ten—gum again!
It's WRIGLEY'S.

As I was going to St. Ives
I met a man with seven wives,
Each wife had a fine clear skin,
All were fat—not one was thin,
And each had a dimple in her chin:
What caused it?—WRIGLEY'S!

The Mother Goose booklets, written when relatively few were concerned with dieting, were filled with reminders that Wrigley gum steadied the nerves, sweetened the breath, soothed the throat, relieved thirst, quickened the appetite and aided digestion. "Have plenty of chewing gum on hand," one

From the beginning, William Wrigley Jr., who revolutionized gum advertising, offered thousands of premiums to dealers to get them to carry his gum. The premiums were as varied as a coffee percolator, a slot machine, and an "Iroquois hatchet." *Wm. Wrigley Jr. Company*

"eminent physician" advised readers. "Begin chewing shortly after meals and chew until all 'fullness' disappears from the region of the belt." Dental benefits were stressed, too, and throughout the booklet, readers were reminded about the United Profit-Sharing Coupons wrapped around each Wrigley gum pack, these redeemable for over 1,000 premiums.

During World War I, Wrigley decided to continue advertising even though rationing of sugar and other problems limited gum production. Once the man made up his mind, he became an autocrat. "Suppose your board of directors don't agree with you?" a reporter asked him on one occasion. "Then we'll get a new board of directors," he replied. And so gum was advertised when there wasn't much gum to sell, the Wrigley name kept before the public. Wrigley ads on billboards and in print urged Americans to buy Liberty Bonds and War Savings Stamps, to contribute to the Red Cross. The company even paid its dividends in Liberty Bonds.

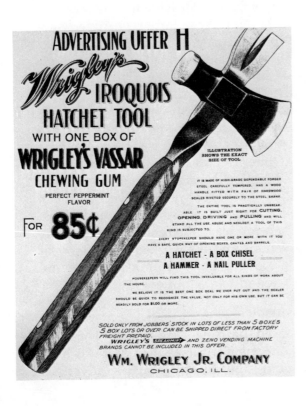

ROLLO FILMS, PHOTOGRAPHER, SAYS_"IT'S A SNAP. I FOCUS THEIR ATTENTION ON WRIGLEY'S AND DEVELOP A PICTURE OF CONTENTMENT, ENLARGED. I'M NEVER IN THE DARK ABOUT THIS GUM. IT SATISFIES ALL, WITHOUT A SINGLE NEGATIVE".

"Tell 'em quick and tell 'em often!" William Wrigley Jr. insisted. Humorous ads like this appeared in newspapers and magazines throughout the Roaring Twenties. *Wm. Wrigley Jr. Company*

Wrigley plunged so deeply into advertising that he acquired a controlling interest in the New York Subways Advertising Company. His son, Philip K. Wrigley, who had already set up a company plant in Australia, finally persuaded him to advertise on the radio. The Wrigley Review—the first nationwide musical show—was by 1927 bringing us songs like "Chloe," "Making Whoopee," and "Ah, Sweet Mystery of Life," while another company show introduced Guy Lombardo and His Royal Canadians for the first time. Wrigley was for a long time the largest advertiser in America and up to his death in 1931 had spent over a hundred million dollars on ads of one kind or another. His advertisements, and those of his heirs, have been criticized by some admen as unimaginative and repetitious. But a company spokesman replies: "We're advertising to the masses, not Madison Avenue. And it's worked year after year after year and we've sold a lot of gum. Our philosophy around here is still 'Tell 'em quick and tell 'em often' . . . "

Gum's Ambassador of Goodwill

Full-shouldered, full-faced, flashing a big mouthful of white teeth without a carie among them, Wrigley the Great was himself a living ad for his gum—the country's biggest advertiser was the world's greatest self-advertiser. A good case could be made that gum's goodwill ambassador even won out by sheer force of personality. Perhaps his chief asset was gregariousness—his friends ranged from Tommy, the Chicago Cubs' batboy, to kings and presidents. Red-faced and beaming, he looked like a jolly bartender and acted like a boy awed and delighted with everything under the Christmas tree. Everything Wrigley did seemed to propel him and his gum into the news, from his building of the Arizona Biltmore in Phoenix to his purchase of Catalina, "the isle with a smile" off the California coast that he had bought sight unseen for $2 million, extensively developed, and refused to sell for $30 million. The $25,000 marathon he sponsored for swimmers of Catalina Channel made good copy, as did the $20 million he spent developing the island, the $2 million dance hall (the biggest in the world) that he erected there, and the island aviary he stocked with over 6,500 birds . . . No doubt he worked hard for much of this publicity. There is one story, possibly apocryphal, that when Wrigley was furnishing his Chicago apartment on Lake Shore Drive he said to his secretary: "Measure those bookshelves with a yardstick and buy enough books to fill 'em . . . plenty of snappy red and green books with plenty of gilt lettering. I want a swell showing." True or false, the tale is symptomatic. When Wrigley decided that a Wrigley Company skyscraper would improve its image, he contacted the best firm of architects in Chicago and asked them to design a shiny white terra-cotta building which would look like a luscious birthday cake down whose sides someone had drawn his fingers. Still Chicago's most spectacular skyscraper, its white facades glistening under floodlights at night, the house that gum built was up in record time. It stood, too, as Wrigley's characteristically optimistic prophecy of Chicago's business growth—the first large office structure built North of the river outside the Loop.

Wrigley's purchase of the Chicago Cubs and subsequent building of Wrigley Field were also inspired in part by the publicity his gum would garner—men were the chief target of his sales campaigns and being mentioned on the sports pages could only help sales. But baseball was a great love, too; the man never did anything he didn't have unbounded enthusiasm for. Wrigley first bought into the Cubs in 1916 and

The Palace That Gum Built—the famous Wrigley Building
in Chicago. *Wm. Wrigley Jr. Company*

eventually became controlling stockholder. There was nothing he liked better than a good old-fashioned slugfest, "watching the boys sock that apple," and he'd often sit in his box seat handing out cigars for home runs. It's said that one summer afternoon he cancelled the signing of a million-dollar advertising contract. "The hell with it today!" he boomed. "The Giants are in town!" Wrigley brought in his great hero Roger ("Rajah") Hornsby to manage the Cubs, spent $300,000 trying to find a good third baseman, and went through $6 million over the years in strengthening the team—though he never realized his dream of a World Series championship pennant. He also made the Cubs profitable with such innovations as free passes to women on "Ladies' Days" and broadcasting games (with the idea in mind that distributing free samples worked as well with baseball as with gum). On his death there were testimonials from practically all baseball greats, ranging from Commissioner Kenesaw Landis to a grizzled old baseball man who called Wrigley "the finest God-damned club owner in the business." Wrigley was so good-natured that Marx and Lenin might even have played for him. When the Cubs won the 1929 National League pennant, he told his players to go out and celebrate, on him, warning them that no expense account under $50 would be accepted.

The Great Wrigley probably never once in his life doubted his own abilities. "With such confidence," a contemporary held, "the wonder is not that he created by far the biggest chewing gum company in the world . . . but that he did not also become President of the U.S. and dictator of Russia into the bargain." Self-doubt was an alien concept to the overlord of gum. "Fear saps more men than almost anything else in the world," he maintained. "Thousands are ruled by it. They're afraid they'll oversleep in the morning . . . afraid somebody in the office is talking about them, afraid they'll lose their job or money. Anyone with such a program of life is running on about fifteen percent engine power and wearing out his machinery. I've been broke three times since I started business. Nobody knew it except myself and it didn't cause me loss of a minute's sleep. There's nothing in life that can really hurt you except yourself."

Nothing sapped the chewing gum king of kings. Bankrupt three times, wiped out by factory fires twice in the early years, his astounding vitality saw him through." NOTHING GREAT WAS EVER

ACCOMPLISHED WITHOUT ENTHUSIASM," read one of the inevitable black-framed mottoes on his office walls. Zest, enthusiasm, energy—what others try to do with amphetamines came naturally to Wrigley the Great. He couldn't wait for another day to begin, so sorry was he that a day had ended. Late to bed and up at five every morning, when the air seemed "less breathed out," Wrigley kept in top physical shape by riding, swimming, playing tennis and boxing almost daily. Money was never his chief preoccupation. "The only real joy in business is the joy of creation," he said. "Making money in itself doesn't amount to a hill of beans." The joy of creation, as he saw it, kept him close to his business at all times; there were few conventional vacations. Often he'd call Chicago from across the country and spend hours on the phone, speaking to everyone in the office. Once, on a world cruise, he left his family and disembarked when the ship reached Egypt, catching another boat to England, where he plunged into the European end of his business. The aimless, slow tempo of the trip had bored and depressed him.

But for all his freewheeling and dealing the Great Wrigley was basically a decent man who played by the rules. Another motto over his desk read: "WHEN THE ONE GREAT SCORER COMES TO WRITE AGAINST YOUR NAME, HE WRITES NOT THAT YOU WON OR LOST BUT HOW YOU PLAYED THE GAME." His credo, this platitude. There seemed to be no deception about the man, he talked candidly to anyone who wanted to see him. Involved in numerous charities, he was the first manufacturer in the country to give his employees the freedom of Saturdays off and offered women employees free manicures and shampoos once a month on company time. Work clothes were laundered free at Wrigley and a cafeteria provided food at less than cost; there was free medical care for those injured or taken ill at work, and paid-up life insurance for every employee. In the depths of the Great Depression Wrigley pioneered a form of guaranteed annual wage, when there was no government unemployment insurance. Such gestures, of course, made good business sense and engendered goodwill, but they were dictated by compassion. Wrigley simply liked and trusted people; his optimistic faith was what separates him in history from great showmen and con men like Barnum, Bet-a-Million Gates and Diamond Jim Brady. Nothing angered him more, he said, than learning that someone wasn't "playing the game," or was taking advantage of another person. Once a millionaire acquaintance of his set out to acquire a city block of property for the erection of a sky-scraper. On one corner stood a widow's home that was mortgaged by the local bank and when the widow refused to sell at his price, the millionaire pressured the bank not to renew the mortgage. Learning of this, Wrigley bought the mortgage himself. Before the millionaire was able to get it, he had to pay so high a price that the widow lived on the proceeds the rest of her life.

One time Wrigley built a food-at-cost cafeteria on his Catalina Island when local merchants were gypping Mexican workers there. On another occasion he threatened to turn his Michigan vacation cottage into a home for orphans if local residents refused to sell property to his friend the famous, or notorious, politician "Big Bill The Builder" Thompson. But not a scintilla of scandal seems to have touched the man through-out his long career, despite his varied friendships. The worst anyone who remembers will say is that it is scandalous that the Chicago Cubs haven't had more winning teams. Maybe great gum people chew all their temptations away.

Wrigley died, when his great parade drum of a heart burst, at his winter home in Phoenix in 1932, aged 70. He was buried on his beloved Catalina, near Mount Ada, which he had named for his wife. The chewing gum king of kings, a grammar-school dropout who started with 35 bucks of his own, left behind an estate of over $200 million and a congrega-tion of chewers ranging from English noblemen to rickshaw drivers and coolies. As early as 1910, when he established a plant in Canada, Wrigley had foreseen the world market for chewing gum and less than 20 years later there were Wrigley factories everywhere; his little green gum packages were being printed in 37 languages, his plants were producing 40 million sticks of gum a day—at a time when raw materials and wages represented only 35 percent of gum's wholesale cost, the re-maining 65 percent almost pure profit. "Nothing is so much fun as business," this incorrigible optimist once said. Life was "a joke, a fine rich joke." The last of the nickel millionaires had taught the chewing gum people everything they needed to know about selling gum and though his death marked the end of an era in American business—the Age of the Great Showman—due to him what had once been considered a minor vice was now either a major vice or a universal custom.

CHAPTER 8

The Great Chewing Gum Orgy

"IF Mr. Wrigley has become one of the ten wealthiest millionaires in America," the *New Statesman* observed in 1928, "it is because humanity has instinctively recognized that he was helping to restore it to the lost art of chewing." The Great Wrigley and his wary competitors, soon eager to learn from his every lesson, taught America and the world to chew gum without guilt and with considerable passion and vigor. By the time of his passing, posters, billboards, car cards, newspapers and magazines carried snappy gum messages about all the leading brands. American Chicle introduced attractive "sampling girls" dressed in orange-colored satin who in teams of four to eight moved from city to city passing out sticks of

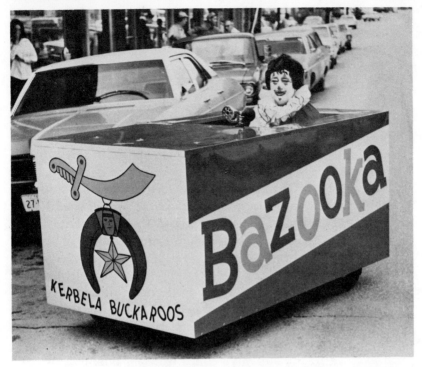

Gum used to be advertised in the streets from the sides of horse-drawn wagons. Today the operation is motorized. *Topps Chewing Gum, Inc.*

Adams' Blackjack, Dentyne, Clove and other favorites. Sampling was done on a large scale. Each girl was trained to give away 5,000 sticks of gum a day and in one year alone over a million and a half New Yorkers tried American Chicle products.

Gum girdled the globe, without stretching, and chewing became so popular that one anonymous satirist even proposed using it as the basis for a tongue-in-cheek "universal tongue"—a language which "could be understood without the speaking of a word in any place at any time." Following is the efficiency expert's specific plan for his gum-chomping Esperanto:

> You have doubtless observed how a large variety of motions are employed by gum chewers, depending upon

their mood. There is the contented man or woman who chews his or her gum legato, or smoothly, with the slow, rotary, ruminative motion of a cow assimilating its cud. Then there are those excited ones who chew staccato, with quick up and down jabs into the unoffending mouthful. Others employ the andante movement, a moderate time-spaced nibbling. Still others worry their gum, like a hungry dog with a bone, in the allegro or quick manner. Some, while thinking deeply, keep their jaws going scherzo without a second's rest. All that is necessary is to work out a code in which these various chewing motions represent certain words or phrases. You will readily see that each single motion or combination of motions employed in gum chewing represents a letter of the alphabet or a phrase of our universal language. We get up this universal code, print it on a card, and sell it to the gum chewers . . . How many millions of gum chewers are there? How many billions of packages of gum are sold in a day? Talk about profits! Billions! It has Volapük and the deaf and dumb language beaten to a frazzle . . . People traveling in the subways could transact business or conduct social amenities without straining their voices or rasping their throats. Lovers could quarrel in public without attracting the police, or arrange an elopement while father and mother were in the same room. Our universal gum language would make for national quiet and repose of manner. A complete waste of energy would be directed into channels of untold usefulness . . .

But most die-hards didn't take "the chewing gum menace" quite so lightly or tolerantly. A snaggle-toothed sermonizer summed up the chief products of the good old U.S.A. as "the cud-chewing cow, the swill-swigging sow—and the gum-chewing girl." Another extremist vowed that there was nothing "so organically repulsive as the animal-munching of gum-chewers," and a confirmed elitist insisted that only "self-conscious peasants" chew gum to make themselves look natural. Instructed this last lock-jawed Comstock:

Ninety percent of the idiotic chomping and facial contortions incidental to the chewing of gum is due to the characteristic peasant trait of overweening self-consciousness. All those futile muscular movements are merely the outward, visible expression of the shameful self-consciousness they are intended to conceal; and so long as adequate physical training, for the purpose of eradicating this trait, is not taught in our public schools, so long will we have a large peasant population, with gum-chewing as the characteristic stigmata of the class.

Emily Post, for her part, still refused even to mention gum chewing in edition after edition of her *Etiquette*. Chewing gum continued to be used in the theatre and early movies as a prop for streetwalkers, gangsters and car hops—you never noticed it in the mouth of a leading man or lady. The puritan wit was in evidence everywhere. "The difference between a secretary and a stenographer," intoned the dean of the commercial department at one state university to each beginning class, "is that a *stenographer*, my dears, *chews gum*." A literary critic on a Chicago newspaper alluded to gum chewing in describing popular novels of the day, his words further besmirching the name of chicle and perhaps explaining in part why no one dared to write much about the greatness of gum. "These books," he noted, "are the chewing-gum of literature, offering neither savor nor nutrient, only subserving the mechanical process of mastication."

Chewing Gum Goes to War

Overseas, chewing gum's foes were stronger, if anything. As early as 1898 crusty Britishers were inveighing against American chewing gum. In that year the New York *Daily Tribune* carried the following dispatch from London: "Health authorities here have issued a warning against the use of American chewing gum, which is fast becoming a rage among the children of the East End. The authorities consider it more dangerous than the 'ice cream' which the Italians sell in the street, and which has been the subject of a rigorous crusade." European abstainers ranged from staunch royalists to revolutionaries like Leon Trotsky, who proclaimed that chewing gum was just another capitalist opiate to make the masses munch away their misery instead of doing something about it.

When chewing gum was supplied to American Expeditionary forces during World War I and offered for sale in quartermaster canteens, the protest was so loud everywhere that one might have thought the Yanks had sacked the Louvre or pitched tents in Westminster Abbey. The respected American novelist Gertrude Atherton, author of *The Californians*, added her voice to the French resistance. Wrote Mrs. Atherton:

> It had been my fond hope that the contact of our boys with the politest nation in the world would send them home vastly improved in manners . . . On the contrary, all France has fallen victim to the vulgarist of American habits, not excepting the justly renowned toothpick. The French jaw is working as one. Great and famous generals promenade the boulevards grinding away like the historic cow on its cud. Duchessess have learned to flirt gum agiley from one jaw to the other or to paste it on the underside of the table. Children may be seen on the street any day pulling out a long string from their lips and chuckling with glee as it snaps back again . . . The soul writhes.

Mrs. Atherton concluded that even "the savage and unhumorous Hun" would guffaw at the spectacle of gumchewing Frenchmen. She implored Herbert Hoover, then head of the wartime Food Administration, to place an embargo on all gum exports so that we could give the French "our lives and our billions, but not our filthy habits," even if gum chewing had "already fastened itself upon them like a pernicious drug."

Gum had its legions of defenders, though. "Chewing on gum," a British writer reasoned, "is at least a hundred times more natural than cigarette smoking or the use of lipstick. It is more natural than playing lawn-tennis or driving a motor-car or writing with a fountain pen. Prime Minister Gladstone attributed his long life to determined chewing and by chewing Mr. Fletcher preserved himself from an early grave so that at the age of sixty he was able to turn a back somersault."

Patriots also rushed to gum's aid. American newspapers featured headlines like CHEWING GUM BOLSTERS COURAGE WHILE SHELLS ARE FLYING. The War Department didn't go so far, but issued a lengthy statement that the gum people publicized for years: "It has often been found that on long marches, where troops are unable to get sufficient water, *chewing gum is very effective in relieving thirst* . . . Recently the

commanding officer of a regiment of field artillery . . . stated
that 250 pounds of chewing gum would save several hundred
gallons of water when most needed. He pointed out that chewing gum is cheap and that there are times when water is very
expensive and almost unobtainable . . . "

GOD BLESS DEAR DADDY WHO IS FIGHTING THE HUN AND SEND HIM HELP,
World War I posters pleaded—and chewing gum answered
their plea. A French representative of the American Red Cross
cabled an urgent demand for chewing gum for use in recon-
quered territory where retreating Germans had poisoned the
water and where allied soldiers came upon the bodies of dead
German soldiers every time they dug a well. Such requests led
the Red Cross to send abroad 4.5 million packs of chewing
gum in 1918, each one labeled "Gift of the American Red
Cross." The Quartermaster Corps placed orders for 2.3 million
packs of chewing gum in 1918 alone, a Canadian retailer sent
30 thousand packs of gum to Canada's soldiers as a Christmas
present, and British press tycoon Lord Northcliffe urged
people to include gum in the parcels they sent to the boys over
there.

As a result of the Great War gum chewing was permitted in
the American Navy for the first time. The Air Corps, equally
enthusiastic about the virtues of chewing gum in soothing the
nerves and relieving air pressure on eardrums at high al-
titudes, included generous gum allowances in their rations.
Other nations didn't let this "secret weapon" or "revolu-
tionary innovation in military equipment" pass unheeded and
quickly permitted their soldiers and fliers to chew on duty. "If
it is generally recognized that chewing gum can be of assistance to the bravest men on earth," someone observed, "then it
is clear that derisive laughter at the mere mention of chewing
gum is misplaced and unintelligent. Chewing gum may be
said, indeed, to have acquired a new dignity in recent years. If
Dr. Johnson had been living today . . . he would have said,
not 'Brandy for heroes,' but 'Spearmint for heroes.' "

As for Gertrude Atherton, she didn't escape unscathed, one
constant reader taking her to task in the letters columns of the
New York Times. Tongue in cheek, he wrote:

> With Mrs. Atherton, I too should tremble lest France
> live to curse us, her myriad brave jaws working on myriad
> lumps of chewing gum. Perhaps General Sherman had

chewing gum in mind when he said, "War is hell!" It is nothing to me that Columbus, in telling of things of great value he had discovered in America, mentioned chewing gum. Christopher was only a sort of semi-American roughneck, whanging eggs butt-end down on tables, and no doubt he was low enough to chew gum . . . But every one has spoken of the splendid quality of men we have in our forces. They are the gum chewers. They have good teeth and can chew gum, and good teeth mean good health. If every Frenchman is chewing gum now, it is a sign that every Frenchman has better teeth than he used to have. There was a time when we thought the Frenchman was effeminate and effete; now we can admire him—we know he can fight like a hero and chew gum like an American . . . I hate to say such a thing, but it seems to me that when war is making a hell of a huge portion of the world . . . a worrying thought about gum chewing is about as important as fretting because our soldiers do not manicure their nails every morning . . . If our boys, over there to rip the hides off the Germans, want to chew gum, let 'em chew! If they want ten tons of gum, send 'em eleven tons! Even if Mrs. Atherton's soul—and it is a perfectly good soul—does 'writhe'.

Though chewing gum turned out to be no more of a "secret weapon" than it did a "corruptor of culture," its consumption increased a hundred-fold among fighting men. A New York doctor urged that no gum be chewed at home, outlining a complicated plan for the rationing of chewing gum so that our troops could get all they needed. When Queen Sophia of Greece found no chewing gum could be had in her country, she cabled a New York paper asking that a shipment be forwarded to Greek troops. The mystified editor cabled back for an explanation, the order was confirmed and a consignment of chewing gum was forwarded with the compliments of an American firm. The donors soon received the following note from the Queen's lady-in-waiting:

Dear Sirs:
    Her majesty the Queen desires to convey to you her sincerest thanks for your most generous donation of chewing gum for the use of our army. Her Majesty fully ap-

preciates your promptitude to offer such a liberal quantity
of an article so useful to our soldiers in the field.
  Believe me,

Sincerely yours,
ANGELICA CONTOSTAVLON

The Greek lady-in-waiting may have felt it imperative to
sign off with a "believe me." But others had no reason to
doubt that the distribution of millions of packs of chewing
gum would mean "a relief from nervous tension, an aid to
digestion, a substitute for tobacco, and in the absence of water
fit to drink, a mitigant of thirst for the doughboys in France."
Our troops soon spread *le vice Americain* wherever they went,
"*Chewing gomme, s'il vous plait* (chewing gum, please)" a familiar request from French children, who introduced their elders
to the delicacy. By the time the war ended the French were
such dedicated chewers that their government bought a vast
quantity of gum from U.S. Army suppliers. However, the gum
had been exposed to the weather for months and the canny
French demanded that the maker, Wrigley, take it back as im-
perfect and send over new gum. Wrigley did so rather than
have his reputation spoiled in a new market . . .

When Johnny Came Chomping Home Again

  To Wrigley and the other gum makers who followed his
lead, World War I proved to be the turning point in making
peoplekind a universal gum-chewing machine. Gum chewing
now knew no national boundaries. "People chew harder when
they are sad," the chewing gum king had predicted and the
Great War also proved this beyond a doubt. Since then gum
sales have always risen sharply with every war or depression,
or whenever people have been deprived of something, as was
the case during Prohibition and after the 1964 Surgeon's General report linking cancer and smoking. Some enterprising
sociologist might well represent increased tension of any kind
on a graph showing the increase of gum chewing. In any
event, the value of chewing gum exports to all countries was
less than $200,000 in 1914—by the end of World War I it to-
talled well over $2 million, America herself spending more on
candy and chewing gum combined than on the peacetime
army. Sometimes this was due to factors like the rationing of

other confections utilizing far more sugar, or the use of gum in places like munitions factories where smoking was prohibited, but generally the habit caught on simply because people liked chomping on gum. England, France, Belgium and Italy were the big chewers at the war's end. Germany, for her part, ordered only one dollar's worth in 1918, leading a few gum chauvinists there to charge that this was the reason she had lost the war. Yet she quickly corrected her strategic error. Germany agreed to let an American concern set up a chewing gum plant in Frankfurt at the end of the hostilities, taxes on profits from the enterprise helping her to pay her reparations. She too began chewing with a vengeance, and may even have taken all the chewing gum propaganda too seriously. Could be, someone suggested, that the Germans chewed themselves into believing they were a "master race."

Gum chewing had increased tremendously on the home front during the war years. Woolworth's Five & Ten Cent Stores alone sold over 10 million packs of gum in 1917. Going into the postwar period Americans mumbled on close to 100 sticks a mouth annually, compared to 39 sticks in 1914. Though gum was now being shipped to 75 countries around the world, we masticated some 20 times more than the rest of mankind combined, close to a pound a year for every man, woman and child in the country. The gum makers were only disappointed about domestic male chewers, who had declined in number with the advent of Prohibition—men no longer needing to camouflage their breath.

American women continued to nibble and gnaw on their cuds, despite Cassandras who warned that chewing gum made the modern girl's face hard and unfeminine. "Many a modern woman has a face as hard as the crockery of a railroad lunch counter," Mrs. Ruth J. Maurer told a convention of cosmeticians in 1926. "And the reason is chewing gum. Human beings were not meant to be ruminating animals, and when we try it there is some kind of rebellion of nature and the muscles become unduly enlarged." Replied a renegade: "Surely there existed hard-faced, large-jawed women before the invention of chewing gum. Jezabel lived some thousands of years before Mr. Wrigley . . . Beauty, besides, is a spiritual as well as a physical thing, and that state of blessed calm which is induced by chewing would, I am sure, aid a lovely face to be still lovelier. Who knows but that we may eventually find in chewing gum the great remedy for the unrest of these days."

But there was no putting down the preachers for long. Most of the Immovable-Jawed blasted gum for what they considered esthetic reasons. The attorney William Rand, for instance, was examining a witness in court in 1923 when the judge interrupted him in the middle of a sentence and asked: "You are chewing gum, are you not, Mr. Rand?" "Yes, your Honor," Rand replied. "I didn't intend to offend the court. My throat is dry, and I would keep an attendant busy carrying water to me." "Stop chewing; it is offensive to me," the judge ordered. "If you need water, court attendants will bring it to you." At least one New York paper headlined the story on the front page.

Children were urged to stop chewing gum by most health experts. An ascetic addressing parents in a *Hygeia* article called "Gum and the Graces" had all the answers. "Gum chewing in its most virulent form is nothing less than an addiction," she was sure, "and the poor unfortunate who becomes an addict in childhood is only too likely to grow up into a gum-chewing woman or a tobacco-chewing man . . . The perpetual public chewing of gum cannot be classed as a crime, but the child who depends on the mastication of a wad of gum for his sense of wellbeing cannot be expected to develop the desirable graces of adulthood."

Though few of us, save Nijinskys, "develop the desirable graces of adulthood," no matter what we chew on, the same writer observed that "anxiety, perturbation and anger" can be noted in the gum chewer by "a jerky chewing rhythm accompanied by occasional sharp snaps," while a contemplative mood or deep depression found expression "in a retarded tempo and the circular motion employed by the ruminating cow." This wasn't the first or last time the gum chewer was compared to a ruminating cow, the most famous example probably being an anonymous poem circulating around the country in the late twenties:

> The gum-chewing girl
>   And the cud-chewing cow
> Are somewhat alike,
>   Yet different somehow.

And what is the difference?
I think I know now—
It's the clear thoughtful look
On the face of the cow!

Chewing gum rolled on against the intangible opposition of manners. Often it had to roll uphill. In England, for example, the head of Scotland Yard got so disgusted seeing his Bobbies "incessantly masticating" while they controlled traffic or pounded their beats that he banned all gum chewing by policemen on duty. This evoked much laughter in the Commons when the Home Secretary was questioned about the regulation. Lady Astor wanted to know if the Secretary himself found it more difficult to answer questions while on duty when he was chewing gum. The House came down when the Home Secretary explained that one of the reasons why a policeman wasn't allowed to chew gum was because when he blew his whistle he might blow gum into it and fail to get the aid he needed.

England, with her strong tradition of civil liberties, responded admirably on the whole to the scandalous Scotland Yard chewing gum ban. "The world has groaned under many tyrannies in the past," a *Times* editorial noted. "There was Pharaoh, and there was Nero, and there was Oliver Cromwell; but under none of these rulers, despotic though they were, was a member of the police force forbidden to chew while on duty. Even Mussolini, who enjoys forbidding people to do things as much as any man living, has never taken so extreme a step as this." Another observer saw the prohibition as the act of "kill-joys who hate to see the human jaws moving in enjoyment, who dislike the very movements of the human face with the jaws slowly moving in quiet ecstasy, who would forbid eating anything anytime anywhere." Some Englishmen did say good riddance to policemen "standing in the middle of London streets, moving their jaws like cattle in a field" and others added that bloody American slang and cocktails ought to be banned along with gum. Then there was the London magistrate who on seeing a witness chewing gum, commented: "Come, young man, haven't you finished breakfast, or are you an American?" But most Britishers agreed with the columnist who held that if chewing gum was horrible "it must

surely be equally horrible to see people chewing salmon and
fish and strawberries at a dinner table . . . ''

Chewing Our Way Through the Depression

Despite all the nasty nonchewers, Americans were spending
well over $100 million yearly for some 700 million pounds of
gum before the roaring twenties went out whimpering and
crying—more than $2 million a week. At a meeting of the
National Association of Chewing Gum Manufacturers in 1928,
L. W. Hoskins, president of the organization, told members
that sufficient energy to light a city of 600,000 was released
daily by the facial calisthenics of America's gum-chewing
population. Mr. Hoskins, of the chewy-sounding Walla-Walla
Gum Company, asked his audience to visualize a band ½-inch
thick and 3 inches wide which (without stretching) would circle the globe at its widest circumference. Such a belt, he assured everyone, represented the annual output of chewing
gum in America. If apportioned among the world's population
it would give every living person four sticks of gum a year.

Gum used to be a seasonal item, sales beginning in the late
spring when the drugstores opened their fountains, putting
out gum at the same time, and ending in the autumn. The
advertising of Wrigley and the other gum magnates changed
all that, though, and by the time of the Great Depression gum
was a year-round proposition. One leading advertiser was
Philip Knight Wrigley, who took charge of the Wrigley Company when his father died and still heads it today. Wrigley
proved to have as much of a flair for gum as his predecessor.
"I, and no one else, can ever hope to fill his shoes," he once
said of his father, but he also remarked that "My father was my
college," as far as the chewing gum business was concerned.
Since the younger Wrigley took charge in 1932, company assets
have increased from $61 million to $231 million (1973); add to
this the Wrigley-owned Chicago Cubs, Catalina Island, large
interests in many airlines (United, for one), and even the
unique Wrigley herd of Arabian horses, and the size of the
empire that gum built becomes apparent.

A brilliant chip off the old chicle block, though a far more
reserved man than his father (few people call Mr. Wrigley
"Phil" and he detests the designation "P.K."), Philip Wrigley
from the beginning instituted many national campaigns that

boosted sales. In 1932 he undertook to learn why people chewed gum and was typically candid in relating the results of his poll. All over the country during the depths of the Great Depression, P. K. Wrigley's Mr. Spear and Miss Mint gave a dollar for an answer from anyone who had an open pack of Wrigley's in his pocket. The campaign ran a full three years and Wrigley admitted that the leading reasons for chewing were always those which his advertising was stressing at the moment. It seemed impossible to say "relieves nervous tension" millions of times without people believing it.

The Great Depression meant good times for the gum people, despite unscientific enemies like the electrical genius Nikola Tesla, who claimed in 1932 that "by the exhaustion of the salivary glands, gum chewing puts many a foolish victim in the grave!" Besides breeding more anxious people who chewed more, no doubt in the "retarded tempo and circular motion" we are told indicates a deep blue funk, the Depression brought the end of Prohibition in 1934. As men took to drinking again, they turned to chewing gum to disguise their breath from bosses, Thurberesque wives and ministers making their calls. Male gum chewers began to increase for the first time in a long while, men encouraged by virile examples like Lou Gehrig, the pride of the Yankees, who seemed to always have a wad in his mouth, and many other athletes. American Chicle's Adams' Clove gum was a particular favorite with drinking men. Adams' Clove hit the market the year Prohibition was repealed, its ads promising users that "It takes your breath away!"

Chewing gum grew so popular in the thirties that it became the instrument used in another popular Great Depression pastime—murder. In 1934 a ghastly gum murder plot was uncovered in Sacramento, California when Mrs. Georgia McKenzie found four innocent-enough-looking sticks of chewing gum near her door on coming home from work one fine June evening. Each stick had been carefully wrapped in a small brown envelope bearing the typewritten word SAMPLE. Mrs. McKenzie, a divorcée living with her mother and her two teen-aged sons, knew that identical envelopes had been delivered to three other residences adjoining her home, and the next day decided to try a sample. Taking an envelope from her pocket book, she opened it, unwrapped the gum and popped it in her mouth. But she quickly detected a bitter, burning taste and spit the gum out. When police analyzed the wad Mrs. McKenzie brought to them, they found it coated with enough deadly poison to literally kill a dozen people. The gum had been treated by spreading poison over it much like icing would be spread on a cake and then dusting it with powdered sugar to make it appear natural. On determining that the gum delivered to adjoining houses wasn't poisoned, police concluded that someone had diabolically plotted to kill the entire McKenzie family. The proprietor of an automobile camp nearby soon reported that he had become suspicious of a woman who rented a cabin a few hours before the gum was found—especially when he peered into the cabin to see her dusting a white powder over pieces of gum. But although police searched everywhere, the abominable gum fiend was never found and remains unknown to history.

The case of the Poisoned Spearmint was about the only bad news for the gum people during the Great Depression. Increased revenues throughout Depression years enabled the gum companies to invest almost as heavily in overseas expansion as they had in the boom times of the twenties. America now had what the Department of Commerce called "a practical monopoly" of the chewing gum industry. Our gum exports were well over ten times what they had been before World War I and went to 80 or more countries—Great Britain, the Netherlands, Italy, Canada and Mexico and the Philippines being our chief customers at the time. Gum wrappers by 1930 were printed in at least 50 languages, this in itself strong evidence that chewing gum had become a permanent fixture everywhere. There was a chewing gum factory in Egypt in the shadows of the pyramids; the "chewing gum habit" caught on in Africa; all South America switched from raw chicle to *chingongo* (this word the result of young hawkers on Panamanian streets attempting to say "chewing gum"). Throughout the world, chewing gum broke down linguistic and social barriers, only the inscrutable Orient remaining to be conquered . . .

Gum Invades Asia

Chewing gum launched its attack on the Orient when the restless William Wrigley Jr. took his first round-the-world cruise in 1913. At the time only a few hundred dollars' worth of gum was sold there yearly, but Wrigley saw the possibility of developing a great market. Noticing that thousands of natives in India, Ceylon, and Burma munched on the addictive betel nut that turned mouths, walls and floors carmine, he decided to convert them to chewing gum. Wrigley spent large sums in India on an unsuccessful campaign (Indian betel chewers still remain a large potential market) and then moved on to more fertile ground in Japan and China. In his endeavors he was aided immensely by his nephew, Byron Wrigley, and a mysterious Englishman by the name of W. H. Stanley, who headed Wrigley's overseas operations for almost 40 years and was so secretive that he destroyed all his files when he retired in the 1950s. Wrigley executives like these men have been characterized as missionary workers. Says one company officer:

> Young Byron Wrigley could chase down 500 glass jars of stale stick gum circulating throughout the East Indies or enjoy a little polo with an Indian maharaja and his court. Dressed in white suits and broad rimmed hats, the Chicago missionaries spread the name of Wrigley's chewing gum to all the far points of the world. Whether they just nailed tin signs up to bamboo posts or organized children to operate as street vendors costumed as Spearmen, they made the Wrigley's brands world famous.

When American chewing gum made its appearance in Japan, the Japanese press didn't take kindly to this sticky grey devil brought by the white devils. Editorial writers emphasized the bad habits alleged to result from habitual gum chewing. The remains of used gum left in conspicuous places were condemned as disease carriers and in districts of the Izu Peninsula, police were ordered to suppress what had become not only "a nuisance but also a menace to the public health." Yet advertising changed everything in the island kingdom. Brass bands were hired, banner-carriers commandeered, lecturers employed. Throughout the land of the Mikado the gospel of gum was carried from village to village. Customers first had to be taught not to swallow gum. Once a crowd had gathered in answer to the airs from the chewing gum band, a lecturer would demonstrate just how gum should be treated. Usually a university student, or another respected figure, he would gravely unfold the wrapper, hold the stick of gum aloft, then just as gravely place it in his mouth, working his jaws furiously to show the crowd that chewing was the thing.

Two kinds of advertisements were used for gum in The Land of the Rising Sun, one for the educated class and another for the semi-illiterate. Billboards went up along the Ginza in Tokyo. No carnival or fair was complete without its chewing gum booth, and at baseball games, which were fast becoming a national mania in Japan, scoreboards first told people what gum was and, secondly, the score. These methods worked and Japan came into the fold. One society matron on a trip to the Far East noticed that her rickshaw man, dressed in the traditional attire, was moving his lips rhythmically as he jogged along. "Doubtlessly he is intoning some prayer to the patron saint of the rickshaw men," she observed, until she saw him take a big wad of chewing gum from his mouth and stick it on the underside of one of his shafts.

It was Wrigley, too, who solved the price problem in Japan, where few people could afford a five-cent pack of gum when a day's pay was often only ten cents. "The Japanese coolie buys from us not in packages, or even in penny-sticks, but in half-sticks," he once said. "He goes into a shop, planks down a sen, or the equivalent of half a cent—and that is what he gets. The shopkeeper cuts a stick in two for him." The same applied in China, where not one Chinese in 10,000 could afford to buy a whole stick of gum and Wrigley provided retailers with special shears for cutting sticks in half. Needless to say, youngsters who could afford half a stick treasured it with a spirit of economy that put to shame that of an American kid with an "all day sucker." A half-stick of gum lasted a week, even a month, and one cynic declared that the first package of gum sold in China is still in the active possession of the family that purchased it.

China presented even more difficult problems to the gum hucksters than Japan did. Although the ad campaigns were carried on in much the same manner as in Japan, great care had to be taken in the type of advertising used, for the Chinese peasant feared "demons" and believed that any figure represented on printed matter might be a sinister visitor of evil. A happy device, however, swept away all doubt. It seems that the outlines of a prominent gum maker's trademark not only coincided with the peculiar peaked architecture of the

Chinese, but also with the makeup of the characters of the language. The peasants accepted this as a reassuring omen and gum sales boomed when the countryside was billboarded with such signs or "bulletins," as the Chinese called them. Yet contrary to all principles of American advertising, local agents demanded signs covered with copy and showing only a small picture of the gum pack. Ad men bewailed the lack of force in the pictures, but finally realized that this was the way things were done in China.

By 1935 the Chinese were being told, like Americans and people everywhere, that gum whitened the teeth, dissipated halitosis and hastened digestion. Chomping on favorites like Wrigley's Spearmint, Sweetie Spearmint, Rose, and Bubble Gum brands, all made in America, the Chinese became a gum chewing nation, consuming well over a million dollars' worth of chewing gum annually. Only Japanese aggression in Manchuria ended the progress of the American gum moguls. Anti-Japanese sentiment resulted in boycotts of Japanese goods all over China and somehow the rumor got started that chewing gum had been invented by the Japanese and was manufactured in Japan. Soon after, Chiang Kai-shek managed to unite the Chinese for self-defense against invading Japanese armies and World War II began in Asia. Whether chewing gum was invented by the Japanese or not didn't matter at all anymore. The future of mastication in the Orient, and around the world for that matter, would have to be postponed for another decade. Nevertheless, the outcome was plainly visible. Wrigley and his competitors had proved that we are all alike under the lips, that we all have teeth there custom-made for chewing gum.

Stretching It Till Chewsday

CHAPTER 9

BY the beginning of World War II gum had become universally accepted—save for a few pockets of ideological resistance like the Soviet Union—and Emily Post had finally deigned to sanction its limited use in her awesome *Etiquette*. But Americans, who were easily chewing some 130 sticks a year per mouth, and fellow gum fiends around the world had to sacrifice their cuds for the war effort. Few people realize that gum was regarded as an essential product during World War II and that its manufacturers voluntarily rationed it. Thirst-quenching, soothing, practical where cigarettes weren't, a tooth cleaner where toothbrushes couldn't be used, tons of it were shipped to servicemen overseas. At night on the front lines, where the glow of a cigarette might betray a position, chewing gum was found by the military to be an adequate substitute for quieting nerves. Packed in K rations and survival kits, gum also served to patch jeep tires, gas tanks, life rafts, radio connections, and to fix machine guns, submarines and even the hydraulic landing gear on bombers. Some of these tales are P.R. puffery, but almost every ex-serviceman tells one and no doubt many are true.

The Yanks again spread the popularity of gum—to the earth's farthest reaches this time. "Any gum, chum?" was hurled at American troops in every country they entered, by people who often knew no other English. In Australia parents complained to the constabulary that soldiers were turning their children on to the vile chewing habit; natives on the remotest of Pacific islands emerged from the Stone Age chomping on gum or blowing bubbles. The relaxing effect of chewing gum on people under stress had been well-documented in scientific studies such as the one undertaken by Professor H. L. Hollingsworth of Columbia University (see Chapter 14), and World War II proved this beyond a doubt. Gum consumption among military personnel was *almost six times as great as for civilians during the period just before the war,* rising to an incredible 630 sticks a year per man—a statistic that even the gum people checked twice, believing as they did that sales had reached a saturation level when they hit around 100 sticks per capita.

American gum plants produced over 15 billion sticks of gum for the armed forces during World War II and everyone seemed to feel that chewing increased morale, eased tension, and promoted alertness, saving lives in the process. Gum was more than once used as a propaganda weapon to aid our allies. Early in the war, for example, the entire output of Wrigley's Australian factory disappeared. Nobody at Wrigley headquarters understood why and the Australian gum makers kept their lips sealed. Only later did it develop that the gum had been decked out in special wrappers—one side bearing the crossed flags of the United States and the Philippines and the other carrying the immortal words "I Shall Return—MacArthur." Thousands of packs of this specially wrapped gum were dropped from planes over the occupied Philippines.

On the wartime home front chawers did without. There just

Wrigley made a number of gums for the armed forces, including this legendary gum pack, which was air-dropped by the thousands behind the lines in the Philippines. *Wm. Wrigley Jr. Company*

weren't the raw materials available to make enough gum for everyone. Flavorings like peppermint and spearmint, essential oils that flavored 90 percent of U.S. chewing gum, were strictly rationed by the War Food Administration to assure amounts required for lend-lease to England. The war virtually dried up the supply of Central American chicle used to make gum base, as well as the supply of thousands of possible natural substitutes that botanists had discovered around the world. Shipping was so scarce that the usual supply of coffee could not be imported from Brazil, so it was impossible to expect that any gum base would be imported. The gum manufacturers did turn to a synthetic base known since the invention of bubble gum at the turn of the century—but sugar was drastically rationed, too, and gum has always been more than half sugar. As a result, black markets in gum thrived—kids commonly paid as much as 50 cents for a penny piece of bubble gum sold under the counter, and there were bubble gum lineups after the war that stretched around the block in many towns across the country.

Some gum fiends were incensed by the shortage. One outraged woman hauled a chain store into court for alleged violations of General Maximum Price Regulations because she said she got fewer pellets of candy-coated gum for more money than she paid when the regulations went into effect. Although the case was tossed out of court, the chain pulled all of the small-count packages off its counters and the manufacturers subsequently discontinued the item.

Any brand of gum—no matter how bad—sold during the war. Small neighborhood stores that used to sell a box of gum (20 packs) over a period of two weeks, found their supply exhausted in a day or two, and nonadvertised brands that once grew stale on dealers' shelves were snatched up readily. But a few companies, after going through their often extensive reserves of raw materials, decided that they couldn't make enough top quality gum to meet the needs of both servicemen and civilians. Wrigley, most notably, took Spearmint, Doublemint and Juicy Fruit off the civilian market in a move calculated to aid the war effort and protect the quality reputation of its brands. For civilians the company developed a wartime brand called Orbit, frankly telling the public that this product, though pure and wholesome, wasn't good enough to carry a standard Wrigley label. Orbit, made without the proportion of Far Eastern gums needed for a first-class product, tasted something like Juicy Fruit, and was advertised as "a plain but honest wartime chewing gum." The company was flooded with letters extolling its honesty and the Calvert Distillers Company took out a unique full-page ad in 60 major newspapers "to salute Wrigley, where honesty is still the best policy."

Honesty ultimately paid off for Wrigley. First, all company advertising was overhauled to fit gum's new role as an essential product necessary in the war effort. Frothy ads depicting people who chewed gum simply because they liked it were out; Wrigley advertising, which constituted an enormous 25 percent of its revenues, concentrated on serious messages to war workers and servicemen. Soon after Pearl Harbor, and long before Broadway itself was blacked out, the spectacular million-dollar Wrigley electric sign on Times Square (which burned enough electricity to supply a town of 20,000 people) was dismantled for the duration. The floodlights that had kept the Wrigley Building in Chicago glowing like an enormous wedding cake all night long were turned off. Wrigley voluntarily surrendered its entire half-million pound inventory of aluminum ingots reserved for wrapping foil, and gave the government free use of its mailing list of nearly a million retailers. All of the company's radio time—$20 million worth for two network programs alone—was devoted to selling not gum but war.

In order to drive home the idea that chewing gum was essential to the war effort, Wrigley made a fifteen-minute recording called a "mind-conditioner." The little opus was laid in a factory. The cast: assembly-line workers; the company president; an eager, insinuating voice called Monotony; a soft, tempting voice called Thirst; an alluring voice called Lady Nicotine; and, of course, Hitler himself. Hitler laughs nastily and says that he has trusty spies slowing down production in every factory in America. Then the three temptresses are depicted seducing the workers into inefficiency. The narrator follows with: "Monotony . . . fatigue . . . false thirst . . . nervous tension. Yes—*these are the agents of the Axis.*" Finally, the company president asks one bright foreman how come his department is producing so much more than the others. The foreman confesses that chewing gum is the hero, explaining false thirst and other related phenomena. Says the president, forcefully: "Make chewing gum available to every person employed in this plant!" After a stirring coda, the recording ends.

Another Wrigley ad very specifically recommended "five sticks of gum a day" for every war worker. Typical copy used on car cards and in industrial publications read: GUM . . . A DELICIOUS TRIFLE ALWAYS . . . AND TODAY A BLESSED TRIFLE—BRINGING BLESSED RELIEF TO NERVE-STRAINED WAR PRODUCERS . . . FACTORY TESTS SHOW HOW CHEWING GUM HELPS MEN FEEL BETTER, WORK BETTER.

Wrigley gum was used in the first K rations for soldiers overseas; several sticks were inserted in trial rations by Colonel Rohland A. Isker of the Quartermaster Corps, who remembered how as a cavalryman in the Southwest he chewed gum to relieve thirst. The gum became a great favorite and was

Refusing to compromise on quality, Wrigley took its most famous brand off the market during World War II when gum ingredients were scarce. But the company kept the brand name before the public with ads like this. *Wm. Wrigley Jr. Company*

thereafter added to every ration pack. However, top-grade materials finally became so scarce that prewar quality gum could not even be produced for the armed forces. Philip Wrigley took his three world-famous chewing gums off the market entirely in 1945; in fact, he so strongly supported this move that he resigned the company presidency when older directors opposed him, being elected chairman of the board after his policy had at length prevailed. Orbit gum was supplied to the Armed Forces, too, a unique advertising campaign launched to keep the name and quality of Wrigley gum in people's minds—even though they couldn't buy it. The campaign succeeded, in great part due to dramatic ads featuring a picture of an empty Wrigley's Spearmint pack complete with the slogan REMEMBER THIS WRAPPER . . .

The Toothless Gum King

When World War II ended, the success of Wrigley's visionary Essential Gum Policy became apparent to all. Production lines everywhere were soon working overtime to meet the tremendous increase in gum consumption that World War II wrought, and now Essential Gum could be sold not as a minor pleasure but as a minor necessity. "No more need the masticating jaw be regarded as a sign of vulgarity," an observer noted. "No more need schoolmarms reprimand their charges for chewing gum in the classroom." World War II virtually ended iron-clad social taboos against gum and effective social criticism of the chew food all but disappeared. The rear-guard "spit it out" schoolteachers still prevailed, but they were fighting a losing battle and gum properly chewed and handled became acceptable almost anywhere—in fact, in one New England school it was even given to students to relax them during exams. There would still be gum cleanup campaigns like the one instituted in the late thirties by New York's fiery Mayor Fiorella LaGuardia, and teachers would brag in print that any student caught chewing gum would be assigned to scraping old wads off the undersides of desks. But on the whole gum had acquired a respectability Thomas Adams would have thought impossible.

The major criticism of gum came from dentists now and the gum makers quickly moved to counteract this. Wrigley financed studies at Northwestern University which supposedly found a way to cut down on the effects of sugar, 60 percent of gum, by making calcium carbonate 3 percent of the base—a practice every gum maker adopted. Other studies showed that it isn't the amount of sugar consumed that causes tooth decay but the amount of sugar in the food film adhering to the teeth. Investigations proved that candy, cookies, jam and ordinary white bread were worse offenders than gum and that gum chewing after eating even reduced the acid in the film over the teeth by stimulating saliva flow.

By virtue of such pioneering public relations work and astute advertising policies, the Wrigley firm emerged from the war as the world's chomp champ, a position they still hold, shipping their gum to 119 countries around the globe and controlling a huge 45 percent of the domestic chewing gum market (American Chicle is number two in U.S. consumption with 35-40 percent). One management professor does feel that Wrigley is too family-dominated, that its top executives spend too much time making day to day decisions. And advertising people can't fathom why Wrigley traditionally puts all its massive advertising spending (low at $23.8 million in 1974) to work for only one of its brands at a time for as long as six months. But the ad policy has been successful for over half a century. As for Wrigley's personal approach, it too has certainly worked in the past and is at least refreshing in today's largely impersonal business world. At Wrigley every executive still answers his own phone. No secretary screens the calls of anyone—from William Wrigley, grandson of the founder and company president, or his father, board chairman Philip K. Wrigley, to the lowest vice-president. Philip Wrigley, like his legendary father, has always stayed close to people. P. K. Wrigley has his own brand of consumerism. He kept his gum priced at a nickel as long as he possibly could, for his father raised him, as he says, "to have a five-cent point of view." The modest millionaire (the longest speech he ever made was "Thank you") is just as democratic as regards his baseball team, the Chicago Cubs. The Cubs are the only major league club that doesn't play night baseball games at home and Wrigley Field is the one major league ball park not equipped with lights. This is because Phil Wrigley believes baseball is a daytime game and should be played in the daytime—not even a lawsuit by a Cub stockholder could alter his belief, despite

$40,000 in legal costs. "For another thing," he adds, "the ball park is in a residential neighborhood. I believe in being a good neighbor. Most of these people can't afford air conditioning and their windows are open in the summer. A guy that works all day shouldn't have to listen to a blaring loudspeaker and 50,000 people yelling at night."

In *Veeck As In Wreck* baseball maverick Bill Veeck claims that Phil Wrigley refuses to play under lights simply because "he blew the chance to be first with lights" in the majors, and is exceedingly stubborn, but that controversy will rage for years in Chicago. As far as is known, P. K. Wrigley, a quiet man of the people, has just one real defect, for a chewing gum king— he doesn't chew gum anymore. "I've got a new set of plastic teeth," he explains, "and I can't chew a damn thing." But now that Wrigley has started making a gum that doesn't stick to dentures perhaps the 80-year-old chairman of the board can once again set us all a good example . . .

Chewers in Outer Space

The gum makers, from Wrigley on down, now supply chew food to everyone from the formerly reluctant commissars of the communist bloc to people in outer space (and maybe even visitors from other galaxies). Great gum beaters around the world today would include General Foods, whose Hollywood Gum is the biggest seller by far in France, a $30 million business that dwarfs all other competitors. General Foods also owns a Netherlands company called Maple Leaf, so named because the Canadians, great gum chewers all, liberated parts of Holland and the company adopted them as its North American image. Their Pingi Pongi brand is the largest selling bubble gum in Brazil. Translated the name means Ping Pong, a favorite Brazilian sport.

An even odder-named brand is put out by the Perfetti Company in Milan, Italy. This is called Brooklyn Gum and has the Brooklyn Bridge pictured on the label above the legend "*Di Gum Di Ponti,*" "the gum of the bridge." Elsewhere, however, western images and flavors are forsaken. In Japan, where some 43 native manufacturers are now turning out *gamu*, as gum is called, 150 flavors have been introduced, including such taste sensations as green tea, pickled plum and gin fizz. Japanese manufacturers have prescribed a code of gummanship (Example: never chew when addressing your elders), have installed over 1,000 wad removal boxes in convenient public places, and not long ago introduced the official gum chewer's anthem quoted a few chapters back extolling the grandeur of gum.

Gum managed to nibble some holes in the Iron Curtain shortly after World War II. European communist countries were the last pocket of resistance against chewing, officially anyway, until Poland's *Cultural Review* called gum chewing "a perfectly harmless recreation." Then East Germany, which had always followed the communist party line that chewing gum should be much reviled as a symbol of the American debasement of European culture, permitted a large synthetic rubber plant to take out an ad for gum in a leading magazine. "An old and always new game that gladdens the heart of every child," the ad said. It featured a drawing of children pulling thin threads of *kaugummi* from their mouths and winding it around their fingers.

Actually, there was for many years an active black market in Eastern Europe for chewing gum, that typical product of capitalist decadence. In remote villages people didn't know what to do with gum and swallowed it out of deference to the stranger presenting them with it, but in most Eastern European countries children begged comrade foreigners for sticks of gum. Toothless elderly people with relatives in the states asked them to include plenty of gum in their packages—so that they could turn a big profit selling it on the black market at up to 30 cents a stick. Chewing gum or *zvykacka* (pronounced *zhveekachka* and literally meaning "cud-chewing") enjoyed great popularity in Czechoslovakia, no matter what the commissars had to say about it. The craze was illustrated by a group of seven enterprising young people, mostly students and other intellectuals, who produced a brand called Breezy Chewing Gum (made from paraffin candles and other domestic products) which sold well at 14 cents a stick until the authorities intervened and threw them in jail. The situation got bad enough for a teacher to complain in the newspaper *Lydova Demokracie* that chewing gum "is flowing into the schools from unknown sources and by unknown roads." Finally in 1957, the communist authorities decided to give up and rehabilitate chewing gum. The national plan for that year, covering every last Czech product, provided for the manufacture of 20 tons of gum. Distribution was reserved for sale to coal miners in the hope that chewing gum would wean them away from the habit of chewing on hunks of tar to ease the strain of their underground work, but the move opened the door to gum manufacture in other communist bloc countries.

Russia herself was the last communist nation to accept chewing gum. When Mrs. Richard Nixon traveled with the then Vice-President in 1959 she carried a trunkful of candy and gum to give away to Soviet youngsters. The kids gobbled up the sweets, but wouldn't touch her gum. "My daughter loves it; she chews and chews," Mrs. Nixon told one little boy in the waiting room of a public clinic. But the boy nearly burst into tears when she handed him a pack of gum and he refused to put it in his mouth even after she unwrapped a piece for him. The Vice-President's wife quickly dropped her plans for distributing gum. Whether the negative reaction was out of fear of some Young Pioneer restriction or just plain bewilderment was never established, but at any rate the Soviet Union has just this year announced that it is going into the chewing gum business with production of 28,000 tons a year of *Zhevatelnaya Rezinka* as a start. Officials have decided that "chewing gum cleans and strengthens the teeth and helps blood circulation in the mouth," so it looks like Ivan will soon be chewing on his spearmint,too—though the great Soviet department store, GUM, doesn't carry any gum yet.

Chewing gum was officially taken into outer space for the first time by the Gemini 5 astronauts in 1965. Here American Chicle triumphed over its competitors when their Trident sugarless gum was chosen by the National Aeronautics and Space Administration for space vehicle use on the basis of environmental testing. In each of the food packages consisting of a meal for the Gemini 5 astronauts two sticks of Trident were included. But although it was used officially for the first time by Lt. Colonel L. Gordon Cooper Jr., and Lt. Commander Charles Conrad Jr. on the Gemini 5 mission, Trident had been smuggled on board the earlier Gemini 4 flight. After that flight, Major James A. McDivett said: "At some point Ed's (Major Edward H. White II's) toothbrush got lost. We don't know whether it floated out of the spacecraft along with his glove when the hatch was open or what. Anyway, I didn't try to brush my teeth, so they got a little furry. We had gum on

Certainly not...

Clearly, no one in his senses would use chewing gum at a time and place such as this.

However there are times and places where the use of chewing gum can be most beneficial; in fact its discreet use is a mark of tact and consideration for others as it is a definite aid to oral hygiene.

Doublemint chewing gum is especially made for such people. Its ingredients are carefully selected throughout, even its flavour has been double distilled; in fact, as its name implies, Doublemint is double good and gives you double benefits in many ways.

Try some at the right time and in the right place and see for yourself.

Hailed as a unique approach to advertising, the Wrigley "Certainly Not . . . " ads set out to change negative British "upper class" attitudes about gum chewing and succeeded to a great extent. *Wm. Wrigley Jr. Company*

One set of the ubiquitous "Doublemint Twins" seen in commercials and ads for a quarter of a century. *Wm. Wrigley Jr. Company*

board to freshen up our mouths." There is only a remote possibility, however, that beings from another planet are now chomping on gum that they found floating in outer space. Asked what the astronauts on both flights did with the gum when they finished chewing it, a spokesman for NASA replied, "They swallowed it." Such is the official explanation, anyway . . .

"U" Chewers and Great Gum Gougers

Gum may not have conquered other galaxies yet, but social taboos against it have broken down everywhere on earth. In 1962 P. K. Wrigley (believing that "the masses follow the classes") launched a British Doublemint campaign to turn the last of the Immovable-Jawed—stiff-lipped "upper-class" Englishmen—into gum chewers, running ads in such upper-case "U" publications as *The Times* of London, *The Economist* and *The Guardian*. One ad depicted a gracious young lady descending a stairway, and an elegant young man in tails greeting her. The headline on the picture read: "Certainly not—

Wm. Wrigley Jr. Company

Wrigley Fun Facts, "painless ads" that appear in hundreds of Sunday newspapers. *Wm. Wrigley Jr. Company*

clearly, no one in his senses would use chewing gum at a time and place such as this." But, just below, the ad asserted: "However, there are times and places where the use of chewing gum can be most beneficial; in fact, its discreet use is a mark of tact and consideration for others as it is a definite aid to oral hygiene." The "Certainly Not" series used the same copy under 13 different situations in which gum should not be chewed—including business conferences, cricket matches, various social events and public occasions. In essence the ads said, "We agree with you—the indiscriminate use of chewing gum is to be deplored, but this should not blind you to the advantages to be gained from its use at the right time . . . " Great editorial interest in the campaign developed, it was hailed as a "daring, unique approach to advertising," and the strong upper-class prejudice against gum was to a large extent overcome. Over the past 20 years annual British sales have increased from 160 million to over 400 million packs. William Wrigley Jr. had learned many years before, when advertising his gum to the British workingman, that big, lavish ad campaigns shocked the English and this successful soft-sell merely extended his discovery.

Peoplekind has been persuaded to chew gum by every advertising gimmick under the sun; every slogan from "increases efficiency"and "helps industrial relations" to "relieves boredom," "keeps lips young," and "stretches your coffee break" has been trotted out. Wrigley has gone through three sets of Doublemint Twins since the original Boyd twins (who doubled sales) debuted in the early sixties, bringing the twins back after tests showed that consumers still associated the brand with them despite a ten-year absence. There have been unique promotion campaigns like the Clark Gum Company program in 1970 which contributed 2.5 cents to UNICEF for every Clark Gum Wrapper returned to the manufacturer—close to half a million wrappers were received. But most gum advertising hasn't changed much since the twenties. Wrigley's "Carry the big fresh flavor" T.V. ads are typical. Here a long giant-sized pack of gum is carried around by an assortment of ordinary-looking people. Viewers like the ads, though— Wrigley has been deluged with requests from people who want duplicates of the big packs used in the commercial. The Wrigley "Fun Facts" column in the Sunday comics is also

The Juicy Fruit Tree   *Wm. Wrigley Jr. Company*

popular, and so is the Juicy Fruit "Pick a Pack" commercial. "Pick a Pack" probably has its roots in Eugene Field's "Sugar Plum Tree" poem, where sugarplums, chocolates, gingerbread, marshmallows, gumdrops and peppermint sticks grow on a marvellous tree. Wrigley has just substituted Juicy Fruit for all the other sweets on their tree and filmed a group of revellers picking off packs. The tune, however, is the thing. It has that quality that makes people hum or whistle it later, what advertising people call the "hook" and invariably aim for.

Wrigley still spends more than any other gum company on advertising, with American Chicle a close second. Industry ads may or may not be entertaining, and are often banal and repetitive, but they are generally truthful. Recently, a couple of

seventh graders in Spring Valley, California decided to find
out for themselves whether American Chicle's Trident slogan
"Four out of five dentists recommend sugarless gum for their
patients who chew gum," was accurate. They wrote to the
manufacturers that they had surveyed 50 dentists in their area.
"We found out that 40 dentists we called chose Trident or any
other sugarless gum," they testified. "We didn't think your ad
was true, but when we thought about what you said in the
commercial ad, it was true, but next time try not to make it so
confusing."

Aside from American Chicle, Wrigley's major competitors
today are publicly held companies, including Beech-Nut, a
subsidiary of Squibb Pharmaceuticals; Clark Gum, now
owned by the Reed Candy Company; General Foods; Gum
Products of Boston; and the Ford Gum and Machine Co. Other
rivals include the Frank H. Fleer Corporation, Topps Chewing
Gum, Philadelphia Chewing Gum, Leaf Brands, Inc., and the
National Chicle Products Company. The one area in which
Wrigley is clearly not dominant is in the new sugarless gums
and some analysts say they have turned their back on this big
growth sector, which can only hurt in the long run. The sugarless entries—such as American Chicle's Trident, the leader,
and Beech-Nut's Carefree—have been experiencing fantastic
growth over the last ten years. Sugarless gum, favored by dieters and other health conscious consumers, has more than doubled sales in that period and now accounts for 15-20 percent of
the gum market. There are even sugarless bubble gums available.

Most gums today are made not from chicle but from a synthetic base (see Chapter 13), but few people can tell the difference. No one can make any gum better or more economi-
cally than American manufacturers, either—chewing gum is
possibly the only product we can still turn out cheaper than the
Japanese. We've come up with almost every gimmick but the
five-course gum introduced in *Willy Wonka's Chocolate Factory*.
In that film the revered candymaker passes out a chewing gum
that changes taste in the mouth from minute to minute, providing the chewer with each course of a meal from soup to
nuts. Unfortunately, the gum hasn't been perfected yet and the
little girl who tries it turns into a huge, round blueberry, the
last course of the meal, and has to be rolled away for flattening.

About the only flavor the gum people haven't been able to perfect over the years is chocolate. Freshen-Up Gum, an American Chicle product with a refreshing liquid center that is released upon chewing; ice-cream flavored gum; lollipop gums; gum with nicotine in it to help curb smoking—there's no end to the combinations and gimmicks the artful flavor technicians have come up with. And we chaw them all with confidence, assured by aggressive advertising that gum chewing is no longer vulgar. Today Americans are chomping over 500 sticks of gum per person annually, according to one estimate. Worldwide, gum is a billion dollar business, and some $800 million in chewing gum passes over counters at the retail level in the U.S. alone. Australia, England and Latin America follow in that order, but our consumption still dwarfs that of any other country. There has been nearly a 500 percent increase in gum chewing here since World War II thanks to such factors as tensions caused by warfare, nuclear bomb explosions, the population explosion, the hectic pace of modern life and the increasing practice of substituting gum for cigarette smoking.

World records beyond belief have been set by Americans for "gum gouging," but the chomp king title is a little clouded. A young Multilith operator named Sue Jordan first won the crown by chomping on 80 pieces of Doublemint 15,600 times in five hours and twelve minutes, but she was quickly dethroned by 17-year-old Clyde Steward "Mighty Mouth" McGehee, a North Carolinian who masticated 105 sticks of Juicy Fruit for a full six hours, stopping only when he became hungry. Then Richard Walker, a Tarheel Boy Scout, set a new record of 135 sticks and eight hours. "Mighty Mouth," however, refused to be outdone. No matter how much gum anyone might chew, he boasted, "I will chew at least one more stick one more minute." And so the "Mighty Mouth Sweepstakes" munches on. A more appetizing record is that held by two Long Island, New York teenagers, Randi Grossack and Barbara Malkin. They have assembled a chewing gum wrapper chain that thus far measures 196 feet, 8 inches long, almost two-thirds the length of a football field and the equivalent of 4,720 wrappers . . . or 944 packs of gum . . . or $141.60 in gum money . . . But then gum wrapper chains have been popular from the beginning, as have "baseballs" fashioned from metal foil scraped off inner gum wrappers. In fact, during World War II, children collected gum metal foil discarded in the street, rolled it into balls and turned it in to the "war effort."

A Wrigley demographic study has found that more than 50 percent of all Americans chew some gum, although other studies show that 10 percent of the population accounts for 75 percent of the gum chewed. At any rate, if rolled into one piece, the $800 million in gum we pay for each year would result in a stick some 5 million miles long. Among all the greatest penny delights of youth and old age: the nonpariels, lollipops, jelly beans, chocolate babies, Canada mints, and licorice whips (red and black) . . . the sour balls, orange slices, sugar cones, peppermint canes, malted milk balls, Mexican hats, and marshmallow bananas . . . the jujubes, Tootsie Rolls, Sugar Daddies, Baby Ruths, Hershey Bars, Mary Janes, and "buttons" on white paper strips . . . Among all of these gourmet delicacies of the many, gum is now indisputably the favorite. Clearly every day is Chewsday.

CHAPTER 10

From Blibber-Blubber (Smack!) To Double Bubble (Thwack!): Bubble Merchants & Bubble Blowers

HISTORY doesn't honor the anonymous genius who invented the knot or nail, or even such relatively modern contrivances as the screw or button, but the name of the man who invented the first successful bubble gum, that ubiquitous pink stuff we all blew bubbles with or stepped on or sat in not so long ago, is writ large for posterity on the pages of time.

To be sure, the prime maker's wasn't the very first bubble gum. Nobody knows who got the original idea (or even why anyone would get the original idea) to blow a bubble with *ordinary* chewing gum—probably it was just an accident. But ever since chicle immigrated to North America, grown men had been trying to devise an elastic gum that would pump up

The Inventor of Bubble Gum. Walter Diemer, still
blowing bubbles at seventy. *Fleer Corporation*

into bubbles one hundred times the size of those that can be
snapped with commonplace gum. The first known appeared in
1906, when Frank Henry Fleer, founder of the Frank H. Fleer
Corporation, developed a synthetic gum with the wonderful
name Blibber-Blubber, a trademark that, inexplicably, hasn't
been used since. Fleer, an essential gum figure who also concocted candy-coated Chiclets, later selling the product to
American Chicle, worked long and hard on his pet project, and
it certainly had bubbleability enough; but, alas, it was too
sticky, too brittle and hardly held together. Reluctantly, Frank
Fleer had to abandon Blibber-Blubber to Bubblegumdom's
Hall of Great Globule Failures.

Yet Fleer workers went right on searching for the ultimate
bubble gum. The company changed hands, taken over by
Frank Fleer's son-in-law Gilbert Mustin, and the quest continued. Finally, one August morning in 1928—unfortunately

no one is certain of the exact date or time—the age of bubble gum rose like a pink sun on the horizon.

On that memorable morning, a young cost accountant named Walter Diemer, inspired by his employer's search for a large dry bubble that wouldn't explode and stick so fast to young faces that parents would forbid it in the house, was experimenting with a new batch of bubble gum mix. The 23-year-old Diemer had no knowledge of chemistry; for over a year he'd been trying through trial and error to come up with the magic formula that would turn gum into gold. This morning he noticed something different, nothing he could logically explain. He put a generous chunk of the mix in his mouth and blew a bubble. The bubble rose, rose higher. It was a big beautiful bubble, a supercalifragilisticexpialidocious bubble, the bubble of all bubbles anywhere; Diemer had never before seen one anything like it. And then it popped. Softly it popped. It popped and . . . and it . . . damned if it didn't peel right off his prominent nose!

"I had it!" Diemer, a merry little man whose eyes snap and crackle behind his spectacles, recalls today. "Everybody tried some. We were blowing bubbles all over the office. Everyone said: 'What a great product!' and it really went to our heads. We were blowing bubbles and prancing all over the place!"

The stuff went to their heads like the bubbles in a glass of champagne—but there is a little more suspense to the tale, a bit more discouragement that Diemer had to overcome, further obstacles he had to surmount in the best tradition of Bells and Edisons everywhere. The next morning his five-pound batch of gum just wouldn't work, "wouldn't blow a bubble worth a darn." Diemer tells me this probably had something to do with the room temperature—he doesn't really know, he isn't a chemist. In any event, he had to work another four months on the sticky stuff before perfecting it.

Bubble, bubble, toil and trouble. But sometime in early December of that same year Walter Diemer made an immense 300-pound batch of bubbly that didn't fizzle out in the vats overnight. "I was young and self-conscious," he recalls, "and all the help was standing around, looking skeptical. The Mustins, who owned the business, were Germans and many of the people who worked at the plant were recent immigrants who didn't speak much English. They just stood and stared—

disapprovingly, I thought. I was sure they were all thinking, 'Crazy kid. That stuff of his is going to pull the teeth off the blades in our mixing machines.' Well, the machines were groaning, and the stuff started popping and then . . . I realized I'd forgotten to put any coloring in the gum.''

Diemer remedied his mistake the very next day, when he made a second super batch. "Pink food coloring was the only one I had at hand," he says. "And that's the reason ever since, all over the world, that bubble gum has been predominantly pink. After World War II, in fact, when there was a black market in bubble gum, it was dubbed 'the pink market.' "

The Dom Pérignon of bubble gum refuses to reveal the formula for the original bubbly, except to say that "the standard ingredients, all natural ones, no synthetics," were employed in those days and that his invention introduced no new substances, his happy discovery rather a unique combination of materials that had been used all along. Bubble gum, however, is made much like all chewing gum (see Chapter 13), being mostly pink wads of sugar and rubber, and is different from its older brother mainly in the elasticity and firmness of its base, which produces a film strong enough to hold more air and thus create bigger, better blobs. A harmless rubberlike tree latex— similar to the one used for making girdles—was the ingredient that gave the first bubble gum its elasticity, though synthetics like vinyl resins and microcrystalline waxes are used today. The new synthetics can best be described as "thermal plastics," Diemer says, because they are soft at room temperature, and they "definitely aren't like rubber tires." At any rate, the prime maker didn't even patent his invention, fearing as all gum makers still do that "patents can be a license to steal" and that in doing so he would be "exposing trade secrets to others."

The day after Christmas in 1928 the first Dubble Bubble, as Diemer's boss dubbed his invention, was test marketed in Philadelphia. A little Mama-Poppa candy store on Susquehanna Avenue in the 1400 block became the first emporium in the world to sell it, though, sadly, the location is still unmarked by any commemorative plaque or pink globe. Dubble Bubble was an instant success, so much so that within three months imitations were on the market. Diemer feels that industrial spies may have had something to do with this treachery, but Dubble Bubble far outsold its competitors anyway. Marketed kiss-wrapped, like salt-water taffy (wrapped, in fact, on taffy-wrapping machines Diemer scrounged from Atlantic City), Dubble Bubble quickly surpassed Tootsie Rolls in sales, became the world's biggest selling one-cent confection, an American institution, almost a synonym for bubble gum itself. Diemer modestly feels that it was all a lucky break for him, "just the turn of events," and isn't bitter about not receiving royalties on a patent that would have made him a millionaire many times over. "After all, I was a Fleer employee," the begetter of bubble gum says. His discovery did move him up the corporate ladder to a vice-presidency, and he has remained a member of Fleer's board of directors since his retirement in 1970. The former Philadelphian now lives with his wife in Ocean City, New Jersey, where he is enjoying his relative leisure and still blowing a few bubbles occasionally. He has no qualms about bubble gum and hardly gives a thought to the parents, teachers, dentists and fundamentalist preachers who have condemned him over the years without even knowing his name. "I have no regrets inventing it," says the father of bubble gum of all countries. "It brought happiness to millions of kids and if I could do that I'm happy."

Diemer isn't one to blow his own horn, but he does seem a bit perturbed when his invention is accredited to someone else. A few months back the son of an early bubble gum maker (the son is active in the birth control movement, something like heresy for the scion of a man so dependent on the youth market) attributed the invention of bubble gum to his father in the course of a news magazine interview. "I had to write them to set the record straight," Diemer says a little testily. "It turned out that they didn't know what they were talking about . . . " There ought to be a monument somewhere to Walter Diemer . . .

The Pink Market

Fleer helped sell Dubble Bubble by distributing free samples of the first successful bubble gum to grocers, druggists and candy stores. In no time at all it became the chewing sensation of the country; everywhere one turned in 1929 a kid seemed to be blowing a bubble or have the torn pink rags of one wrapped around his mouth. Soon over 20 other companies were competing for a share of an apparently inexhaustible market composed mainly of three- to fourteen-year-olds but including many adult "connoisseurs" who say they find bubble gum a better chew than regular brands. Dubble Bubble's chief competitor was the now defunct Bowman Company, which first made ordinary By Gum gum but soon came up with their famous Blony, advertised as "the biggest piece of gum available for a penny" and guaranteed to produce bubbles "twice as large as any other." Bowman inserted picture cards in their bubble gum packages, becoming one of the first firms to do so. At the outset these cards depicted the traditional cowboys and Indians—until J. Warren Bowman, the company's colorful founder, included pictures of war heroes. A full set of his 240-card war series is a collector's item today, worth well over $500, but they created an international incident at the time. Most of them centered on the Sino-Japanese war and when 100 million of the cards had been issued, the Japanese embassy in Washington protested that "peace-loving Japan" was being done an injustice. The State Department, however, coldly replied that there was nothing unjust about depicting the sinking of the U.S.S. Panay in the Yangtze River and the furor only gave Bowman welcome publicity. Some reasoned that the Japanese had more than one motive for going after him, too, that he may even have given them a motive for Pearl Harbor. Bowman had been the first man to install bubble gum plants in Japan, Japanese youngsters soon driving their elders to near hari-kari as a result. In 1937 "King Bub" had been denounced as an "enemy of Japan" and banned from the empire because of his good works.

In prewar years kids were spending close to $4.5 million a year on bubble gum, but during World War II the bubble burst when a shortage of essential Siamese jelutong forced gum makers to halt domestic production. GI's, however, blew bubbles all over the globe—in Europe, Africa, Asia, Borneo, even on Pitcairn Island, where descendants of mutineers on the Bounty took to bubbling over at the mouth. Servicemen introduced Dubble Bubble to the Eskimos and the Eskimos soon preferred it to their previous favorite chew—whale blubber. In Africa various tribes accepted large quantities of bubble gum as payment for a wife, in lieu of sheep and oxen. Headhunters

in Borneo kidnapped a diplomat and held him for a ransom of
Dubble Bubble. Unfortunately, bubble gum didn't see wartime service in bubble gum guns and bubble gum bombs, but
it had at least some value in counterespionage. Here on the
home front the Topps Company, which entered the gum field
in 1939, coined a variation on the "slipped lips sink ships"
slogan that became a great favorite. "Don't talk, chum; chew
Topps gum," was heard so often that it made at least one slang
dictionary.

The postwar years marked a bubble gum boom that has
never been equalled by any plaything anywhere. To kids, the
return of bubble gum was second in importance only to the
return of their fathers and brothers. Almost as soon as they
could buy the pink prize, students in Longview, Texas conducted a contest and crowned local chewers for bubbles that
had the loudest pop, were biggest, messiest, smallest,
"cutest," most geometric and most "glamorous." At first bubble gum manufacturers could not meet the demand for their
product and all over the country emerged the "pink market"
named for the color of the bubbly, a pint-sized black market
mainly operated by kids (so far as is known the Mafia didn't
get into the act). Manufacturers continued to supply what
penny gum they had at regular prices and retailers sold it at
five cents or so a piece, but the kids themselves made such 500
percent markups seem conscionable. "I remember four people
best from World War II," Robert McShane, a high-powered
salesman, recalls today. "Hitler, Mussolini, Tojo and Cynthia
Bolo. Cynthia Bolo used to sell me bubble gum at *one dollar* a
piece! I don't know where she got it from, but someday,
somewhere, I will catch up with Cynthia Bolo!"

Frequently sweating out lines that stretched around the
block, kids in the pink market would buy up whatever gum
they could and resell it at anywhere from a dime to 50 cents.
There were times when penny pieces of Dubble Bubble, then
regarded as the bubble gum nonpareil, did go for one dollar
each, and those lucky enough to get it kept it "alive" in glasses
of water nights and chewed it for as long as a month. Some bubble gum entrepreneurs made fortunes in those years. A short
while after the war, Andrew J. Paris, a young candy importer
from McAllen, Texas, sewed up the output of four Mexican
factories and dumped some 5,000 tons of bubble gum on the

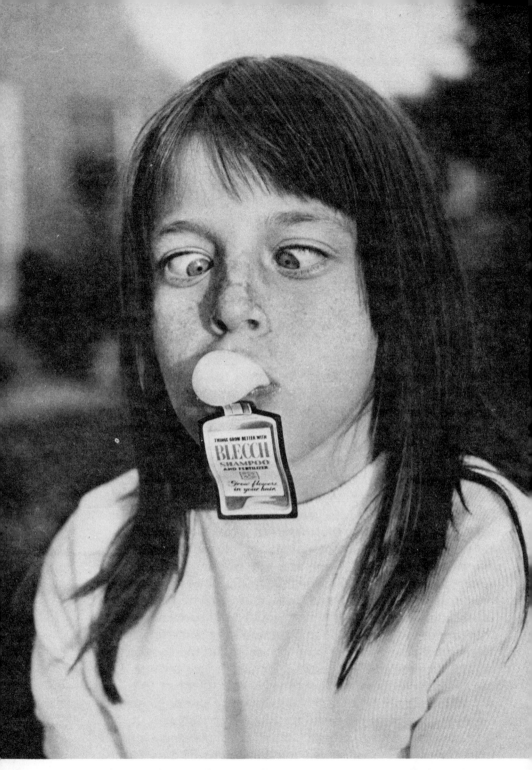

Topps Chewing Gum, Inc.

market, winning a temporary corner of the business. The spiffy Paris, dressed to the nines with a good-sized bubble obscuring his mustache, rated a full page in *Life* as the "pigtail's set Man of Distinction."

Parents of bubble gum addicts firmly believed that the popularity of the new product was based largely on its capacity for driving them crazy. "Bubble gum differs from ordinary chewing gum," one father held, "in that it possesses a fantastic elasticity which permits Junior to blow a large bubble with it . . . This bubble, covering his mouth and at least keeping him quiet for a moment, may grow larger than—and just as empty as—Junior's little head, before it bursts with a loud, ghastly, vulgar, thwacking sound. This, the kiddies insist sadistically, is great fun, even if the remnants of the bursting bubble should cling to hair, new Sunday suit, or innocent bystander."

Bubble gum did indeed achieve its eminence despite protesting parents. This wasn't due as much to the evangelical fervor of the bubble gum businessmen as to kids themselves. Kids braved lines to get it, paid outrageous prices for it, fought among themselves for it, and nothing as reactionary as a parent or teacher could stop them from chewing and detonating it. Bubble gum is still spirited into the house or schoolroom tucked safely in little cheeks and is sometimes passed from mouth to mouth. Bubbles are snapped when the teacher's back is turned; bubbles the size of gall bladders are blown to tatters whenever there's a safe ten seconds, and if there's any danger that teacher will confiscate a mouthful, it's moulded around a pencil eraser or a wristwatch for use at another time. Kids, for their part, love to flatten their pink wads twixt tongue and teeth, separate the teeth slightly and exhale slowly against the gum until a prodigious bubble forms and explodes. Parents, for their part, hate the way bubble gum looks being chewed or blown, loathe to step or sit in it, and dread washing it off clothing, peeling it off faces and cutting if out of hair. The problem will never be resolved . . .

The Great Bubble Gum Epidemic

At least one parent believes that bubble gum blowing has made ordinary gum chewing far more acceptable. "After one has seen bubble gum blown into an ugly balloon, popped,

sucked, stretched, chewed and blown again, ad nauseum—
then mere chewing gum may seem relatively good form," she
contends. But no one has ever been able to make a good case
that bubble gum is harmful to youngsters on other than shaky
aesthetic grounds; it is only dangerous when sadistic adults
coat it with lye and give it to kids on Halloween, an all too
common occurrence. In June 1947, for instance, a puzzling
epidemic of sore throats, vomiting and headaches spread
among youngsters throughout America and anguished parents
blamed it all on villainous bubble gum. The U.S. Food & Drug
Administration promptly collected 4,000 samples of the gum,
in all flavors, and subjected it to scientific tests unlike any ever
performed before. Seventy-five human guinea pigs, including
25 kids, chomped and blew bubbles for periods of up to eight
hours, the test wads composed of anywhere from one to six
pieces. In the laboratory investigators analyzed the gum ingredients, implanted gum in the skins of guinea pigs, attached
wads of chewed gum to shaved rabbits, fed the stuff to monkeys, cats, dogs, and even chickens. For comparison paraffin
wax was also chewed. Finally the F.D.A. concluded that
"There is no basis for legal action against bubble gum" and
dismissed the complaints. No toxic ingredients were found in
the bubbly and except for aching jaws, which were acquired
from chewing either gum or wax, there were no bad reactions
to the tests.

Some kids have certainly tried chewing too much bubble
gum at a time—one boy wadded so much into his mouth that
he dislocated his jaw. On the other hand, dentists and speech
therapists have recommended chewing bubble gum to
strengthen weak jaws. As for dental caries, Walter Diemer ar-
gues that his invention *prevents* them, noting that a German
scientist introduced bubble gum to a group of people previously on a very soft diet and that caries decreased as a result of
all the hard chewing. All gum manufacturers seem grievously
injured at the mention of dental troubles and gum in the same
sentence, but the bubble gum people are particularly sensitive.
"I've chewed more gum than any ten people I know," Diemer,
aged 74, says, "and I've got all but four of my teeth." Diemer
blames bubble gum's troubles with the dentists not on sugar
but on the dental profession's need for a scapegoat. "When a
dentist fills an adult tooth," he says, "he can undercut the

cavity to anchor his filling. But a child squirms around so that this isn't possible. As a result, when the child chews—candy, a caramel, a piece of gum, anything—the filling might come out and the dentist, consequently, is a bum as far as the parents are concerned."

Though medical men obviously don't agree with Diemer (see Chapter 14), even they will admit that bubble gum is not made from horses' hooves, old girdles and inner tubes, or used gum scraped off the street. Furthermore, it will not cause buck teeth, won't snap and pop in the stomach, give you appendicitis, clog up the intestines, dwarf you, or seal the lips so that Junior can't breathe, as hysterical parents have claimed over the years. Actually, it may even be of some help in the adult world. An authority on natural foods has proclaimed that liquified bubble gum makes a useful insecticide, far better than DDT—it seems that bugs nibble on it and their jaws stick together so that they can nibble on nothing else no more. But kids, who are hard to intimidate, like it just because they like it. In fact, that is the essential answer all ten kids I interviewed gave when I asked why they chewed bubble gum and blew bubbles: "Cause I like it." Nothing more. All you can do with ordinary gum is chew it, snap it, stretch it, sculpture it, fish coins out from below gratings with it, and leave it on theatre seats; so bubble gum opened up new vistas for the younger set.

Kid power, and an economic prosperity that has lined children's pockets, has brought bubble gum up to the point where it now accounts for 20 percent of all chewing gum sales, compared to 10 percent in 1955. The bubble gum tycoons are blowing bubbles all the way to the bank. Fleer alone turns out five million pieces of Dubble Bubble every *day*, over five times what it did ten years ago, gum that is exported to some 50 countries, including several behind the Iron Curtain. Bubble gum, which only turned 50 in 1978, has blown up into a big business that has quintupled in the last 15 years, Americans chewing on over $100 million of the stuff annually. Five-and ten-cent slabs are now common on the candy counters and even Topps has raised its price to two cents, which regrettably leaves a few small gumballs and Tootsie Rolls as the last remaining penny confection anywhere. Bubble gum now comes in many shapes and sizes, however, and chews out into colors ranging from red, white and blue to orange, yellow and ecru—though pink is still everybody's favorite. There are sugarless bubble gums—sweetened with sorbital or similar chemicals—and dietary bubble gums low in calories. Topps sells brands like Bazooka, Wacky Packs, Jeepers Creepers, Hot, Rocks O'Gum, and Big Tooth in addition to its famous baseball card gum. Fleer has, among others, Dubble Bubble, Razzles, Happy Stickers, Gum Balls and Fantastic Quicksand (little purple granules). Philadelphia Chewing Gum makes Swell and many more. All are manufactured with a care equalled only by baby food makers. Topps brags of its "spotless factory" in Havertown, Pa., "big enough for six football games on six regulation size gridirons played under one roof," where "there are 118 steps of manufacture, including 23 checks for quality" and where "not once is the gum touched by human hands." The bubble gum makers have always been so sanitary and conscious of quality, at least in recent times. When the now defunct Bowman Gum bought a gum base from a New York firm in 1930 and it developed that a new base on the market was much better, the company brought the matter to court. During the trial, Bowman's attorney, former Pennsylvania State Senator Harvey Shapiro, arranged for the judge to sample gum made with both bases. The gum with the old base stuck to his honor's dentures; the gum with the new base didn't. Clarence Darrow couldn't have done better . . .

The Clown Prince of Bubble Gum
And Other Royalty

Something like seven billion pieces of bubble gum are turned out in American factories every year, but competition in the industry is so intense that today the only major firms left are Fleer, Topps, Philadelphia Chewing Gum Company (all with their sweet-smelling plants in Pennsylvania, making that state the bubble gum capital of the world) and the Donruss Company in Memphis, Tennessee.

The Bowman Chewing Gum Company was taken over by Topps in 1954, but its memory will live long in Bubblegumdom. Its founder, J. Warren Bowman, a big, hefty Pennsylvania Dutchman with a booming voice, was known throughout Chewsville as the Clown Prince of Bubble Gum, or, for short, King Bub. The glib Bowman got into the bubbly business after careers as a used-car salesman (he often sold parked cars to people and then persuaded their owners that they had the chance of a lifetime to dispose of them), green turtle egg hunter, exotic fruit hauler, donut salesman, and policeman (fired because he was found parked in a squad car filled with women). Down to his last $25, Bowman borrowed $300 more from a finance company, bought some ancient chewing gum machinery, a barrel of sugar, a barrel of glucose and a minimum of other essential ingredients and went into the bubble gum business. His inspiration was William Wrigley Jr., whose Wrigley Building he visited in Chicago just after it had been built—it's said that he stared at it so long, with the reverence of a Moslem at the outskirts of Mecca, that a suspicious policeman finally ordered him to move on.

King Bub, married five times, had more the dashing lifestyle of a William White than a William Wrigley Jr., though he did adopt many of Wrigley's sales practices. Premiums were his forte, and according to Diemer, he gave out coupons redeemable for almost anything with his gum—once awarding an ardent coupon collector a pedigreed bull. But it was his picture cards of the early West, war and professional sports that put his products over. At one point in his career, the clown prince manufactured four times more bubble gum than any other company; Blony and his later Bub were selling at the rate of one million dollars a month in postwar years. King Bub, a 6'3" 220-pound giant, really lived it up. In his reception room visitors were announced over an intercom. If he wanted to see them, he threw a switch on his desk, the door to his office unlocking electrically and opening like Ali Baba's cave. At home he lived just as flamboyantly. In his Miami vacation palace he had an electric organ and an amplifier pointed out to sea so that he could hear a professional organist playing for him while he fished. Bowman was an original, a Barnumesque character bubbling over with flamboyant ideas. Branching out into plain chewing gum he invented the eight-stick gum pack long before Beech-Nut, and he even made a valiant attempt at manufacturing pinball-machine gum vending machines—which would have been a marriage of two great public favorites. King Bub, like most gum magnates, thoroughly understood the principles of advertising and public relations—

maintaining a full-time Congressional lobbyist, among other publicists. Once, Lady Iris Mountbatten, Queen Victoria's great-granddaughter, was happily endorsing one of his gums on subway posters everywhere when she got some undesirable publicity by bouncing a few checks on a Washington, D.C. dress shop. King Bub's advertising directors urged him to get rid of her immediately. "Nothing doing," Bowman said. "Now people will really look at our ad." He sat down and wrote a check for $10,000 payable to Lady Iris and instructed his P.R. men to notify her and the press that this was to make good any further checks that might bounce.

There aren't any bona fide Bubble Gum Kings around today, but there are a lot of fascinating characters with weird, creative glints in their eyes and wild games in their hearts left in an industry whose history is fraught with tales of big blowups, burning jealousies, closely guarded secrets, industrial espionage and heated lawsuits. One bubbly manufacturer refuses to discuss its business at all. The Donruss Company, a division of General Mills and the maker of Super, wrote to me declining to contribute any information whatsoever about their operation, "due to the very competitive nature of our market." Ask certain questions (about formulas, various lawsuits, etc.) and anybody in this "children's entertainment business," or "food with play value field" at best snaps a bubble at you.

The multimillion-dollar Philadelphia Chewing Gum Company in Havertown, Pa. is probably third in bubble gum sales, behind Topps and Fleer, which both claim first place today. It is headed by Edward L. Fenimore, whose chemist father, Dr. Edward P. Fenimore, founded it in 1948. The junior Fenimore doesn't claim to be a chemist, but there is pictorial proof that he can flex his big bubble gum-made mouth muscles and blow a bubble inside a bubble inside a bubble (3!) at the same time from the same wad of gum. This makes E.L.F. about the only executive in America who can blow three bubbles simultaneously—though I knew two big kids who could perform the same feat when I was under ten. Philadelphia's Swell Gum is noteworthy, but their Striped Buttons, six to a pack with a thin strip of gum, seems to be their best seller presently. Striped Buttons include such gems as "Out to Lunch (permanently)" and "You've Got A Winning Smile—But A Losing Face." The company has also included picture cards with some of its gums: a Tarzan series, National Football League cards and various war cards—the Green Berets, among others. In 1968 they offered "A complete memorial series of 55 cards on the Story of Robert F. Kennedy" with their bubble gum. A *New York Times* reporter checked out this Kennedy Bubble Gum. "A spokesman for Senator Edward Kennedy . . . " he wrote, "said that he thought it highly unlikely that the Kennedy family had authorized the bubble gum pack. Edward L. Fenimore, president of the Philadelphia Chewing Gum Corporation, leaving for Europe tomorrow, was unavailable for comment. In a call to the office, J. H. Daly, vice-president, R. E. Arnold, sales manager, and Jack Gobler, promotion manager, were also unavailable for comment, a secretary said, following a three-minute delay." I tried to check the story several times myself and couldn't get through to anyone but a secretary, either.

At the Fleer Fun Factory in Philadelphia, Pa. entertaining the kiddie subculture with food with play value is paramount, too. Fleer may or may not be the biggest bubble gum maker, but bubble gum was definitely invented there and Fleer is one of the oldest gum companies in the country or world for that matter (you can ask for "Dooblee Booblee" in Spain). The company itself has been in the same family since 1849, when founded by Otto Holstein, father-in-law-to-be of Frank Fleer, as a flavor factory. Frank Henry Fleer organized the present corporation in the 1880's and began making gum about 1885. Fleer executives today are as big on novelties as anyone in the bubble gum business. Signs, stickers, horoscopes, little statues of monsters, Smileys (grinning colorful little characters that can be tatooed on skin or clothing) are all included with their gums. Sometimes the search for appealing novelties—whose average life is only six to eight weeks for the short attention span of whimsical youngsters—can lead to unexpected trouble. Fleer once gave away little rubber "Zulu darts" which some kids put in their mouths to blow, inhaled and swallowed.

Fleer makes Razzles, the world's only patented gum formula, but its biggest seller is still old reliable Dubble Bubble, which has a color comic insert that millions of Americans were brought up on and has probably been read more than any native literature save for the copy on cereal boxes. The tiny

Comics enclosed in bubble gum are more widely read than any American literature—save the copy on cereal boxes. Here's an original of the Fleer Funnies, starring fat Pud.
Fleer Corporation

one-sheet comic includes Your Dubble Bubble Fortune, these even more innocuous than those in Chinese fortune cookies: "Good days are ahead of you," "Safety is catching," "Food for thought is not fattening," "Sharing is caring," "A smile can make a friend," etc. The comic itself is the main attraction, though. Featuring fat Pud in his striped shirt and his freaky friend Rocky Roller, Walter Diemer says it was created "to make our product distinctive" after competitors barged into the bubble gum markets. That it did. Pud's adventures can now be read in almost any language, the comics distributed with Dubble Bubble all over the world, although Pud has been slimmed down in recent times to appeal to the calorie-conscious everywhere.

In recent days corpulent Pud has been slimmed down to appeal to a diet-conscious generation. *Fleer Corporation*

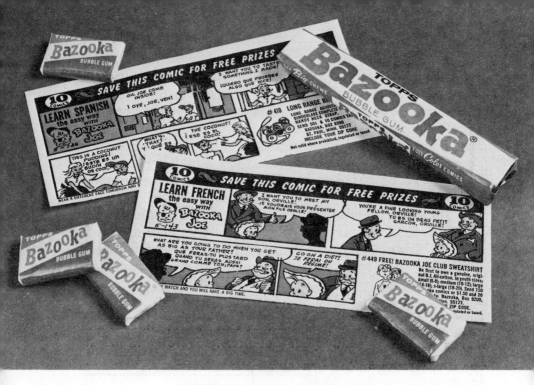

Bubble gum comics, printed in 50 or more languages, are sometimes educational. Here Topps' Bazooka Joe teaches kids French and Spanish. *Topps Chewing Gum, Inc.*

Topps' Bazooka also features a tiny color comic, its character Bazooka Joe speaking several foreign languages as well as English. There is even a bilingual "Learn French with Bazooka Joe":

—*Tu sais, Joe, il ya beaucoup de filles qui
  n'aiment pas sortir avec garcons!* (You know,
  Joe, lots of girls don't like to go out on dates.)
—*Comment sais-tu, Mort?* (How do you know, Mort?)
—*Je leur ai demandé!* (Because I asked them.)

"I don't make much on one piece of Bazooka," says a New York candy store owner. "But 3,000 pieces a week! Kids buy 25-50 pieces at a time." Topps sells more than a billion and half pieces of Bazooka annually and had sales of some $44 million last year, enough to pay its president Joel Shorin over $114,000, not including profit-sharing and stock options. Out of the pockets of little children, gum millionaires are made. The company sells its products in 55 countries, has licensed manufacturers in 10 of these and has the Bazooka Joe trademark

Billions of pieces of Bazooka, which made its debut after World War II, when there was a shortage and a "pink market" in bubble gum, roll off the production line. *Topps Chewing Gum, Inc.*

registered in 30 countries. While it didn't get into the gum business until 1938, Topps goes back a long way, having its antecedents in the American Leaf Tobacco Company, which was founded by Morris Shorin, grandfather of the present company president. During the Great Depression, Morris' sons diversified into chewing gum, coming out with a one-cent fruit-flavored cube long popular as a change-maker in small stores. Toward the end of World War II, Bazooka bubble gum was introduced. This was the biggest chew around—a large Tootsie Roll tube affair that sold for a nickel and was soon followed by the one-cent square of Bazooka. Topps, too, considers itself in the "children's entertainment business," as opposed to just making candy, its many gums and novelties reflecting this. The company even distributes a brochure with instructions on how to give a "bubble gum birthday party." But Topps is most famous for baseball cards, which it reinvented in 1951 and hit the jackpot with shortly after (see Chapter 11), "insuring the company's niche in American boyhood immortality . . . "

Big Bubbles and Famous Bubblers

Most lamentably, no one knows who has blown the biggest bubble with a piece of bubble gum, or even who has chewed more bubbly than anybody else at one time. Many contests have been held around the world, but no accurate records exist—so the most superfantastic bubble blower ever won't receive any kind of immortality. Philadelphia Gum's jumbo triple bubble is certainly an accomplishment for any child or child at heart to aim at and I've been told that one bubble bellowed several years back dwarfed the blower's body, yet the biggest example I could document is a monster created by Fleer worker Reinaldo Gutierrez. You've probably seen photos of animals, especially horses, blowing bubbles, too, but these are always balloons supplied by P.R. men. The champion bubble gum blower among ball players is Kansas City Royal utility infielder Kurt Bevacqua, who received a trophy and $1,000 for himself, $1,000 for his favorite charity, and a life-size Kurt Bevacqua baseball card when he beat the Phillies' Johnny Oakes to win the first Joe Garagiola/Bazooka Big League Bubble Gum Blowing Championship in 1975. Bevacqua, who didn't even expect to make the majors that spring, blew an

Reinaldo Gutierrez, a Fleer worker in Santo Domingo, has blown what may be the world's biggest bubble gum bubble. *Fleer Corporation*

Joe Garagiola measures All-Star Johnny Bench's bubble with a caliper provided by Topps, sponsor of the 1975 Big League Bubble Gum Blowing Championship. The winner received $1,000 and a gold trophy. *Topps Chewing Gum, Inc.*

18¼-inch bubble that was measured with special calipers by National League umpire Dick Stello. "I feel like the bases are loaded and it's the last half of the ninth and I'm at bat," he said as he stepped up to blow his prize-winning entry. "You wouldn't have to worry," said M.C. Garagiola. "They'd send in a pinch hitter."

Though some think it is the symbol of all that is vulgar and gauche, what one writer called "the pernicious bubble" is slowly enveloping the adult world. Seventy-five percent of the pink market is kids, but that leaves a whopping 25 percent. Several years ago it was reported that at least three members of Congress are known to be surreptitious gum bubblers and that the House restaurant keeps a supply of bubble gum hidden on a lower shelf. Then there was Ava Gardner, who fed a chimp some of her bubble gum in the film *Mogambo*, only to have Clark Gable, the great white hunter, reproach her. In *WW and The Dixie Dance Kings*, Burt Reynolds blows a giant bubble to conclude the picture. Nowadays, even movie idol Robert Redford chews the stuff, as does Telly Savalas (at least he blows an occasional bubble to punctuate his remarks as Kojak on his T.V. show). Joe Namath has his omnipresent wad in his mouth whenever he lopes out on the field, and there is a classic picture of Mickey Mantle blowing a bubble while he awaits the next fly ball. It is of course the athletes that kids admire most and as long as they keep on popping, bubble gum sales will doubtless continue to rise. There's no danger that the stars will stop effervescing, either—bubble gum is almost an integral part of sports today, one columnist observing that it is as much a part of baseball as the rhubarb. So the bubble shows no sign of bursting—no matter what any self-appointed His Meaniness says, kids will go on striving for that balloon bigger than a mushroom cloud, maybe even one that can carry them away to a far better world. (Tip from the experts: chew gum five minutes before trying to blow a Brobdingnagian bubble). A word of admonition to all, however. Remember that major league catcher who blew a mighty bubble during the pitcher's windup, popped it all over his mask, couldn't see, and let the winning run score on a passed ball.

CHAPTER 11

Flipping, Topping, Matching, Banking, Farthies, Dubs & Shades: Bubble Gum Baseball Cards

BEETHOVEN couldn't really be great, Lucy once told Charley Brown—because his picture isn't on a bubble gum card! One bubble gum baron claims the cards would sell well with spinach-and liver-flavored brands, or with no gum at all. In fact, even today some kids buy them and throw the bubble gum away—it has definitely become a case of the tail wagging the dog. Youngsters trade, flip, pitch and knock for cards, nickel and diming parents to distraction in the process. Collectors pay up to $1,500 apiece for the sweet smelling 3½-by-2½-inch cardboards squares, subscribe to special periodicals devoted to them, amass 200,000 card collections that museums proudly display. Billions are sold throughout the world inside packages containing thin, pink slabs of bubbly, the Topps Company alone turning out more than a quarter of a billion every year. Baseball trading cards are surely the biggest bubble gum novelty ever and seem destined to survive as long as baseball itself. Everything but a famous batboy's series has been printed.

Card collecting goes back over a century ago to the early 1870's, when cereal and cigarette makers enclosed pictures of flags, ships, Civil War generals and Indian chiefs to lure buyers. The first baseball trading cards were issued in 1886 by Old Judge cigarettes, who were followed by a number of cigarette manufacturers, including such forgotten brands as Sweet Caporal, Piedmont, Turkey Reds, Polar Bear, Fatima, Mecca and even Tolstoi, a Russian mouthpiece brand. Non-tobacco firms like Tip Top Bread and Cracker Jack also got into the act, as did candy companies and at least one newspaper. The earliest cards were usually stilted, studio-posed shots of ball players swinging at a ball suspended on a string that gave players a pop-eyed expression because of the tremendous charge from the flash powder used, but a number were made with expensive imported dyes and beautifully colored.

Some of the early stars depicted were Mordecai "Three Finger" Brown, who lost his other fingers in a mining accident . . . Cy Young, a pitcher so revered that he was once presented with the entire receipts of a ball game . . . and Charles Street, his card revealing, somewhat cryptically, that he was the first player ever to catch a ball dropped from the Washington Monument. All the pioneer greats were photographed in the strange-looking uniforms of teams that wouldn't be recognized today—teams like the Brooklyn Superbees and the Boston Rustlers. One ancient series features a foldover card that is one player when open, another player when folded in half. A few old cards are very valuable, indeed. A Sweet Caporal entry with "Ty Cobb Cigarettes" printed on the back is worth a lot, and so is an entire 1920 set issued by the Zeenut Co., as well as the whole 1915 Cracker Jack series. But most prized of all is the Honus Wagner card issued by Sweet Caporal in 1908. The Pittsburgh Pirates' "Flying Dutchman" was a confirmed nonsmoker adamantly opposed to children smoking and got into a Dutch dudgeon when he learned that his picture had been included in a cigarette pack without his permission. Fearing that his portrait would be taken as an endorsement, Wagner demanded that Sweet Caporal recall all of the cards. This was done, but not before an estimated 60 smokers had corralled a few of them. Only 11 Wagner cards are known to be in existence today, the rest, like the 1913 Liberty nickels that supposedly went down with the *Titanic*, seem to have disappeared from the face of the earth. Not long ago a New Jersey college student paid $1,500 for the head and shoulders view of the popular slugger. All the other rare Wagners are worth the same.

Baseball cards weren't the only collector's items in the early days; also popular were pictures of movie stars, boxers and other athletes. Similarly, the first bubble gum cards issued in the thirties included many types, such as Bowman Gum's famous war series, which created an international incident when the Japanese protested that they were depicted as barbaric warmongers. Bubble gum cards have ranged all the way from

Bubble gum baseball trading cards, a multi-million dollar business, derive from cards that used to be issued with packs of cigarettes. This old Honus Wagner card is worth $1,500. *Topps Chewing Gum, Inc.*

A recent fad in gum novelties is Topps' "Wacky Packs," takeoffs on advertising. *Topps Chewing Gum, Inc.*

Topps' World War II plane spotter series for civil defense (these went well with their slogan "Don't talk chum, chew Topps Gum"), and the Davy Crockett series so popular in the early sixties, to the Wacky Packs that are the rage today. Davy Crockett's name was once magic, and Topps alone sold 300 million packs of its Crockett series. Elvis Presley and the Beatles had their days, too, as did such diametrically opposed political candidates as Barry Goldwater and Lyndon Johnson. Every conceivable type of card has been done, even series on popular television shows. When Topps came out with an anticommunist series called Freedom's War in the sixties, a competitor answered the challenge with Fight The Red Menace Gum.

Aside from baseball cards, the biggest recent craze among the fickle kiddies is Topps' Wacky Packs, which went through six series in its first year. Wacky Packs, put-downs of advertising, consist of three Wacky stickers and a piece of gum. Among the stickers, which kids paste on doors and all over the

house, are Fruit of the Tomb (clothing), Sneer (laundry deter-
gent), Peter Pain (peanut butter), Footsie Roll ("the candy bar
with sole"), Sailem Cigarettes ("Better to sail 'em than to
smoke 'em"), and Neverready Batteries. Kids often buy a 48-
pack carton of these at one time and in parts of New York City,
store owners have separate cash registers just to handle Wacky
Packs sales. Youngsters clearly have an antipathy toward the
advertisers that interrupt their T.V. programs. Capitalizing on
this, many companies have flooded the field with imitations.
Fleer, showing more originality, has its Crazy Covers series,
featuring *U.S. Booze and World Report, Slime* and *Newsleak.*

Horror cards are about the only bubble gum novelties that
have been denounced by the experts. These include pictures of
the Frankenstein monster telling a youngster, "I'm your new
baby sitter," or the picture of a monster captioned "You
should see the other guy." Psychiatrist Dr. Frederic Wertham,
who forced sweeping changes in the comic-book industry with
his book *The Seduction of the Innocent,* feels that horror cards
pander to a child's basest instincts, warning that "the average
youngster can become callous to the beauty in the world and
fail to see the evil in horror." Most cards, however, are harmless, especially the perennially top-selling sports series. Small
fry even learn from these, after a fashion, like the five-year-old
Minnesota youngster who can recite the vital and professional
statistics of over 400 baseball players—all learned from the
backs of bubble gum cards . . .

The Cardboard League

Bubble gum cards cover all sports from football and basketball to hockey and soccer—and will doubtless someday include
chess players from Russia and Ping-pong players from China.
But baseball cards outsell football cards, their nearest competitor, by 2½ to one. According to Seymour "Sy" Berger,
director of Topps' sports department, kids prefer baseball
cards for three reasons. "First there is the identification," Berger says. "The baseball player is typical of the man walking
down the street, unlike the football player who is a very big
man, or the basketball player who is a very tall man. With a
baseball player he can see himself. He can identify. In addition, because of the game's pace, the youngster has the opportunity to learn to imitate baseball players—to hold his bat like

Stan Musial or spread his feet like Joe DiMaggio. And he can familiarize himself with the facts of the players. It's all within his grasp."

Though most kids pass the card-hoarding stage before they turn thirteen, some pursue their passion into their nineties. It isn't a hobby that can be immensely profitable, like coins or stamps, but the cardophile's love of sports makes it more than worthwhile. There are baseball card fanatics all over the world—a man in Great Britain named Worton-Tiger recently purchased an extensive collection from an American. The largest collection ever assembled belonged to the late Jefferson R. Burdick of Syracuse, New York, the father of baseball card collecting. Though his fingers were crippled with arthritis in his later years, Burdick managed to correspond with other fans around the world and amass more than 200,000 cards extending from the 1880's through the 1950's. Burdick developed card collecting, swapping and cataloging to a science and was responsible for the American Card Catalog, published by the Nostalgia Press, which is the bible for serious collectors. In 1963 he donated his immense collection to the Metropolitan Museum of Art, where it is now on display. It's said that he died a day after mounting the cards, which are included in more than 100 scrapbooks.

Collectors advertise in periodicals like the *Sporting News* and specialized publications such as *The Sports Hobbyist* (P.O. Box 3731, Detroit Michigan 48205), *The Trader Speaks* (3 Pleasant Dr., Lake Ronkomkoma, N.Y. 11779) and *The Collector's Bulletin* (Box 293 Franklin Square, N.Y. 11010). There are also several books on baseball cards, including Gar Miller's *BASEBALL CARDS: Everything You Always Wanted To Know, But Didn't Know Who To Ask* and Brendan C. Boyd and Fred Harris' *Baseball Card Flipping, Trading And Bubble Gum Book*. The *Card Collector's Bulletin* holds quarterly mail auctions, bids sent to the magazine on cards listed by their owners and the magazine awarding the cards to the highest bidder. Baseball card conventions, which often draw over 1,000 people, allow collectors to keep up to date, too.

At least one enterprising young lady is working her way through college selling baseball cards. Renata Galasso, a junior at Fordham University, started dealing when she bought about 10,000 pieces of bubble gum containing about 130,000 cards.

She sorted the cards into sets, advertised and sold them at $8.99 a set, and gave the bubble gum away to neighborhood youngsters. Not long ago Topps decided to sell her the cards without making her buy the bubble gum and now she's doing even better.

But most collectors are still kids up to age twelve who store their baseball cards in cigar or shoe boxes, ready to take out whenever there is the prospect of a trade or flipping match. The kids are quick to spot possible collectors' items today; they aren't totally absorbed in the moment as they were in the past, when old cards, even last season's, weren't worth a slab of gum. Today's kids have more of a sense of history and are always looking for errors. There have been a good number of these in recent years on the Topps cards alone. In 1952 photos of pitchers Joe Page and Johnny Sain were reversed and the mistake wasn't discovered until several cards had been distributed. In 1969 the Topps photographer mistook the Angels batboy for Aurelio Rodriguez. The most notorious error oc-

The photograph of this 1969 Topps card mistakenly shows the batboy of the California Angels. *Topps Chewing Gum, Inc.*

curred in 1959 when Milwaukee Brave pitcher Warren Spahn convinced fellow pitcher and right-hander Lou Burdette to pose as a southpaw. Burdette had his picture taken with his glove on the wrong hand and as soon as his card hit the market, hundreds of calls and letters started pouring into Topps offices. Too many of these Topps cards were printed for them to be worth much, but the Page-Sain reversal, for example, is worth about $5 today, as is a card showing home run king Hank Aaron batting from the wrong side of the plate. Some of the first Topps cards from the year 1951, however, are worth $10 to $50 apiece.

Topps is by far the leader in the baseball card business, which has been invaded by firms as diverse as Red Heart Dog Food, Kahn Franks ("The Wiener The World Awaited"), and Johnson Cookies. There have been cards printed on bottle caps and milk cartons, even cards built inside of marbles, but Topps bubble gum cards dominate the field. Last year the Card King sold 20 million packages of baseball cards accompanied by

On this 1957 card, Hank Aaron's photo was reversed and he was shown batting from the wrong side of the plate. *Topps Chewing Gum, Inc.*

almost 200 tons of bubble gum: a quarter of a *billion* baseball cards (a cool $8 million retail) that include over 700 different cards, one on each major league player, plus team and specialty cards like the series "Boyhood Photos of the Stars."

Topps claims its gallery of color photos of baseball players is the most extensive in the world and no one has challenged them yet. So thorough is the company in signing up players for their series that in 1964 the Federal Trade Commission charged that the Card King was illegally monopolizing the baseball picture card industry. The bubble gum people have been no strangers to the courts in regard to baseball cards. In 1949 the now defunct Bowman Gum Co. sued to prevent Leaf Brands of Chicago from using pictures of players under exclusive contract to Bowman, and last year, in more bubble trouble, good old Broadway Joe Namath filed a $750,000 suit charging that his picture had been used without his permission on bubble gum cards. But the F.T.C. case had to be among the most ridiculous in history. After eight weeks and 4,075 pages of transcribed testimony, including sampling of bubble gums and discussions of "bubbleability," F.T.C. examiner Herman Tocker ruled that Topps did not have an illegal hold on the market, exonerating the company of any wrongdoing. Its dominance, he said, seemed to be due to the incompetence of the competition, but he did recommend a curb on Topps baseball contracts. To this the *New York Times* snorted in an editorial reply: "In effect, the company is being penalized for building up its business by efficient management, simply because it has not had competent competition. That seems a strange doctrine to the layman; one inclined to remind him of Mr. Bumble's dictum: 'The law is a ass, a idiot.' "

At one point during the hearing the president of Topps was asked in an aside why he didn't come out with a series of cards showing former chairmen of the F.T.C. "For the same reason that Custer didn't publish pictures of Indians," Mr. Joel Shorin replied testily. That must have summed up Topps feelings exactly, although Mr. Tocker's statement that Fleer had employed "subversive efforts and espionage to obtain copies of Topps' contracts" must have been some consolation. Fleer did set out to develop other types of novelties, but apparently the hatchet hasn't been buried yet, as Fleer has recently filed suit in a Federal District Court accusing Topps of illegal restraint of trade—taking an unfair bite of business because of its near-exclusive control over pictures of big league players. Topps, which has a purported income of $6 million from just its baseball card operation, denounces the charge as baseless. In any event, aside from revealing the sharp teeth and tongues of the bubble gum people, the entire affair has thus far yielded no more than the only legal definition of bubble gum ever made. Bubble gum, ruled the F.T.C., is "that commodity which is offered, sold or advertised as a chewing gum for the making of bubbles and not necessarily a gum which, by the ingenuity of a child, could be used to make bubbles." Questioned on this tortuous opinion, one precocious ten-year-old bubble gum chewer later stated: "The law is a ass, a idiot."

Topps now turns out its cards and bubble gum at its new 400,000 square foot plant in Duryea, Pa., where over 1,000 people are employed, but its executive offices are still in the waterfront Bush Terminal section of Brooklyn, the kind of place, one visitor observed, that Joey Gallo might have found unnerving. Sy Berger, Topps' sport card director, who with enthusiasm and sincerity holds down a job every other kid in America covets, heads a staff of associates here that includes statisticians, writers, artists, photographers and scouts in the field. The card operation begins with the Topps scouts (the late Brooklyn Dodger scout Turk Karam was the first to work for the company), who convince minor league players to sign options with Topps for cards if they make the majors. At first only promising players were signed up, but this bruised too many egos (imagine being told that a bubble gum company doesn't think you're good enough to make the majors) and now all minor leaguers are given what is called "steak money," a $5 binder that they can "go buy a steak" with. Then, if and when they make the majors, Topps signs them for $250 and a share of royalties, for a total of about $400 annually.

Players are photographed for the cards in spring training, which accounts for an occasional palm tree in the background. Eight photos are taken (with and without a cap in case the player is traded before the card reaches the candy store), action shots interspersed with the traditional head shots. Everything from the photography to the compilation of statistics on back of the cards and the complicated distribution of each series is done with great care and professional pride, putting Topps in a cardboard league all by itself compared to the competition. "In this business, we have a tremendous responsibility to the

Players get about $400 a year for appearing on Topps cards. Free gum, too. *Topps Chewing Gum, Inc.*

kids," says Berger, a former collector himself. "The baseball card is the gospel, the Talmud. They have nothing else to go on. If we made a mistake it would be like giving a kid an erroneous primer to read." Besides, there are all those letters and phone calls—the youngsters are uncannily knowledge-able.

Players can be very touchy about their photos and the Topps photographers try to depict them at their best, though as Berger says, "You can't make a silk purse out of a sow's ear." As for the player statistics, sometimes these, too, are immutable. "You don't know the agony of trying to think up something nice to say about some guy who hit .176 last year and made 25 errors," Berger laments. "What can you say—'This guy stinks'?" Everything is done as fairly as possible. The only concession made to the stars is that any card ending in zero is likely to be a big-name player—Henry Aaron, for example, is 400. But most of the players wouldn't expect preferential treatment, anyway. It's enough just being on a baseball card and some would appear there for love alone. "It's like the actor or movie star who makes it to the top and gets his name up in lights on a theatre marquee," Berger says. "When a player reaches the majors and gets his picture on a baseball card, he feels he has made it. I've had many of them tell me it was one of their biggest thrills." As former major leaguer Jim Bouton put it in his *Ball Four*: "Someone once asked Al Ferrar of the Dodgers why he wanted to be a baseball player. He said because he always wanted to see his picture on a bubble gum card. Well, me too. It's an ego trip . . . "

Cardboard Players

Baseball cards can be an ego trip for their collectors, too, especially those who trade and flip their cards. Trading can't be explained, values depend on the season or yesterday's game, and if you don't have an instinct for this early stage of horse trading, it's something you can't possibly learn—it would be no surprise to find that J. P. Morgan or J. P. Getty was an accomplished baseball card trader in his youth. As for flipping, it appeals to the instinct for gambling that is with us from the instant we choose to emerge from the womb. Some kids are such born losers at flipping that they are candidates for Gamblers' Anonymous before turning ten, but they keep buying new baseball cards and coming back for more. Fortunes (in cards) have been won or lost on the toss of a baseball card, long-lasting friendships have been dissolved, more noses have been bloodied and eyes blackened over the years than ever were violated by school bullies who got kids for tattling after school. But still the cardboard players keep playing.

Kids seek out pigeons and flip for their cards in a number of ways, which seem to subtly change with each generation of little nippers. In case you want to get down the old Garcia Y Vega Cigar box from the attic, if your mother didn't throw it out long ago, or buy a few packs of baseball cards and join the kids out on the street, here are the latest variations on the sport, which should be recorded for posterity anyway. Various youngsters were bribed with bubble gum cards for these and I've included a glossary of more obscure terms that might be obsolete by tomorrow, like the games themselves. Remember that coating cards with candle wax to make them more flippable is strictly illegal and that all rules should be agreed upon before you play. You can, however, sandpaper down calloused fingers.

MATCHING

Here players simply take turns matching their cards against their opponent's—the "heads" are the ballplayers, the "tails" the statistics on the back of each card. The odds are about 50-50, but can be overcome, experts say, through the skillful use of body English when flipping the cards and careful consideration of prevailing winds. No one can teach you how to flip a card in matching—except to say that ideally the card is held with the thumb on the long bottom edge and the other four fingers on the long top edge. The rest, like blowing a bubble, can only be learned through trial and error. As is often the case in life, luck is far more important than skill.

FARTHIES

Also called skimming, pitching and scaling, farthies requires a totally different flipping motion than most other baseball card games. It is similar only in that it too can only be learned by experience and mastered with luck. Sometimes heavy losers are given the chance to switch a matching game to farthies. Here the player who skims, scales or otherwise pitches his card the farthest from a given point (usually toward a wall) wins, no matter whether the card comes up heads or tails. This game can be played with one card each or a number of cards each. When a number of cards are used, the one card farthest away from tossing line wins all. There are many elegant variations on farthies. For example, a card leaning against the wall can sweep the field, according to agreed upon rules. This is called "Make A Leaner." But if two cards lean against the wall, the side with the player's colored picture facing the participants wins over a card leaning with data-side out.

KNOCK DOWN THE LEANER

A number of cards are arrayed on edge against a bottom porch step. The opposing player tries to knock them down with his cards and keeps any cards he does knock down. If he misses, he loses the card he throws, my informants say.

TOPSIES AND TIPSIES

This game consists of topping a card in the pot with the card flipped. Topsies is often played off a stoop. Players shoot their cards down onto the sidewalk, trying to cover their opponent's cards with their own. Often a rule called Tipsies is in force in Topsies and as a result Topsies is then called Tipsies (it gets confusing sometimes). Tipsies just means that when a card barely touches another, it wins that card.

BANKING

Banking is the simplest game of all and depends completely on luck, unless you cheat. A group of five cards is shuffled by each player and the two packs turned over. The numbers of the back cards are compared and the higher one wins all of the cards.

SINGLES, FLIPS, FIVES AND TENS

In singles, no matching is involved. The flipper has to flip a card either heads or tails, whichever his opponent orders. If he flips a tail when his opponent calls for a head, he loses the card; if he flips the head, he wins a card from his opponent.

When four cards are used in this game, it is called Flips. The flipper here has to flip his cards in the exact order given by his opponent. If he doesn't flip, say, tail, head, tail, head, he loses all.

Flips is called Fives or Tens when five or ten cards must be flipped in order.

UNMATCH OR ODDS

Here the challenger rapidly names an order, ie. tail, tail, head, tail, that the flipper must *reverse* as he flips. This is about the only baseball card game that requires quick coordination between the fingers and mind.

GLOSSARY

Lasts—means "you go first" by the player who calls it.

Winning first or lasts—a rule specifying that cards matching the first or last card take the whole stack.

Winning on dubs—second card of a kind ("doubles") wins.

Shades—different shades of the same color banner win.

No sport—no cards will be returned at game's end.

No split—cards won't be divided at the end of the game.

No crap (or worse)—don't think up new rules that benefit you while the game is in play, or throw in out-of-date, value- less baseball cards.

CHAPTER 12

The *Anatomy Of Gumballs*

"YOU can set your gumball machine down in the most unlikely place—say, the middle of the Sahara—and someone,
possibly a camel, will come along and play it," writes James
Nelson in *The Trouble With Gum Balls*. "You can lock a machine
up in a trunk, weight it with stones, and drop it through a hole
in the ice at the North Pole, and when you pull it up, there will
be a penny in the coin box. This doesn't mean, however, that
the North Pole is a good location, because a second penny may
never come along to join the first. It is merely a demonstration
of the supernatural nature of gum machines."

Almost from the chewing gum industry's inception have
gum machines been so mysterious and omnipresent. They've

been around since at least the late 1880's, dispensing tab gum (miniature pieces of famous brands) and the bright-colored gumballs treasured for nearly a century by everyone from those in their nonage to nonagenarians. Tab gum has always sold well and the machines vending it in public places have played an important role in popular culture. "They have contributed greatly to the neatness of the personal appearance of the nation," the *Literary Digest* noted half-seriously back in 1914, "as it is estimated that in the mirrors on gum machines there are 345,659,256 cravats and 756,586,589 wisps of hair adjusted during the calendar year." This is not to mention the trillions of lips painted, faces powdered and narcissists rewarded over the last century in tab gum machine glasses catering to the fairest of us all. Yet it was the mirrorless gumball machine, not the tab dispensers, that won the heart of America. Gumball machines, despite the many kids who have got their fingers stuck in them, are a triumph of Yankee ingenuity—as few as possible moveable parts operating with unerring precision. Many were intricately designed—one old model called the Pulver had a little man in it who held a gumball in his hands and turned and dropped it down the hatch when you inserted a penny. Most simply had a vivid fire-engine-red base that no one could miss and a sparkling glass dome filled with gleaming multi-colored gumballs. Some are collectors' items today. A wooden Zeno machine brings up to $200, and a Climax with a curved glass dome sells for $250.

Vending machines themselves go back at least as far as the first century, though the earliest ones to survive are eighteenth century English "Honor Boxes" that unlocked with a coin to provide snuff and tobacco. In the late eighteenth century there were fascinating machines like the model with a clucking hen that laid a hard-boiled egg for a dime, and the noteworthy Bull's Head, which snorted a squirt of perfume into your handkerchief when you inserted a penny and pulled down on the horns. Although no one seems to know who invented the first gumball machine, the Frank H. Fleer Company was one of the first to sell gum in penny vending machines. In the 1880's the company's founder agreed to an experiment proposed by a young vending machine salesman. The salesman argued that vending machines were so great a sales gimmick that people would actually drop a penny in them for nothing. Frank Fleer agreed to buy several machines if the young man's pitch proved true, and the experiment was conducted at New York's old Flatiron Building, a popular tourist spot noted for the strong gusts of wind that constantly blew around it. The salesman set up a vending machine there, with printed instructions to "drop a penny in the slot and listen to the wind blow." He got Fleer's order when hundreds of people dropped pennies in the slot and continued to do so until New York's Finest hauled the machine away.

Since Fleer's time, gum and vending machines have become inseparable. There have been scores of types, even an attempt to combine a gumball machine with a pinball machine. The latter was the brainchild of the irrepressible J. Warren Bowman, America's bubble gum king during the depression years. King Bub bought 180 forerunners of the present-day pinball machines—without electric lights, buzzers, gongs and all the other gaudy lures—intending to convert them so that an attachment on the machines would reward high scorers with gumballs. He and an old friend named Charles Fellenbarger, who had invented gum machinery for Wrigley, worked on the machines, but lost thousands when they couldn't come up with the right attachment.

Mr. James Nelson, aforementioned author of *The Trouble With Gum Balls* (Simon & Schuster, 1956, but unfortunately out of print), spent a few years as a gumball vender trying to realize a part-time profit of $100 a week ($1 profit on each of 100 machines). A former editor at *Business Week* magazine, Nelson quit his job and moved to California in hopes of making his fortune. Con men suppliers told him that gumballing was a precise science, the routes chosen by experts who spent hours pinpointing the perfect locations for machines—near schools, bus stations, wherever foot traffic is particularly heavy. After he bought his route, Nelson found he had locations where two pennies never met in his machines. Some storekeepers left the machines out in the rain: "A tiny rivulet of colored water poured out and spattered the toe of my shoe . . . I lifted the vending mechanism, and a brightly colored, semisolid mass of bubble gum began to ooze gently out of the merchandise slot. It got on my right hand, and when I withdrew my hand, it stretched out in long sagging sticky strings." Then there were kids who jammed machines with slugs, buttons, play coins, *groschen und pfennings*, cardboard yen, hacksaw blades and even gumballs that they chewed up and forced through the coin slot to completely gum up the works. There was gum that went stale before being sold, storekeepers who insisted on counting all the pennies in figuring their commission (instead of weighing them on a spring-type penny scale that registers the pennies in dollars and cents), and customers who complained that the gumballs were hollow (they weren't), or that the free charms in some machines were glued to the glass (which was never the case). Nelson tried every gimmick conceivable, even mixing striped gumballs with the solid colors and awarding "free five-cent candy bars" (available from the storekeeper) for each striped ball, but he never became a gumball machine tycoon. He never even cleared $50 a week and after a harrowingly hilarious time, retired from the field . . .

The Hallowed (Though Hollowed) Last Penny Candy

From the time gumball machines came on the market every kid has known what to do with a penny: dash off to the nearest dispenser . . . put in the coin . . . turn the handle . . . and pop the chewing-gumball that rattles out into the mouth. For many years Tootsie Rolls were the favorite penny confection of American youngsters. These chewy chocolate logs honor the sweetheart of Austrian candymaker Leo Hirshfield, who came to New York in 1896 to pursue his fortune, invented them, and named them after his old flame. In the 1930's, however, penny bubble gum and gumballs (which are usually made from a bubble gum base) wrested the title from Tootsie Rolls. Today gumballs and a bite-size Tootsie Roll are just about the only penny items left in the world.

Gumballs now account for about three percent of the chewing gum market. They are sold to vendors as "hundred-count gum," one hundred gumballs to the pound, and are available from many manufacturers large and small throughout the country. New marketing techniques have cut down machine sales somewhat. East Boston's Gum Products, Inc., for example, believes that the old Mom-and-Pop stores with gumball machines in the front are phenomena of the past. Gum Products is pushing a 29-cent item called the "Chewmore" strip—a length of cellophane about a yard long containing a multi-hued

For over a century, dispensers like this original Ford Gum Ball Machine have attracted kids and pennies like magnets all over the world. *Ford Gum & Machine Company*

25-ball chain of gumballs that is sold in supermarkets. There are also specialty items like the bright orange mass of gum just slightly smaller than a tennis ball that is perched on the desk of Gum Product's president, Ned Caruso. This behemoth costs a full 25 cents, treasonable to the gumball faithful, but some kids do buy them. Gum Products hasn't given up hope on machines, though; their vending division still accounts for 63 percent of sales. Instead, as is the case in the whole industry, new outlets are being sought. These include the entrances of Woolworth-like variety chains, discount stores and supermarkets—anywhere there is traffic and an empty space. Supermarkets are particularly good spots; some stores have as many as 32 gumball machines pouring out thousands of shiny, colorful gumballs every week. "They're a fixture now and the reasons are simple," Ned Caruso says. "The machines utilize that empty space in front of the market and they cut down on the opening of candy bags by kids shopping with their parents."

Gumballs may be acquiring more class by being dressed up

in cellophane or clear plastic, but the gumball machine won't disappear until teeth do. At least not according to John F. Fry, vice-president of the Ford Gum and Machine Company, which Mr. Fry calls "the Cadillac of the gum ball industry." Ford is the only gumball concern that makes both its own gum and machines and was the first company to brand its name on its product in mass quantities, long before the popular M & M candies were so marked. Two billion gumballs a year are produced in its Akron, New York and Ponce, Puerto Rico plants—6,000 tons of gum, 5½ million pounds, a quarter of a million Ford gum machines dispensing enough gumballs to circle the globe in just 18 months.

Ford was founded back in 1918 by an itinerant roofing salesman named Ford S. Mason, who gave the company his prenom with the thought in mind that he would be linking his product with Henry's Model Ts. Only a handful of men were in the gumball machine business when Mason borrowed the money to lease 102 machines and placed them in various stores in western New York. Most gum was so poor then that people only bought it once, and most vending machines so unreliable that they generally took coins and failed to deliver merchandise. Ford Mason changed all that. His father, a Baptist minister, urged him to manufacture his own machines as well as gum ("Make your own machines, my boy, and share your profits with God.") and proceeded to design a dependable vending machine for him, one that remains basically unchanged today. Later the son perfected formulas for texture and flavor until he was certain his gumball was the best on the market, helped perfect a stamping machine that could brand 250,000 gumballs an hour with the Ford trademark, and spent ten years devising a method of coating each gumball with a thin layer of water-repellant glaze. "In the old days," Mason says, "a drop of water would ruin the colors of a barrel of gum balls. Of course the gum still tasted good, but nobody wanted gum balls that looked stretched and spotty." As a result of his innovative process, moisture condensation inside the glass globes of gum machines no longer discolors gumballs. You can take a handful of treated gumballs and hold them under a running faucet without any color coming off.

In days to come chicle chews, aspirin gum and sugarless gum were added to Ford's line, but perhaps the Ford Company's greatest innovation was its fund-raising program called the Fordway Plan. Fordway came into being in 1939 when a ladies' club in Columbus, Ohio was seeking money to outfit a children's ward in a local hospital. The ladies learned that local businessmen were collecting 20 percent of the take from Ford gum machines on their premises and suggested that the merchants donate these earnings to charity. The merchants agreed and in six months the women collected enough pennies to outfit their children's ward. The outgrowth of this experiment was the Fordway Program, which is now sponsored by 3,500 service clubs and civic organizations (such as the Kiwanis, Lions, American Legion, and Boys Town), who make about $2 million a year from the pennies inserted into Ford gum machines carrying their decals—20 percent of the company's total earnings. Sometimes the merchants housing the machines share in the profits, sometimes not; but the Fordway system was one of the first (possibly *the* first) programs to let charities share in the sale of a product on any consistent basis. The machines are insured under a special policy that gives liability coverage to Ford, its distributor, the sponsoring group and the merchant space grantor. Today Ford Gum is sold only through sponsoring service clubs. "Chew for charity" has made the company millions and done immeasurable good, as the many testimonial letters in the Ford archives show.

Ford Mason sold his firm to the Automatic Service Company of Atlanta, Georgia in 1970, retiring to Florida, where he remains active in other businesses and reigns as a kind of unofficial historian of the gumball industry. A venerable, deeply religious man (he has tithed his income to the church since he started working), his place in history will be assured if only because one of his machines has been encased, complete with gumballs, in the cornerstone of a Milwaukee building—a training center for spastic children that penny gumball profits built. Mason has a fund of anecdotes about Wrigley, Adams and many other old-time gum greats, but perhaps the oddest tale concerns a psychology professor at Syracuse University. The professor wanted to train laboratory monkeys to put pennies into Ford's machines and extract gumballs in order to observe their reactions to various colors. The monkeys were no different than most children, he found. They sulked when a white ball emerged from the machine and jumped with glee when they got a colored one.

White, pink, green, red, yellow, black and orange gumballs by the millions literally roll off Ford's assembly lines every day, as do scores of gaily colored self-service machines—their globes of either conventional glass or nonbreakable Lexon clear plastic—that will eventually find themselves perched on store counters and pipe pedestals here and abroad. Ford's spotless plant includes such sophisticated equipment as a sugar dust collector machine that recycles 2,400 pounds of sugar dust a week. The manufacturing process is identical to that of most gums (see Chapter 13), until the gum is formed into balls. For ball gum the forming is done in a pencillike strip. The strips are scored twice, resulting in the ball shape. The shaped gumballs are then stored at least overnight in a cold room (56 to 60 degrees) until they are hard enough to coat. They are next transferred to large drumlike kettles, each holding 300 pounds of gum centers, where they are coated with a sucrose solution (sugar syrup similar to that used for canning fruit) to which flavor and color is added.

Following the seven-hour coating procedure, the gumballs are dried with hot air to drive off moisture and recrystallize the sugar. Then they are smoothly polished with waxes like beeswax in a battery of gleaming tumblers and given their special resinous glaze. The final stop before packing is the branding department, where a series of rolls (similar to kitchen rolling pins) etched with the name Ford pick up a quick-drying edible ink in the etched portions and transfer it to the gumballs passing through on conveyor belts. All that remains is for the penny gumballs to be inspected before rolling out to encounter the jaws of the world.

Penny gumballs are still rolling off production lines by the billions at Ford and elsewhere, and there are gumball machines everywhere man has landed excepting the moon—wherever there is an extra square foot of space near a store. But the penny gumball is in trouble these days. "It's getting smaller and smaller and smaller," says Ned Caruso of Gum Products. "I guess you can call us pioneers with the hollow gum ball." Firms all over are making gumballs with nucleuses of next to nothing in order to hold their penny price line. Two-cent, five-cent and ten-cent gum machines have been introduced, but gumball machines still remain one of the few places where the penny is king. The villain in the story is sugar, whose price skyrocketed at one point from $14 to $40 per 100

Thousands of quadrillions of gumballs that are probably "the only worthwhile penny item left in the
world"—even though they are made largely of air.
Ford Gum & Machine Company

pounds, a finished gumball being 75 percent sugar. The gumball people have two choices: either make the gumballs smaller—which could gum up the dispensers; or keep them the same size, but use less gum and candy coating. Same size has won out thus far. This has been accomplished by making the gumball's hollow center a little larger—making the ball lighter but not changing its outside dimensions. The air of inflation, then, is a major constituent of the new gumball, but the "residual cud," as the chewed-out result is called in the industry, is the same size as before. "We're going to stay in the penny gum business," Ford's John Fry says. "Despite the penny shortage, the pennies are still out there." Everyone hopes he is right and that penny gumballs don't go the way of five-cent packs of gum, five-cent cigars, and nickel beer, et al. Clearly the fight involves more than just corporate profits. It is a battle to save what is surely one of the worthwhile penny things left in the world—the American gumball, an international institution.

Making It— *Kosher & Unkosher Ways*

CHAPTER 13

IN its infancy, chewing gum was rumored to be a wicked brew of any noxious substances parents could conjure up to scare children off the terrible stuff. Many early, highly imaginative accounts of gum making bring to mind the witches in *Macbeth* cackling over their cauldron while stirring in eye of newt, toe of frog, wool of bat, tongue of dog and all the rest to "make the gruel thick and slab."

Some reputable scientists perpetuated this piffle. Not only was chicle "the carrier of influenza" (see Chapter 4), but the "glue" in chewing gum would "cause one's intestines to stick together—resulting in death." Among the wild accusations there were only a few valid criticisms. An article in *The Practi-*

cal Druggist of August 1913 put it this way: "The sweet sticky nature of the chicle sap [sic] attracts and hold countless insects, creeping and flying, after the manner of a strip of flypaper. The native gatherers of the sap are not unduly solicitous over the presence of insects or extremely careful to avoid including pieces of bark and leaves, for they are paid by the pound." The writer, a medical doctor, concluded that gum makers didn't purify their chicle before putting it on the market. "Take at random a piece of gum from each package, wash off the sugar and hold the piece to the sunlight," he warned. "In every case will be seen particles of dirt, making it clear that every man, woman and child user of chewing gum is for the time being a walking washing machine." Professor William Mansfield of Columbia University agreed. "Today the users of chewing gum are refining machines," he wrote later that year. "They swallow the refuse, and about the time the gum is thoroughly clean and pure, they throw it away."

No doubt many "chiclers" did purify their gum by digesting it, and certainly some curious substances were used in chewing gum whenever the supply of chicle ran low due to one South American revolution or another. "Unpalatable *asphalt* is frequently used," a medical writer noted in 1920. "It is boiled in a decoloring liquid containing a flavoring extract and may then be combined with other ingredients. Often other chicle substitutes are boiled in a solution of *caustic soda* and repeatedly washed until the soapy part of the material is removed." As for chicle itself, investigators found that its fermentation yielded a poisonous oil known as furfural, which is also produced during the distillation of wood to form wood alcohol, in the distillation of grain and in the brewing of beer. Furfural, a colorless oily liquid now used chiefly in plastics manufacture and as a solvent in refining lubricating oils, is a harmful substance, and many attempts have been made to free beer and wine from its noxious presence, but it was never really a problem in chewing gum. One writer, however, suggested that it caused the "dreadful occupational ulcer" of the chicle gatherers now known to be caused by the chicle fly native to Yucatan jungles.

Fear of early chewing gum manufacturing methods led British officials to suspect that the impurities in gum might have caused several new diseases which were the subject of notification under the Factory Inspection Act. Yet no exotic diseases were ever conclusively linked to chewing gum and no illnesses more serious than an upset stomach ever resulted from its use (if untampered with outside the factory). Fly-by-night quick-buck operators did put out an unsanitary, un-palatable product, but they were in the minority from the be-ginning. The stories that people died from chewing gum have no basis in fact (at least I can find no record of them) and one suspects that early Comstocks and crackpots who disliked the "chewing gum habit" invented them, just as they concocted the tale that tomatoes were poisonous, or that citrus fruits make the blood acidic, or that sweets cause adolescent acne—to name but a few food myths. Most pioneer gum manufactur-ers were acutely aware of their image and strove to keep their factories and product as sanitary as possible. Close to the truth is an early report on the industry made by a popular magazine: "It will be gratifying to 'gum fiends' to learn that the numerous gum factories throughout the United States are sanitary in every particular and that methods of absolute cleanliness pre-vail in each department. Also that an official report by the Department of Commerce and Labor states that a chewing gum factory was the second cleanest plant inspected in the United States in 1910. The produce is pronounced an article harmless to its vast and faithful army of consumers." An American was taking a far greater risk at the time if he ate a piece of meat . . .

Rubber and Other
Natural Gum Ingredients

Of all the imagined ingredients conjured up by the Com-stocks as the base of chewing gum, only natural rubbers are actually employed to any extent. Although chemical synthetics have become the prime ingredients in the gum base, many rubbers or latexes closely related to chicle are still widely used today. These were added to the blend almost from the beginning—partly to insure a satisfying, uniform chewing quality (smooth, even texture) and partly because the Central American chicle supply was never really dependable. Due to scarcities created by bad crops, political problems, or the like, chicle rose in price from 7 cents a pound prior to 1888, to about 50 cents a pound by the turn of the century. This alone offered impetus enough for the gum magnates to go on safari.

Gum industry botanists here and abroad came up with hundreds of natural chicle substitutes over the years. Just the Sapotaceae family—of which the chicle tree is a member—contains 35 genera and about 600 species, including the genus *Bumelia*, shrubby plants native to the southeastern United States. None of these substitutes equals chicle as a gum base, and all are incapable of forming a good natural base when used alone. But by skillfully blending them with chicle an even better base is achieved, and at a considerable savings.

The modern gum base may be made of as many as 15 latex products, though considerably less are generally used. Most of these latexes are tapped from trees growing wild in tropical rain forests, for every costly attempt at cultivating the trees in plantations has failed. Besides chicle from the sapota tree, the more important chewing gum latexes over the years would include all the guttas: gutta-percha; gutta-katiau; gutta-kayete; gutta-niger; and gutta-siak. Then there are balata; jelutong; the leche caspi of the Amazon Valley that is sometimes called sorva; and leche de vaca from South America. No less important are the milky latex massarandula from the "Brazilian cow tree"; nispero from Central America; South American pendara and perilla; tunu from Central America; and wild fig latex from Africa.

Gutta-percha, the most valuable of the guttas (gutta means "drop" and the surnames merely indicate what specific trees guttas come from), is chiefly derived from various species of *Palaquium* and *Payena* growing in the Malay peninsula. Handsome evergreens with leathery leaves, gutta-percha trees commonly reach a height of 70 to 100 feet and are tapped for their gutta when about 30 years old. The latex is a grayish, milky fluid which flows so slowly that the natives customarily fell the tree to collect it. They then chop off the branches and remove circles of the bark, forming cylindrical channels about an inch wide at various points about a foot apart down the trunk; the latex exudes and fills these channels, from which it is removed and converted into gutta by boiling it in open vessels over wood fires. Gutta-percha, which has the curious property of softening in warm water and of regaining its hardness when cold, was introduced to Europe in the mid-seventeenth century, but the Chinese and Malays had utilized its plasticity for ornamental purposes in the construction of walking sticks, knife handles and the like many years before this. Its hard nonbrittle characteristics have been used in insulation, golf ball covers and dental cements as well as in chewing gum.

Jelutong, also called gutta-jelutong, is another historically important resin used in gums, especially in bubble gum. Closely related to gutta-percha, it comes from the same area and has essentially the same properties, though its latex is slightly inferior. Essentially the same could be said of balata, which is obtained from the "bullet tree" native to the West Indies and South America. Balata is extensively used in machine belting, chewing gums containing it often rolling down assembly lines on balata conveyer belts. Unfortunately all of these natural resins are hard to come by (gutta-percha, for example, yields only 2½ pounds at a tapping) and consequently high in price. In the past, blocks of natural latexes were carried out of the jungles on the backs of elephants on the first leg of their journey to our jaws, but today more prosaic synthetics are taking their place.

At times natural waxes have been used in chewing gum, too, and even today the resin obtained from pine trees in this country plays an important part in the blending of the quality gum base. Known commercially as rosin, pine tree resin is refined by a special process for use in chewing gum, the trees it comes from found in the eight coastal states of the Southeast.

The remaining chewing gum components include softeners, sugar, corn syrup, flavorings and the synthetics added to the gum base. The substances listed on the gum pack as "softeners" are often made of refined vegetable oil products, helping in both blending the gum base properly and retaining moisture in the gum. As for sugar, which composes 60 percent of gum's weight, and cornstarch, contributing 19 percent of weight, only the finest grades are used—this the major reason why chewing gum prices have soared so high in recent times. Flavorings, comprising only about one percent of gum's weight, are far more important than their volume would indicate. Today many artificial flavorings are used, but licorice extract from Turkey is still common; Zanzibar furnishes cloves; cinnamon comes mainly from Ceylon; and the once popular but rarely used balsam of tolu is obtained from *Toluifera balsamum* trees from the province of Tolu in Columbia.

The most popular flavors in America are distilled from mint plants—more than 50 percent of all gum sold is peppermint—but gum company surveys show that the average chewer can't identify his favorite flavor. That is, he can rarely distinguish between peppermint and spearmint, two distinct flavors from two different plants, and almost never knows that teaberry is wintergreen, a plant that grows mainly in the mountains of North Carolina, or that the flavor in American Chicle's Dentyne is cinnamon and the flavor in Black Jack is licorice-anise. The mint gums, peppermint pioneered by William White in 1886 and spearmint fathered by William Wrigley Jr. in 1906, are largely supplied by domestic production. Once over 90 percent of the U.S. supply came from a district several hundred miles square in southern Michigan and northern Indiana. There the A. M. Todd company owned the two biggest mint farms in the world, Mentha and Campania, and also bought the crops of the thousand-odd mint farms in the area, distilling the leaves into oil, packing it in 400-pound drums and selling most of it to the gum companies. Today the Michigan-Indiana area remains a leading producer, but other big mint states include Wisconsin, Oregon, Washington, Idaho and Montana. The mint plants are carefully cultivated for delicate, long-lasting flavor and the gum men buy only top-quality crops.

Fruit flavoring is also supplied by domestic sources, but fruit flavors are one of the biggest secrets in a highly secretive industry. Juicy Fruit, for example, gains its popular flavor "from a secret formula of pure fruit extracts and other essences blended in the Wrigley laboratories," and that is all the company will say about it. It could be completely pure, or the "other essences" might make it partly artificial—and we'll never know which. It's true that natural flavor essences are still widely used in the chewing gum industry, but artificial flavors seem to be edging them out. The entire U.S. strawberry crop wouldn't make enough natural flavoring to supply the annual needs of one average-sized U.S. city, so no less than four chemicals are used to simulate strawberry flavor. Artificial grape flavor is made from five chemicals. Ethyl acetate is used in artificial apple; ethyl butyrate in pineapple; decylaldehyde in orange; benzaldehyde in cherry, isoamyl acetate in raspberry. Even mint flavors can be produced artificially with chemicals. Flavor has always been the big selling point in gum advertising and even in the face of the new dietetic sugarless gums continues to be stressed more than any other factor. Wrigley has always emphasized that its gums "carry the big fresh flavor." Beech-Nut's Life Savers gum is supposed to taste like fresh, fruit-flavored Life Savers even though they "left out the hole." But, in fact, today's "big fresh flavors" come mainly from chemistry labs . . .

Romance in a Test Tube:
Chewing Petroleum, Turpentine and Co.

The gum company executive who observed that "there's romance in a jungle tree's sap and none at all in a test tube" was referring not to flavorings but to the use of synthetics in most chewing gum bases and the industry's efforts to minimize this (though, to be fair, American Chicle, for just one, does admit that its gum base "is made mostly of man-made food-approved ingredients"). Chicle and other natural latexes are used less frequently every year and what we are chewing today is largely synthetic plastics. Inert and insoluble, these synthetics are harmless if swallowed because nothing can be absorbed from them by the body. Most were developed during the chicle shortage created by World War II, but their origins go back almost to the beginnings of gum manufacturing. In the early 1900's, for instance, 30 percent of benzol, an impure form of benzine (which is chiefly obtained from coal tar), was used as a softener for the Para rubber in some gum mixes, and the first bubble gum was made of synthetic rubber. A half-century before this, as noted, the paraffin used in paraffin gum was refined from petroleum.

If you object to chewing on the many natural rubbers or latexes in most chewing gum, the synthetics used may seem even less appetizing. These include such materials as butadiene-styrene rubber, paraffin, polyethylene, and polyvinyl acetate, as well as preservatives such as butylated hydroxytoluene, and the calcium carbonate—three percent of the gum base—that every manufacturer adds to the mix in the belief (or the hope that others will believe) that it helps reduce tooth decay. Then there are microcrystalline waxes and glycerides to control moisture. The truth is that even the manufacturers don't know too much about the synthetics that go into gum bases, as they always buy them from chemical companies. For example, the L. A. Dreyfus Company, a Wrigley subsidiary, makes and sells a gum base to gum manufacturers. Dreyfus (formed when chemist L. A. Dreyfus set up a lab in the Wrigley garage in 1918) told me that they no longer use chicle in their mix, but that some companies buy it on the New York market (from outfits like Herman Weber & Co., and Alcan Rubber & Chemical Co.) and add it themselves. Chicle is far too expensive at $1.25 a pound, Dreyfus claims, and Wrigley is one of the few companies left that does use it.

Dreyfus will only say that they buy a number of gums other than chicle on the New York market and mix these natural latexes with synthetics. Their exact formula is another gum industry secret and they'll only admit to an "under 50 percent natural mix"—though the amount of natural materials employed is more likely in the range of 10 to 20 percent, judging by the company spokesman's intimations. Dreyfus itself doesn't manufacture the chemicals it uses in its base, buying them from other companies. Among the most prominent of these is Hercules, Inc. (formerly the famous explosives manufacturer, Hercules Powder Company, owned by Dupont), which has become a major plastics producer in recent years (their sales totalled $1.5 *billion* in 1974). At Hercules and other chemical companies, styrene butadiene resins (SBR) are refined from crude oil and supplied to the gum base manufacturers who compound them for use in their product and then sell the gum base to the gum manufacturers. Polyvinyl acetate, another synthetic plastic, is also a big seller. Alcohol derived, it is an odorless, nontoxic and water insoluble resin that is an important adhesive in certain paints, and even contains a phonetic spelling for chew in its formula—$H_2CCHOOCCH_3$. But styrene butadiene is clearly the favorite. Styrene, prepared from ethylene and benzene, is combined with butadiene (derived from the gas butane) to form synthetics like the styrene butadiene that we chew on. Hercules, Inc. says that its use increases every year, primarily because it costs much less than natural latexes, the supply being practically unlimited, and because it is far easier to control as to chewing quality . . .

If We Knew What We Chew

The fact that we chew on slickly disguised polyterpene resins made from gum turpentine, scores of artificial flavors, and gum bases conjured from petroleum-derived chemicals doesn't say much for the sensitivity of our 10,000 plus tastebuds. There is nothing unusual about the use of synthetics in modern foods—many beers, for instance, incorporate a foam stabilizer propylene glycol alginate made from refined petroleum and seaweed. But we might expect that we could determine what we're eating (about two-thirds of a stick of gum is ultimately swallowed and goes into the chewer's digestive tract) after reading a gum label. "Under our system," John F. Kennedy once said, "consumers have a right to expect that packages will carry reliable and readily available information about their contents." This is not the case with chewing gum, among many other foods. According to the Federal Food, Drug and Cosmetic Act, administered by the Food and Drug Administration, food ingredients must be shown on labels, and there is even a special provision that chewing gum is a food. But back in 1939, when the law was adopted, chewing gum makers asked for an exemption on the grounds that it would be impractical to list some 25 or 30 ingredients on a gum wrapper or package. Since the law specified that ingredients need not be listed on foods when there is insufficient label space, the F.D.A. ruled that the chewing constituents in gum (both natural and synthetic, numbering up to about 15) could be collectively termed "gum base" on the label. Shortly afterward, again in response to industry demands, the F.D.A. permitted the 3 to 12 materials used as plasticizers in gums to be lumped together under the descriptive name "softeners." The agency also suggested an acceptable labeling which included only two sweetening agents (sugar and corn syrup), although they had earlier said that most chewing gums included additional carbohydrates, such as dextrose, dextrin, starch and maltose (about 75 percent of most gums is carbohydrate, at least half of that plain sugar). Furthermore, the F.D.A. did not require the gum makers to list sugar as the first ingredient on the label, even though it constitutes 60 percent of chewing gum, and didn't compel them to label artificial flavors as such. In this last respect regulation was better *before* the Federal Food, Drug and Cosmetic Act—in 1929 the Department of Agriculture had ruled that labels on chewing gum must not imply that fruit juices or tree fruit flavors were used in gum if the flavoring was artificial. Just the word "flavor," while not a lie, could imply that true flavors were used where this was not the case.

As a result of F.D.A. rulings, the ingredients on a typical gum package today reads "Made of Gum Base, Sugar, Corn

Syrup, Flavor and Softeners"—only 2 of the possibly 30 or more natural and synthetic ingredients that might have been used are listed. The consumer is given no idea that any of the substances discussed in these pages are present, not to mention other gum base ingredients sometimes used, notably: chicquilul, crown gum, masaranduba chocolate, rosidinha, chilte, glycerin ester of partially hydrogenated wood resin, glycerin ester of polymerized resin, sodium stearate, potassium stearate, sodium sulphate, and sodium sulfide. It should be emphasized that there are F.D.A. regulations stipulating what substances can go into a gum base and that no additive not "generally recognized as safe" for many years, or thoroughly tested, can be added to any food. However, lumping together the many ingredients that may be present in the gum base or softener is deceptive. Consumers should be able to determine for themselves what they want to chew and there is no practical way to do so if all ingredients aren't listed. This can lead to problems. As it stands now anyone who is allergic to a certain vegetable gum (and some of these gums are known to be allergens) can't choose a brand that doesn't include that gum in its base.

When the F.D.A. does not require all ingredients to be listed on a gum pack it is clearly not enforcing the law. Especially when it has been proved that the too-little-room excuse is a myth. Over 10 years ago investigators for *Consumers Bulletin* showed there is plenty of room on a gum pack to easily list 25 or more ingredients, by having their printer print in small type, in a space equivalent to one side of the wrapper of a stick of gum, the number of components of an "average" chewing gum. More than enough room remained for the manufacturer's name and address, in large letters like those customarily used. Still, the F.D.A. did nothing to change the status quo. My own inquiries about the label were answered with the usual bureaucratic logic and double-talk. I was told "there are many other foods that use inclusive terms like gum base," that "the gum base is defined here at the agency," that "allergy-prone individuals shouldn't eat *any* food unknown to them," and that "so many substances are being used today that it wouldn't be possible to sell anything if all the names were listed— completely impractical." No matter how they hedge, the law says "full disclosure" and the F.D.A. administrates its evasion . . .

Secret Formulas

If chewing gum makers are secretive about the ingredients used in gum, they are almost paranoid when it comes to their gum formulas and manufacturing processes. The brain work in making chewing gum is mostly confined to the compounding of new mixing formulas, but it may be that more brain power is expended in protecting "secret formulas." Predictably, nobody would discuss this subject, and one company representative refused to discuss anything else after being asked about it. The most I could get was a statement from a gum base supplier, which he warned he'd deny if attributed to him. "Maybe we're all jealously guarding the same secret formula," he said only half-jokingly.

Only industrial espionage could reveal the exact recipes for gum—it was hard enough discovering the true ingredients. I can just add that, traditionally, there have been two schools of gum makers: the "Little Chicle" and the "Big Chicle" people (in these days of synthetics, substitute "Little Chew" and "Big Chew" people). The Little Chicle partisans argue that people don't like their gum too chewy and the Big Chicle people take the opposite stand. Beech-Nut gum used to be a staunch member of the hard-chew school; in fact, its 1932 advertising keynote was "There's more chicle in it!" The chewiness of gum still varies greatly (Black Jack, for instance, is slippery, while Dentyne is stiff), but recently most gum makers have moved toward a softer chew "to reduce jaw fatigue."

Research to insure a good chew plays a very important part in every company's activities. Wrigley, for example, supports six research labs in the United States and six more in other countries where it has factories. Gum research scientists work toward two main goals: quality control and future development. In the field of future development, experiments are constantly under way to search out and test all possibilities for producing new and improved products and packages. Quality control specialists carefully inspect and test ingredients at every stage of processing to make sure that each day's gum batch is pure and wholesome, and that texture and flavor are always of the same high quality.

The manufacture of chewing gum is an immaculate operation, one in which a human hand never touches the product before it is packaged. The American gum industry employs some 7,000 workers in 19 establishments (compared to 74 establishments with under 2,000 workers in 1914), its payroll about $55 million annually. Today men and women in clean, white uniforms guide the gum making operation in all chewing gum plants. Working in spotless, air-conditioned rooms, they operate ingenious machines whose movements are also controlled by electric eyes. Aside from the exact formula, most chewing gums are manufactured in essentially the same manner. The blocks of solidified chewing gum base, whether they be natural gums, synthetics, or a combination of each, may often chew as smooth as any piece of finished gum, but must undergo several additional refining processes before chewing gum is made of them. First the crude materials are ground to the texture of coarse meal in a crushing mill and spread on trays in a "hot room," where excess moisture is removed by passing warm currents of air over the trays for a day or two. These ingredients for the chewing gum base are then carefully inspected and cooked together in large steam-jacketed kettles which heat the mixture to about 240 degrees, until it achieves the consistency of thick maple syrup. This sterilized syrup is filtered (blown by air pressure through fine mesh screens), clarified in a centrifuge at the rate of 15,000 revolutions per minute for further purifying action, and finally filtered through ultra-fine vacuum strainers to remove the last vestiges of any foreign matter and impurities.

The melted gum base, kept hot and in a "running" consistency throughout the purifying process, is next partially cooled and piped through a completely sanitary system to great mixing kettles. The unlovely viscuous mass—a slow-moving stream—generally flows by gravity through great gorged boa constrictor pipes to the level below and the steam-jacketed kettles, which resemble cement mixers. The mixers are capable of holding up to 2,000 pounds each, and are equipped with slowly revolving steel blades. Here the most delicate step in the production of chewing gum takes place—the first additions are made. Powdered sugar is added first. Because sugar's particle size has a telling effect on the brittleness or flexibility of the final product, some companies pulverize and sift granulated sugar for use in their products—the resulting powdered sugar is finer than the powdered sugar available on the market. Corn syrup, or glucose, is added with the powdered sugar, to

Modern gum mixers, where the gum base (chicle or synthetics), sugar, corn, syrup, softeners and flavoring are carefully blended together. *Wm. Wrigley Jr. Company*

keep the gum moist and pleasant to chew and help the sugar combine easily with the gum base. Then come either natural or artificial flavorings and the softeners, such as refined vegetable oil products, which further retain moisture in the gum to insure a flexible, resilient chew. These ingredients must be added at exactly the right time and be cooked neither too long nor too little, the giant steel blades in the mixing vats slowly turning all the while.

From the mixers, the fragrant mass, still an unsightly molten blob, passes onto slow-moving cooling belts and is bathed in currents of cool air to reduce its temperature. After this it moves to kneaders, machines which manipulate the gum to make it much smoother and finer in texture. For hours the mass is churned and kneaded at a carefully regulated temperature by these mechanical hands. Velvety and ready to chew now, the "batch" passes to another machine that gum factory workers call the "loaf cutter." This cuts off chunks of cooled gum and presses them down into a flattened loaf for easy handling in the series of giant rollers which make up the "sheet-rolling machine." In the long sheet-rolling machine, by a process of "step down rolls," the gum is first pressed into a flowing ribbon 18 inches wide and about 2½ inches thick. Each pair of rollers is set closer together, reducing the thickness of the ribbon of gum in stages until it is finally pressed and drawn out to the thickness of a stick of gum (stick gum comes from the thinnest sheets, while candy-coated and ball or bubble gum comes from a thicker sheet). The rolling machine performs a function comparable to a baker using a roller pin to roll cookie dough to the proper thickness, but also contains a series of sugar hoppers that sprinkle the gum with more powdered

On the sheeting machine the gum is rolled out into scored sheets, which are then chilled and later broken into individual sticks before wrapping. *Wm. Wrigley Jr. Company*

sugar as it comes through on the moving belt, this both en-
hancing flavor and preventing sticking together.

Near the end of the rolling process the gum is brushed
lightly to remove excess surface sugar before moving along on
the conveyor belt through the cutting and scoring machines.
Knives here cut the gum into large sheets and score these in a
pattern of single sticks. The scored sheets are powdered with
sugar again and automatically stacked on trays, moving along
to the conditioning room, the final step in seasoning. In the
conditioning room, carefully controlled temperature and
humidity give the chewing gum good keeping quality.

Bubble gum, specialty gums, gumballs and candy-coated
gum vary somewhat from the stick gum manufacturing operation. Candy-coated gums like Chiclets are not rolled as thin as
stick gum. Furthermore, instead of being scored into sticks,
they are scored into little squares or oblong pellets, and broken
up by machines. After a 24- to 48-hour storage period, they are
often undercoated to help the coating adhere more firmly, then
coated with pure liquid sugar. The Chiclets are finally placed
in pans where they are whirled with beeswax or another wax
product. This process, combined with constant rotation in the
whirling pans—each pellet polishing its neighbor by its
friendly nudging—provides candy-coated gum with its characteristic sheen. Specialty gums also diverge a little from the
pattern—with Clorets, for example, various methods are
employed to incorporate chlorophyll into the gum base in such
a way that it will be released upon chewing. As for bubble
gum, it needs a firmer base so that it will form a strong film
when air is blown into it to form a bubble. The machines
shaping and wrapping bubble gum, first sold in 1906, may be
set for a variety of shapes: stick, candy-coated, ball, pencil,
kiss or square.

The packaging of the finished gum takes place in another
large, fully air-conditioned room as immaculate as the mixing
area. In the case of Chiclet-type gums, the counting, boxing
and wrapping is performed completely by machines, one
operator turning out hundreds of boxes a day simply by pouring Chiclets into a hopper and removing the finished product.
Even more fascinating are the stick gum machines. In one con-
tinuous process these high-speed marvels, capable of turning
out hundreds of thousands of sticks a day, break gum sheets

Operators working wrapping machines in a sterile factory where "the gum is never touched by human hands." *Wm. Wrigley Jr. Company*

Funnies are wrapped around bubble gum in a fully automated operation. *Topps Chewing Gum, Inc.*

into sticks, apply aluminum foil and paper wrappers to each stick, and finally gather the sticks together and seal them in airtight moisture-proof packages. The gum packs are then assembled and automatically packed in boxes or cellophane bags.

The wrapping on stick gum is particularly important, contributing in great part to keeping gum fresh and juicy. For this reason metal foil was traditionally used when available to wrap the gum slabs. When it wasn't—during the war years, for example—gum on the market tended to be hard and dry. Today the airtight packages are doing the job of metal foil in most big plants. Dating is also important. Wrigley, for one, is so eager to insure the freshness of all its gum that each 20-package box is dated for the guidance of retail merchants; if the gum is not sold before the date on the box, the company guarantees to replace it with a box of fresh gum . . .

No More Nickel Chicle

After the boxed gum is packed in shipping cases, it is ready for shipment to all quarters of the globe. It is usually handled by confectionary, tobacco, grocery and drug wholesalers, except in the case of large chain stores, where the buying is generally done through central offices. The wholesalers, in turn, supply the gum to a wide variety of retailers. Probably no other product is carried in as many different stores as chewing gum. You can't walk half a block in most cities without passing a place that sells gum, Wrigley brands alone selling in more than one million outlets around the country (including vending machines). There is even a report that gum is sold in at least one "foundation shop" specializing in corsets—certainly as a diet aide rather than because both products contain rubber.

Gum takes up little space in a store and can be displayed by the cash register where people will impulsively buy it with their change. Up until recently, the price has also been a major attraction. Most gums sold for a penny a stick or a nickel a pack for nearly a century, which is a remarkable record for any product. It was only in the early sixties that the nickel pack of gum started to go the way of the nickel cigar and the nickel glass of beer, and some manufacturers held out against price increases until 1970. The bad news that chicle would no longer be a nickel began to be heard in the land back in 1960 when a wholesale price increase, the first by the gum industry in more than 40 years, provided an excuse for smaller retailers with "captive chewers" (in theatres, subways, etc.) to raise the price to six cents despite the fact that they could have easily absorbed the increase because of the higher markup (generally 100 percent) on gum than on other products they carry. It didn't take long for larger retailers to follow suit. Though the manufacturers had no idea that their 10 percent increase on standard 20-pack shipments would do it, nickel gum had soon joined the five-cent cup of coffee, the five-cent ferry or subway ride and the nickel phone call in the museum of good memories.

Gum held its own at the six-cent level until 1971, and then the price really began to rise. Despite a presidential plea that all business hold the line on prices, Beech-Nut gum offered the "Big 8," an eight-stick pack (which Bowman Gum had pioneered back in the thirties) at a suggested retail price of ten cents. Beech-Nut rationalized that on a per-stick basis, for a 20-stick box, "the eight-stick pricing represents a 10 percent price reduction by us versus our current five-stick . . . price," but their move encouraged or forced other companies to accelerate conversion of gum-wrapping equipment to seven or eight-stick capacity and hop on the bandwagon. A number of feuds broke out in the ever sensitive industry. Wrigley, which went to a seven-stick pack it had in fact already test marketed, claimed that Beech-Nut's eight-stick pack was "misleading" because Wrigley weight tests showed that an average seven-stick Wrigley pack ranged from 96 to 98 percent of the weight of an average eight-stick Beech-Nut pack. Beech-Nut replied that it had "more like a 7 to 8 percent advantage" and challenged Wrigley to a public weight test in which gum from a pack of each would be placed on a two-disc scale. Wrigley refused, of course—it wouldn't look good to have Beech-Nut on top and Wrigley on the bottom in public, no matter how slight the weight difference. The larger company said they preferred "to let the consumer settle the matter on the basis of product quality."

Wrigley had always tried to hold the nickel price, believing that "multi-coin pricing is a deterrent to sales, since gum is an impulse purchase." In fact, in the early days, William Wrigley called those who charged more than a nickel for his gum "profiteers." The market did go down when the first wholesale price increases occurred, but it quickly recovered when the public got used to the idea of a ten-cent pack of gum. For the next two years the dime held its own, but then in 1974, largely due to a 100 percent increase in the price of sugar, even ten cent chewing gum bit the dust; Wrigley announced three price increases that year, amazing considering the fact that it has only taken such action five times in 81 years. Other companies did likewise and as a result seven-and eight-stick packs of gum were soon retailing at 15 cents. It has been observed that if the price of gum had increased along with many other prices over the century, today one stick might cost as much as 10 cents. At least gum hasn't shrunk in size the way most candy bars have—a Hershey bar, for example, weighed two ounces and cost a dime in 1965; today it weighs a little over one ounce and costs 20 cents. But this doesn't change the fact that the romance of the penny, nickel and dime are over as far as gum is concerned—and we are working on wrecking the romance of the quarter. The only nostalgic old-fashioned price left in the industry is the penny charged for a few gumball bubble gums—and they are made largely of air.

CHAPTER 14

The Case of The Moving Jaws: Gum & the Gums, Molars, Mind, Stomach, Sex Glands, & Other Subjects You Can Sink Your Teeth Into

OUR whole facial structure below the eyes is falling to pieces," says Dr. James E. Harris, chairman of the orthodontics department at the University of Michigan. "When we see a person with perfect teeth, it's so rare that we take pictures." But despite the admonitions of parents and teachers, chewing gum is not responsible for the human jaw becoming smaller, the chin receding and the teeth getting crooked. This is simply an evolutionary process that chomping gum at a force of from 5 to 160 pounds per square inch has nothing whatsoever to do with. Some two and a half centuries ago when a Turkish pasha visited a peasant family he demanded a free meal and afterwards collected a tax from the poor wights to compensate him for the wear on his teeth. Before someone suggests a similar tax on the gum makers, we ought to record here both the benefits and disadvantages of gum chewing in the light of scientific findings.

The ultimate chew food admittedly has its drawbacks, but in some ways it is a health food: improving dental health, mental health, and (at least to those who think positively) even sexual health. No one would think this by the way didactics have denounced gum since chicle was a nickel. We have been led astray by killjoys who molded the facts to fit their highly indignant theories. The trail of the red herring, we've seen, has many landmarks: groundless accusations that the chicle in chewing gum caused the great influenza epidemic of 1918; charges that mass indigestion is caused by chewing gum because we "weaken our chewing muscles" and don't have the strength left to properly chew our food; pronouncements that gum chewing "hardens the faces" of American women; and intimations that cutaneous leishmaniasis, an insidious disease that eats away the ears and nostrils, can be contracted by gum chewers as well as chicle gatherers.

In the past many people did serve as refining machines for dirty chewing gum—swallowing the refuse and throwing the clean cud away. But today, thanks to the immaculate plants of the gum makers and the skillful work of their P.R. people, nobody believes for an instant that chewing gum causes influenza, beri-beri, rickets, terminal acne, or any other dread or imagined disease (unless the wad is shared with too many friends). Extensive tests by the Food and Drug Administration using gum-chewing monkeys, rabbits, guinea pigs, dogs and young humans, found nothing at all wrong with bubble gum. Chewing gum has received both the Good Housekeeping and Parents Institute seals of approval. Even the Soviet Union has changed its mind about gum, recognizing its benefits as a dental aid and starting to manufacture tons of it for the proletariat.

Much research into the advantages of gum chewing was inspired by the establishment of Wrigley-Beech-Nut Fellowship at Northwestern University during the Great Depression, this industry-sponsored grant made for the sole purpose of researching the physiological effects of gum chewing. Since then a number of independent researchers have joined ranks with the chewing advocates. Dr. Robert H. Veitch, Director of the Deafness Clinic at the Massachusetts Osteopathic Hospital, recommended that anyone experiencing deafness during common colds should try chewing gum several hours daily for relief. Common colds, he said, often result in temporary deafness, retracted eardrums, or tinnitus, and he further stated that there would probably be more retracted eardrums and that the retractions would be greater were it not for the widespread American habit of chewing gum. Similarly, many airlines offer gum to passengers during flights to relieve discomfort caused by varying air pressures. Civilian and military medical authorities point out that the chewing of gum induces frequent swallowing, which opens the eustachian tubes, or air passages, permitting air pressure to be equalized inside and outside the ear. This fact has been stressed in many air force training manuals, along with endorsements of gum chewing.

During World War II, the British Royal Air Force recommended chewing gum to pilots as an "aid to descents." The constant working of the jaws, it was explained, creates saliva and this assists in overcoming the difficulties experienced by many fliers of swallowing, when coming to earth rapidly, because the throat becomes parched. Wartime experiments at a small lab not far from the Wrigley Building in Chicago clearly demonstrated how chewing gum creates saliva and relieves thirst. Wrigley Researchers sat with metal tubes clamped over their salivary or parotid glands, located in the cheeks next to the molars. They solemnly recorded the drip of their saliva from the tubes into beakers, then chewed gum and recorded the drip again. Almost invariably the rate of drip went up 100 to 200 percent. No one tried to determine how long the parotid glands can go on manufacturing saliva if their owner chews gum and drinks no water, but the experiment definitely showed that false thirst is eliminated by gum chewing. As a result many employers now supply free gum to their employees, reducing daily trips to the water cooler.

Studies have also shown that gum chewing is one of the best ways to relieve the craving to smoke, especially for a dieter who doesn't want to replace a compulsion for cigarettes with a compulsion for fattening foods. Though 60 percent of a stick of gum is pure sugar (about a teaspoon to each stick), in food content one stick of chewing gum contains only nine calories and increasingly popular sugarfree gum, made with sugar substitutes like sorbitol (a natural product like most diet gum sweeteners), often contain only half that many. Whether gum chewing is a dieting aid is another matter. Those who say it is claim that if one chews a piece of gum containing a relatively small amount of sugar, this eliminates the opportunity to eat something more caloric, and that the filling of the stomach with saliva might tend to reduce hunger signals transmitted by that organ. On the other hand, it has been argued that chewing gum actually increases the appetite, since it stimulates some flow of gastric juice without providing any food for digestion (unless you swallow the stuff). At any rate, thousands of dieters chew gum as a kind of pacifier. A woman in one Weight Watchers' group chews 96 packs of sugarless gum a week!

Medicated chewing gums on the market include aspirin, laxative, and antacid types. Medicated gums have been around for nearly a century; as far back as 1898 Dent's Toothache Gum

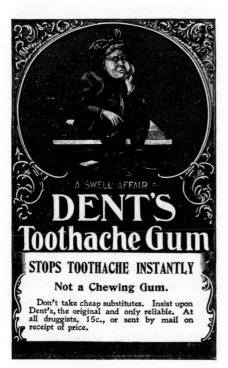

New York Public Library

was prominently advertised "Not a Chewing Gum!" Other medicated brands well established in the first quarter of this century included a laxative gum with the purgative phenolphthalein added to the chicle base, which caused severe inflammation of the skin if improperly used, and even so-called diet gums. As for these last, their makers claimed that they contained antifat properties in the form of various drugs. Often laxatives like phenolphthalein were used—this guaranteed some temporary weight loss, but running to the bathroom constantly wasn't a very practical or healthy way to reduce. Other diet gums incorporated desiccated thyroid, a potent substance that should only be administered by a physician, if at all. Still others contained powerful drugs that so disturbed the digestion to bring about weight loss that the "cure" was worse than the "disease." One such gum, sold under the proprietary name Silph was indeed declared a fraud by the government and barred from the U.S. mails. Two similar brands, Slends and Eljin, were tested by the American Medical Association and found to be useless as weight reducers unless one followed the directions printed on the packages—which instructed the chewer to exercise strenuously, eat prescribed foods, and walk five miles a day! Since that time a number of safe, medicated gums have been developed, but clearly the quacks were exploiting chewing gum nostrums from the very beginning, branching into the field from the fading patent medicine business.

Pepsin chewing gum and other types have been advertised and purchased as an aid to digestion for generations, but there seems to be little evidence for this claim. Over 60 years ago, Dr. T. H. McClintock refuted the theory, writing in the *Medical Times*, and his conclusions haven't been successfully challenged to this day. McClintock noted that "the salivary enzymes produce all the effect on starch that nature requires" and that "there is no evidence that salivary digestion continues to any considerable extent" after food reaches the stomach. "The act of chewing does stimulate gastric secretion," he wrote, "but after a meal the appetite is appeased, and no form of stimulation to the gastric mucous membrane can equal that of food in actual contact with it . . . It is possible that some brands of chewing gum do contain a trace of pepsin. If so, the most that can be said of it is that it does no particular harm." Still, pepsin gum has made millions of people feel better after heavy meals, even if the effect is only psychological . . .

Gum and the Gums, Teeth and Breath

Ever since Ohio dentist, William F. Semple, was issued the first patent on a chewing gum in 1869, chewing gum manufacturers have been claiming that gum chewing is good for the teeth. Semple's gum was supposed to clean the teeth of debris, a claim that is still made, along with many others aimed at those with odontiatrophobia (fear of dentists), or who want sound teeth for sounder reasons. One of Edgar Lee Master's poems mentions a turn of the century sign reading: CHEW FLOSS'S GUM AND KEEP YOUR TEETH. The evidence available today suggests that you won't necessarily keep your teeth if you chew gum, but you won't lose them because you chew it, either.

Chewing gum definitely sweetens the breath, one of the reasons the Greeks began ruminating on mastic gum centuries ago. Gums containing chlorophyll and retsyn, a discovery made at American Chicle's research labs, will pretty well conceal the results of faulty hygiene, halitosis or an all-night binge. It is doubtful that any gum will "whiten the teeth," however, despite the propaganda for many brands over the years. As a matter of fact, the teeth are not naturally white, as is generally believed, but vary from a pale ivory to a more or less definite "cream" color. In any event, the properties of the teeth which determine their natural shade do not reside in the surface layer of the enamel and it isn't an easy matter to change them—which is a task best done by a dentist carefully using agents too strong for inclusion in chewing gum.

Even dentists prescribe firm chewing gum for problem gum conditions and before surgery to strengthen gums and jaw muscles, as do speech therapists. Authorities have long recognized the importance of exercising chewing muscles in order to develop well-formed jaws and straight, permanent teeth in children. Few, if any, dentists today believe that gum chewing causes buck teeth: "You can't blame gum for pushing teeth out," dental expert Dr. James Thomson states flatly. Vigorous chewing also stimulates circulation of the blood in mouth tissues, giving the gums a healthier firmness, which is an impor-

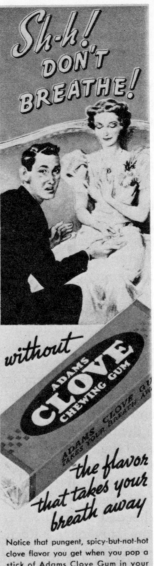

These ads appeared in 1937. Still others promised to take bad breath away from garlic-eaters, secret drinkers, and those who feared dentists. *American Chicle Company*

tant factor in dental hygiene, since gum tissue is attached to the roots of the teeth and walls of the tooth sockets. And gum chewers certainly chaw vigorously enough. Measurements have shown that in ordinary chewing, the front teeth may come together with a force equal to from 30 to 80 pounds per square inch, while the heavier back teeth may register 140 to 160 pounds per square inch (by comparison, the right hand of a strong adult male can be closed with a force of 81 pounds). Gum isn't usually chewed with such a vengeance, though some people seem to manage it, but the 10- to 20-pound force of most chewers is enough in itself.

The biggest controversy over gum is whether it rots your teeth or not—whether it does or doesn't cause caries. The great majority of studies made on gum and tooth decay have shown that chewing gum does *not* cause decay. One 1960 experiment by Dr. P. D. Toto and associates evaluated the effects of gum chewing by 275 schoolchildren as compared to 276 nonchewing control subjects; it lasted over a year and found that caries in both groups were identical. A 1957 Tufts Dental College study also concluded that gum chewing didn't significantly increase caries, and experiments in Greece and England came to the same conclusion. As recently as 1972, Dr. Jeffrey Slack of the London Hospital School of Dentistry claimed that gum was harmful to the teeth. He agreed to make an extensive study of his premise if the Wrigley company would finance it. Wrigley, according to one of its executives, "took a deep breath and agreed." The results of the study, published in the *British Dental Journal*, proved that gum didn't hurt the teeth at all.

A team headed by Dr. Basil G. Bibby at the Eastman Dental Center of the University of Rochester has even established that chewing gum does less harm to your teeth than hard and chewy candies, cookies, cakes and doughnuts. "If you must have sugar," Dr. Bibby told me, "you might as well take it in gum as from a stick of candy or a cookie. A stick of gum is less destructive than a cookie, for instance. And the sugar in a carbonated beverage is less destructive than that in a candy bar. We hope we can encourage people to switch to the safer snack foods. We know we can't accomplish withdrawal from all of them." The results of Dr. Bibby's work, which can be found in the December 1974 *Journal of Dental Research*, concluded that gum is an ideal snack food.

Back in 1942 Dr. Louis M. Fleisch summed up the evidence then available that chewing gum was detrimental to the teeth in the *Journal of the American Dental Association*. "The use of chewing gum may be harmful so far as caries is concerned owing to its sugar content," Dr. Fleisch wrote, adding that "excessive habitual use of chewing gum appears to cause caries in some cases." Dr. Fleisch suggested that anyone who chews gum stay with one piece as long as possible so that less sugar is introduced into the mouth. But the information in his article was to a great extent suppositional and based mainly on a few case reports. In recent years there has been more and more agreement that normal consumption of gum is harmless. Chewing stimulates saliva, which dissolves and washes away the sugar in the gum very rapidly. About 90 percent of the sugar in a stick of gum is chewed out in two to three minutes, and less than one percent remains after ten minutes. Gum chewing (of sugar gums) is of course harmful in abnormal conditions like "rampant caries," where the individual is extraordinarily susceptible to tooth decay, and particularly if the chewing process produces no stimulation of saliva, in which case any sugar in the diet would be undesirable.

It is true that the excess saliva stimulated by gum chewing tends to neutralize harmful mouth acidity. But does chewing gum benefit the teeth in any other way? Gum, especially a firm base gum, is certainly a thorough mouth cleanser, a convenient way to cleanse the mouth after meals when no toothbrush is handy. This has been established in many reliable studies. Experiments by Dr. J. F. Volker at Tufts Dental School in 1948 showed that the chewing of gum removed on an average of 80 percent of residual oral debris. Dr. Arthur Black, conducting experiments at Northwestern University in 1934, had similar results (50 to 95 percent debris removed) and in a 1937 study found that "chewing gum (even if it does contain some sugar) will remove sugar from the mouth faster than if the sugar is left to free itself by natural saliva flow." Similarly, experiments at the Loyola Dental School showed that chewing gum removed sugars and starches from the mouth and recommended the use of chewing gum after eating to help remove these tooth-decay-producing substances. One reason chewing is so effective in cleansing the mouth is that it *steps up* the flow of saliva and thereby hastens the clearing of decay-producing sugars from the mouth. In 1955 Doctors A. Albert Yurkstas and William A. Emerson of Tufts College Dental School reached this conclusion in a series of experiments proving that it is not the amount of sugar taken into the mouth that is significant in normal tooth decay so much as the *speed* with which the sugar leaves the mouth.

The trouble is that although all of these studies show that chewing gum does appreciably reduce the amount of debris in the *saliva*, no experiments have proved that gum chewing removes debris from the *teeth*, where 80 percent of dental disease starts. Chewing gum might force food deeper into the gums, or it might withdraw food particles as a result of the pumping effect of chewing and the inrush of saliva—but there is no conclusive evidence for either theory. Since debris adhering to the teeth is in large part responsible for tooth decay, this is probably the reason why no dental studies have been able to prove that gum chewing prevents decay to any great extent. In 1965, two dentists surveyed all available studies on gum chewing and concluded in the *Journal of the Canadian Dental Association*: "There is no evidence that chewing gum reduces caries; neither is there evidence that gum increases caries." That about sums it up. Chewing gum is neither villain nor great hero when it comes to bad teeth . . .

Gum for Your Third Set of Teeth,
Gum-Proof False Teeth and
Other Great White Hopes

New chewing gum studies may uncover unknown blessings, and new types of gum may become a real boon to the mouths of mankind. "We live in the age of anxiety," says Dr. Marvin Simring of New York University's College of Dentistry, "and people express their intense feelings and frustrations by clenching and grinding their teeth." Dr. Simring feels that this injures the gums and helps spread infections. If such is the case, then chewing gum may well be effective in preventing our teeth from falling out—by relieving anxiety, or as a substitute for tooth-gnashing, or bruxism. There is also hope that future chewing gums will help prevent tooth decay in other ways. This would be accomplished with chemical additives, but the problem thus far is that saliva, which washes away most of the sugar in chewing gum, also washes away the dozens of substances scientists have added to gum since at least 1945. The Wrigley Company has patented an anticavity chewing gum in which one or more aldehydes are added to the gum base, these calculated to inhibit the growth of microorganisms and the formation of acids in the mouth. Other patented additives include various phosphates, synthetic vitamin K, nitrofuran, chlorophyll, fluorides and even an extract from oat hulls. Sidney B. Finn, D.D.S., professor of dentistry at the Dental Research Institute of the University of Alabama recently experimented with a new phosphate—sodium trimetaphosphate—that has reduced tooth decay in test animals by about 60 percent and reduced dental caries on proximal surfaces (those facing each other) in human test subjects. But when he added the substance to gum chewed by 600 children in the Florida School for the Deaf and Blind in St. Augustine over the last two years, he told me, "It was not too effective and didn't significantly reduce decay." Dr. Finn still has faith in some new gum additive helping to eliminate tooth decay. "As for now, I can see no harm in chewing gum if one chews sugarless," he says. "And I can see possible benefits."

Chewing gum will dislodge fillings, but so will candy, caramels, an apple, a piece of steak and almost any hard food. It will also stick to false teeth, although there have been a number of patents for chewing gum that does not stick to dentures. One inventor, Morris C. Leonard of Nashville, Tenn., got rid of the stickiness by adding a silicone to gum, and the Wrigley Company has a patent covering more than 40 formulas for additives that discourage sticking. They have, in fact, recently marketed a new brand, spearmint-flavored Freedent, advertised to be "specially formulated not to stick to most dental work." The problem appeared to have been greatest with the acrylic plastics common in fillings and dentures. Arthur J. Comolio, a chemist for the Wrigley-owned L. A. Dreyfus gum base company, found that tannic acid had an outstanding ability to reduce adherence to acrylic dentures. He noticed, however, that during mastication the tannic acid was extracted and set out to extend its presence for the normal chewing period of 45 minutes to an hour, finding that the addition of polymeric materials, including gelatin and starch, made it last much longer. Wrigley also has a patent for soaking dentures themselves in a strong alkaline solution which would

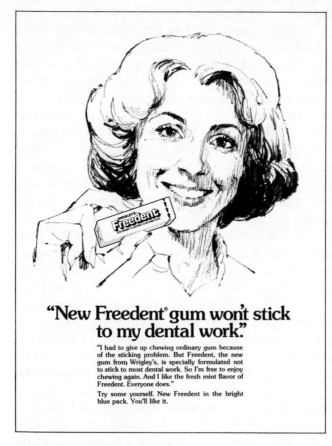

"New Freedent® gum won't stick to my dental work."

"I had to give up chewing ordinary gum because of the sticking problem. But Freedent, the new gum from Wrigley's, is specially formulated not to stick to most dental work. So I'm free to enjoy chewing again. And I like the fresh mint flavor of Freedent. Everyone does."

Try some yourself. New Freedent in the bright blue pack. You'll like it.

Wm. Wrigley Jr. Company

modify their surfaces so that normal gum could be chewed with impunity. But although the company has entered the marketplace with its nonsticky gum, denture manufacturers thus far don't seem to be going in for gum-proof false teeth . . .

The Psychodynamics of Gum Chewing

While no one has proved just why we chew gum, many psychologists have theorized about the mass chomping that has created an industrial giant. It's true that when Wrigley interviewers gave a dollar to anyone who would tell why they chewed gum the leading answers were always those that Wrigley advertising stressed at the moment. And certainly many chewers like gum simply because it sweetens or conceals the breath, refreshes the mouth, cleans the teeth, gives them a pleasant little lift, or tastes good, among other obvious reasons. But so far as is known, the major reasons for chewing gum are psychological. Nothing in gum is habit-forming or creates a compulsion to chew, yet the motives for chewing gum are mainly in the mind. According to one group of psychoanalysts, psychiatrists and psychologists which investigated the unconscious emotional needs behind all our constant chawing, three primary factors prevailed. The most important motive was to relieve a feeling of loneliness, boredom, or sadness. Motive number two was to provide relief from tension by discharging nervous energy. Finally, chewing sublimates rage, providing a quick and socially acceptable outlet for anger and irritation.

In our time tension seems to have replaced loneliness as the major motive for chewing. Wrigley was the first to make studies on chewing gum and tension, back in the early forties. One device put a researcher in a cage enclosed in copper screening. The researcher rapidly dropped steel balls into a tube with his right hand. Tension was induced in the left arm by the activity of the other member. Three electrodes, strapped on the left arm, gathered tiny electric discharges from the arm and deposited them in a condenser. As tension increased, the charge in the condenser piled up and at last registered on a counter. The tests were first made while the subject's mouth was empty, then while he chewed gum. The counter always clicked fewer times while he was chewing.

More important than the Wrigley tests were gum experiments made at Columbia University that extended full scientific recognition and a medical alliance of sorts to gum chewing. These were all the work of the esteemed Dr. Harry L. Hollingsworth, who found that chewing reduces muscular tension and helps people feel more relaxed. He emphasized that it is the act of chewing that does this—chewing on practically anything would give the same result—but that chewing gum provides the benefits of chewing in the most convenient form.

Professor Hollingsworth, who admitted only to chewing on

his pipe, began his experiments because he was amazed at the large amount of gum chewing going on during the "tense" depression years. The results, published as "Psycho-dynamics of Chewing" and "Chewing as a Technique of Relaxation" in such prestigious journals as the *Archives of Psychology* and *Science*, stressed that chewing—whether on gum, pencil, rubber band or toothpick—is a restful form of exercise for the office worker, allowing him or her to put more physical energy into the job at hand and thus aid efficiency. Chewing, Hollingsworth concluded, is not guaranteed to raise the mental standard of the chewer, but it does increase the energy quota. Chewers drop nervous habits such as tapping their feet and twitching about, using the energy saved in more useful ways. Writers pressed harder on their pencils; typists typed faster (and retained accuracy *if they liked to chew gum*). Tension, in general, decreased.

Ten women and ten men ranging in age from 16 to 30 were used in the four-year experiment, and although their education varied from high school through college, the general results were the same. One of the experiments brought in subjects at eight in the morning and put them through a regular eight-hour workday. Observers in the room noted the nervous reactions of nonchewers. Invariably, foot-tapping and similar dispensers of energy ceased when the subject started to chew. One subject was given a more thorough test. Seated in an armchair, he was directed to add columns of figures. As he used his right hand for this, his left rested on the arm of the chair. This was hinged, and when a trigger was released, a weight drew on the left arm, causing the arm of the chair to swing out. There was far less reaction when the subject was chewing gum than when he was not, indicating that the chewing had relieved nervous tension to a marked degree.

Hollingsworth's metabolism tests also showed the degree of relaxation chewing produced. Tests were made of a subject completely relaxed. Then tests were made while the subject chewed. The results showed that the energy required to chew called for the use of 17 percent more oxygen than when the subject wasn't chewing. Finally, the subjects were retested without gum while performing technical tasks. Naturally, the amount of oxygen used increased enormously. Given gum to chew while performing these tasks, however, the subjects showed no further increase in the amount of oxygen consumed. This, the professor concluded, showed that the chewing was cutting off some form of nervous tension which had been draining the subject's energy before the chewing started.

Some of the Columbia tests were tried with candy mints, but these were not nearly as effective as chewing anything at all, even though peppermint oil is a stimulant. No one knows how many sticks of gum were assaulted in the four-year Hollingsworth study, although cynics speculated much on this, just as they pointed out that thanks to this exhaustive experiment one could now identify a gum chewer by the clarity of his second carbons. The professor himself warned that he found hints that "chewing is not a good habit for anyone trying to learn something new," but at least one other researcher had stronger reservations. G. L. Freeman, a psychology professor at Northwestern University, agreed with his colleague in finding that chewing gum reduces tension and facilitates one's major performance, but he found that chewing has no special virtue in tension reduction because of its association with eating, as Hollingsworth had suggested, stating that "foot tapping, nose picking or ear pulling might be equally effective if engaged in appropriately." So, someone added, might fidgeting, coin-jingling, wriggling, twiddling, knitting and grimacing.

Hollingsworth wasn't the only scientist to find chewing gum a balm and comfort to millions. The eminent behaviorist Dr. John Watson called gum chewing an adult pacifier on a plane with biting nails, chewing up pencils or doodling—if there were less gum chewers, it would seem to follow, there would be more adult thumbsuckers, nailbiters, and perhaps graffiti artists transmuting the establishment. The Freudians, on the other hand, regard gum chewing as a carry-over from infancy when babies acquire an oral sensitivity while feeding at the breast. The carry-over is even more pronounced, they believe, when instinctive oral needs go unfulfilled in childhood. "The oral instinct is inherent in all of us—from birth to death," says Dr. George F. Newman, a Dearborn, Michigan psychiatrist. "Without it we wouldn't survive. You only have to observe those around you to see how oral we really are. In tense situations people will pick up a cigarette or a pipe, gnaw on a pencil—or chew gum." He reasons that a mother who doesn't

breast-feed her baby, or who stops the child from thumbsuck-
ing, deprives that child of a way to fulfill basic oral instincts,
and that the child will fulfill these needs by chewing gum or
the like in later life.

Some observers go so far as to call gum chewing "oral masturbation." Though no one has admitted masticating gum for
such reasons in any opinion poll, such links between sex and
chewing gum had led to exotic brands like Love Gum, Forbidden Fruit, and Passion Gum. There is a Korean chewing gum
laced with ginseng, that much heralded herb believed to increase sexual potency, and here in America, Frenchie's
Spanish Fly Chewing Gum is available. Swingers, Inc., a Gary,
Indiana P.O. Box outfit offers the so-called aphrodisiac at a
dollar a stick. Their ad shows a naked man grinding his pelvis
into the pelvis of a naked woman, apparently to demonstrate
Frenchie's effectiveness, though in this gum the dangerous
Spanish Fly (cantharides) is spurious, hot cayenne pepper its
main ingredient. One might as well stick with ordinary chewing gum at two cents a piece. Many flavorings in ordinary
gums, such as peppermint, cloves and licorice, have legendary
reputations as aphrodisiacs. However, gum might make one
lose all desire to do anything but chew. At the least it would be
disconcerting to try and kiss someone with a mouthful, or to
be groping in the dark for a place to temporarily park your
wad. Sex just doesn't seem to be one of those Wrigley situations where gum is socially acceptable, whatever it might do
for you.

CHAPTER 15 *Sticky Problems, Including More Mannerly Mastication*

SMACK! Slurp! Crackle! Snap! Pop! Slurp!

Very few, if any, arbiters of taste have found these basic chewing gum phonetics pleasing over the years. Indeed, up until very recently those who pass on our manners haven't had anything nice to say about gum chewing. Gum chomper Americanus has been compared to the cow, or a herd of cows when a chorus of us chew in unison, and one foreigner supposedly told an etiquette writer that he thought the spastic movements accompanying our national habit constituted a general facial affliction—"a sickness of the face," as he put it so well in broken English. Not to be outdone, the lady replied that it was "a far more serious ailment—a sickness of the mind and character." A quick look at ten or so etiquette books, none dating earlier than 1930, shows just how hard the elitists have come down on gum:

Chewing gum! Ugh! How can anyone indulge in the vulgar habit when seated so close to another? The odor—both of the gum itself and the flavoring—is most offensive. No person of refinement would so violate the rules of politeness!

Don't chew gum in the streetcar, bus, or any other public place. You look disgusting and are repugnant. Just gaze at the chewing brigade every day and notice the type of person who does it. Do you really wish to be of that class?

To chew gum in public classifies you as ordinary. If you do not believe this, observe the chewers in the street.

Chewing gum is an act that should be avoided except by persons in a cheap burlesque house where such things are done.

Never chew gum in the presence of those who do not indulge in this plebeian habit. If you must, at least keep an arms length from everyone.

Chewing gum in public is bad form . . . Personally I do not care for gum at any time!

Chewing gum cheapens both you and your firm! The working of your jaws in that vulgar manner gives you a common appearance.

Chewing surreptitiously prevents you from doing your own job well because your mind is on preventing the employer from finding out that you are engaging in an act forbidden to his employees.

Young people who care to develop pleasing personalities will not chew gum while walking along the street or in other public places . . . for a little observation will show how pitiably ruinous this is to youthful charm.

> Wear rubber-heeled shoes, keep your voice low-
> pitched, never chew gum, whistle, hum or make funny
> noises with your tongue or teeth . . .

Yet chewing gum somehow survived the indignant ser-
monizers sputtering and frothing at the mouth in a display of
manners that might have been improved by a calming slab of
gum. Since the years after World War II a new chewing gum
code has emerged, and at least one observer believes that the
generations in their progress from spruce to sugarless have
forged a common bond by indulging in the gum habit.
"Chewing gum has been in the top ten sin list for the last
hundred years or so," says humorist Erma Bombeck. "It's a
no-no that even grandparents can identify . . . It doesn't blow
your mind, make smoke rings, make you giggle or stagger or
give you adult status. All I know is that educators abhor it and
place it in corruption above failure to take showers and pencil-
ling glasses and mustaches on the aborigines in *National Geo-
graphics* . . . Face it, adults, chewing gum is our last frontier of
understanding where it's at."

At any rate, since the end of the World War II, chewing gum
has made the transition from a major social sin to what writer
Edith Efron calls "the most popular of *minor* human vices."
Once found in the mouths of only sleazy gangsters and
floozies, it is now publicly worked by the jaws of national
idols. "Characterizing the inferior social status of people by
their gum-chewing proclivities is the sign of an outdated
novelist," writes a respected literary critic. Long regarded as a
low-class addiction, gum chewing is now considered a no-
class relatively harmless practice—number ten on the top ten
sin list, if it makes the charts at all anymore. The old morality
does hang on in places. Many still believe that chewing gum is
the symbol of all that is vulgar and gauche in the world. Those
with geniophobia, the fear of chins chomping, or some other
gum phobia, abound in the schools, where the "spit it out"
brigade busily monitors snaps and bubbles. Bosses almost invariably take a dim view of secretaries chomping their synthetic chicle cuds or smelling of attar of Juicy Fruit. Recently a
writer even charged that gum chewing is an infallible yardstick
of intellectual mediocrity. "Habitual gum-chewers," he wrote,
"are invariably of below-average intelligence—no individual
of imagination and culture above the age of 18 is found in this

group . . . Not all dullards chew gum, but all chewers are dullards."

Yet these are generally the last Puritans speaking, the final threads of the hair-shirt mentality. In reality every day *is* Chewsday today. Gum has become, at its very worst, what one critic calls a "classic of trash." How could Chewsday help but make the calendar when millions of people around the world chew and enjoy billions of pieces of gum every day, when Congressmen blow bubbles, when 50 percent of the American people chew some gum? A leading etiquette columnist has instructed her readers that it's perfectly all right to chew gum in public if it isn't done with too much gusto. An antichewing employer has been ordered by the National Labor Relations Board to let his workers chew gum on the job. Teachers who used to admonish their students not to chew gum in class now use gum to reward good work. Gum chewing is even "legal" in many schools today, including one in Florida where students went on strike for its acceptance.

Gum chewing has so much grandeur today that the Japanese invented their prayer, intoned by a Shinto priest, paying homage to the Great Spirit of Chewing Gum (see Chapter 1). "It is still impossible to imagine a lady walking on a city street chewing gum," Emily Post wrote shortly before World War II, when she finally condescended to even mention gum in her *Etiquette* (many etiquette writers never mentioned gum, as though by being ignored the prevalent practice would go away). But this admonition, like so many others, no longer applies. When is it strictly proper to chew gum nowadays? Emily Post herself later answered that question, advising that gum could be chewed "Wherever formal standards of behavior are not in force . . . certainly not in church, during recitation periods in school, or when wearing formal clothes." Other authorities instruct us never to chew gum "during a job interview, while on the telephone, or during the playing of the national anthem," and never to take a wad out of the mouth in public. Aside from this, we are told, gum should be chewed quietly, the mouth kept closed—definitely no popping or cracking. Wrigley further advises: "When in company, it is considered impolite to take a stick of gum for yourself without offering it to others. If you have just one stick, offer to share it with the other person. If you are with several people, it is better to wait until you are alone or until you have enough to pass around."

Just a few more suggestions, based on observations of my own kids, would seem to follow:

- Don't chew three or four packs at a time.
- Don't pull the gum out in long strings and twirl it around your fingers, or toes for that matter.
- Don't store unwrapped chewed cuds in the refrigerator.
- Never trade chewed gum with the kids next door, your brothers or sisters, or people on the street.
- Don't give gum to the dog or cat.
- Don't take back gum if you do give it to the dog or cat.
- Don't park gum anywhere. Definitely not next to the pencil sharpener on my desk where I prop my elbow. Especially not in the summer when I wear short-sleeved shirts.

Chewing kids out any more than that would be unrealistic ("Don't chew like that, damnit!" just doesn't work). Anyway, more important than gum-chewing etiquette today is what could be called the matter of the cud and the ecology—that is, getting people to dispose of chewing gum so that it doesn't eventually wind up on the seat of someone's pants or on the sole of a shoe destined to transplant it to the living room rug. Disposal of gum ranks as a menace only behind beer cans and dog litter, despite the efforts of the gum companies. Wrigley, for example, is an ecology-minded company that installed water and air pollution control systems in several of their plants long before there were any strict legal controls. But try as they have, their attempts to educate the public about gum disposal haven't been conspicuously successful.

Gum wrappers constitute a litter problem, but they aren't nearly as objectionable as chewed gum wads, which are spat out or stuck on park benches, theatre seats, floors, sidewalks, underneath tables and pianos, beneath window ledges, on trees deep in the wilderness, in the lower depths of subway tunnels and far up atop the tallest skyscrapers. Every place visited by man bears traces of his chewing gum habit, possibly even outer space, if the astronauts who chewed it didn't really swallow their wads as they reported. Not long ago a major airline, after spending over $7,000 to remove gum from plane seats, ruled that patrons could no longer chew gum to keep their ears from popping. Theatre associations have found that removal of gum costs thousands of dollars annually. A commercial cleaning fluid manufactured especially for this purpose has to be used and since moviegoers don't respond to signs pleading with them not to park their gum, seats have to be gone over nightly in some large theatres.

Gum removal is a full-time business in several large cities, where theatres, restaurants, ball parks, and even churches contract with skilled professional removers to take care of illegally parked gum. This costs thousands of dollars a year, forcing some firms to employ their own removers. The New York Central Railroad for years had a full-time gum man assigned to Grand Central Station. He averaged a seven-pound harvest every evening (better than a chicle gatherer), the nightly wad swelling to 14 pounds on holiday weekends.

Gum removal isn't a modern-day problem. As far back as 1920 one large department store reportedly spent $3,500 a year on cuds its customers left behind, employing a three-man Gum Removal Platoon for this purpose. The first real action taken against The Great Gum Menace involved New York's fiery Mayor Fiorello Henry LaGuardia, who not only attacked the gum chewers but was the scourge of housewives who shook dust mops out of windows. In 1939 the "Little Flower" declared that there was a Gum Clearance Scandal in New York, the streets and subways clogged with used cuds. Some 20,000 wads were scraped from one spot on Times Square alone and LaGuardia proclaimed a new city slogan: Don't Gum Up The Works. The Mayor declared that a tiny glob of gum might seem a harmless object to the person who has grown tired of chewing it, but that it was no trifling matter to the city since it cost "literally hundreds of thousands of dollars a year" to scrape up the caked gum from public places. In a letter to the major chewing gum manufacturers LaGuardia asked their support in "a campaign of education to induce users of chewing gum to dispose of used gum in a proper manner . . ." He made the specific suggestion that warnings be printed on the inside of gum wrappers and that they be kept as a receptacle for old chewed gum.

New Yorkers responded sympathetically to Mayor LaGuardia's crusade. The *Times* editorialized that "gum decidedly does not rank among the good things of life when it is placed where the innocent will step on it or sit on it" and that "just as a drunken man is a bad advertisement for the liquor industry, so a misplaced wad of gum is a bad advertisement for the gum industry." One New Yorker wrote about how she "stuck to the sidewalk with every step" while out walking and another "non-chewer" demanded that the gum manufacturers be compelled "to make a non-sticking product and also, while they are at it, a non-chewable one." A third observer suggested that gum manufacturers "offer a box of fresh gum free for every so many pounds of exhausted gum turned in." The accumulated wads, he added, "might be disposed of to European belligerents for use in large gobs as tank traps."

LaGuardia's Don't Gum Up The Works campaign had its first success when American Chicle agreed that on January 1, 1940 the company would print on the wrappers of all its gum: Save this Wrapper for Disposal of Gum After Use. However, these historic words were the Little Flower's only success in the war against gum wads. All of the major companies followed American Chicle's lead. "When a person has finished with gum," Wrigley most specifically told its customers, "it should be disposed of carefully. A good idea is to save the inner wrapper from the stick, then wrap the gum in it, and place it in a wastebasket or other container." But although Save This Wrapper For Disposal After Use became the most publicized instructions in the world, it also became the most ignored advice—except perhaps for Close Cover Before Striking. People just did not pay much attention, and still don't.

After 105 years, American ingenuity still hasn't solved the gum disposal problem, but there have been some interesting suggestions. Signs imploring No Gum Parking probably wouldn't work, nor would "individual, attractive jeweled containers to serve when gum loses its flavor in the middle of the street." But then someone has advocated "a gum with nutritive value that could be neatly and expeditiously swallowed," and another inventive genius suggests that clothing manufacturers put "convenient non-stick pockets in all garments so that chewing gum could be deposited there for future use."

Someday a gum company may bring out one of the many patented nonstick gums, or invent a chewing gum that disintegrates on contact with air. It seems unlikely, and perhaps that's the way it was meant to be. Left in the sunlight, gum wads will eventually crumble and disappear, but shellacked or varnished under a chair or a student's desk, a wad could last for all time. Maybe fate has decreed that that's the proper ending. *Man ist was man isst*—Man is what he eats (or chews). Perhaps someday, somewhere, a saucerful of intelligent beings from another galaxy will come upon a wad, the last remains of western civilization, like an insect in amber, telling of *homo chompit erectus*—the anxious, bored, bedeviled, fun-loving creatures who tried valiantly but gummed up the works on a strange planet.

Or will it all end not with a whimper but with a thwack? *Smack! Snap! Pop! Crackle! Slurp! Thwack!* Great masses of the sticky stuff, parked wads from everywhere converging upon our cities like molten lava in the midst of a killing heat wave, inundating earth as it spreads out in all directions. An angry sun beating down harder. Smack! Slurp! More cuds snaking forth from under tables, beneath windowsills, off the soles of shoes and living room rugs. The ground gurgling, families fleeing bubbles that rip up huge sections of pavement in their advance. The great unlovely grey and pink gob seeking revenge on the trillions of teeth that mistreated it, devouring everything in its path, until the heat spell breaks and those same beings from another galaxy glimpse the sculpted remains of our years of glory, the scene as enigmatic to them as all those messages carved on prehistoric stones remain to us today. Spearmint people . . . Wrigley rivers . . . Bubble gum buildings . . . Gumball armies . . . All earth a chewing gum Madame Tussaud's . . .

O Great Spirit of the Chewing Gum, rest in peace!
THWACK!!!

Getting It Off

APPENDIX 1

THE best way to remove sticky gum from clothing, fabric or furniture is to rub an ice-cube over the gum and then gently scrape it off with a table knife when it begins to harden and crumble. Rubbing alcohol and fingernail polish remover will have the same effect as ice. To remove any stain left behind, use a grease solvent. Better yet—make the stain problem your drycleaner's.

Bubble gum stuck to the face can be removed in a novel way, say the experts. Chew the remainder of the gum in your mouth. Then apply it to the remnants on your face—the rags of that glorious bubble will stick to the wad and come home.

One thing that is impossible to remove is gum stored

chewed in a pants pocket and then washed unwittingly by an unsuspecting parent. You have two choices here—cut out the pockets or throw the pants away. For that matter, no dry-cleaner, custodial service or alchemist consulted had any magic formulas for removing gum. All they volunteered were answers like "Hard work," "Impossible," and sad shakes of the head. What America needs is a good self-destructing gum wad! You could make a million.

"Gum's"

The Word

GUM'S missionaries never tried to translate words like spearmint, doublemint, or even chewing gum itself, into the language of any country. They have thus become truly international, making up part of a universal vocabulary that includes O.K., Coke, and Kilroy was here. However, many countries do have their own words for gum. Should you stray far from home, here is a vocabulary to call for gum with:

Arab World	*Elki*
Argentina	*Goma de mascar*
Austria	*Kaugummi*
Brazil	*Goma de mascar*
Canada (French)	*Gomme a macher*

Chile	*Goma de mascar*
China	*Heung How Chu*
Czechoslovakia	*Zvykacka*
France	*Le chewing gum*
Germany	*Kaugummi*
Greece	*Tsikles*
Italy	*La gomme da Masticare*
Japan	*Gamu*
Malaysia	*Shee Yung Tung*
Mexico	*Goma de mascar*
Norway	*Tyggegummi*
Peru	*Goma de mascar*
Portugal	*Pastilka elastica*
Russia	*Zhevatelnaya Rezinka*
Spain	*Goma de mascar*
Sweden	*Tuggumi*
Switzerland	*Chaetschgummi*
Thailand	*Mag farang*
Venezuela	*Goma de mascar*

INDEX

About the author

Robert Hendrickson has traveled with a carnival, dug graves, been a migrant worker, and traveled around the Far East. The author of *The Grand Emporiums, Human Words, Rip-Offs, Foods for Love,* and *The Great American Tomato Book,* he has also published hundreds of articles in *Time, Reader's Digest, Saturday Review, The New York Times* and other periodicals. An honors graduate of Adelphi University, he has also received a Ford Foundation Fellowship. Mr. Hendrickson lives with his wife and five children in Far Rockaway, New York.